LEE COUNTY LIBRARY
SANFORD, N. C.

P9-CMD-674

MAX BRAND

The Big "Westerner"

Frederick Faust at forty-eight.

LEE COUNTY LIBRARY
SANFORD, N. C.

MAX BRAND
The Big "Westerner"

by Robert Easton

University of Oklahoma Press : Norman

By Robert Easton

The Happy Man (New York, 1943)
The Hearing (Charlotte, N. C., 1964)
Max Brand, The Big "Westerner" (Norman, 1970)

As co-author

Lord of Beasts (Tucson, 1961)
The Book of the American West (New York, 1963)
California Condor: Vanishing American (Charlotte, N. C., 1964)

As editor

Max Brand's Best Stories (New York, 1967)
Bullying the Moqui: Charles F. Lummis' Defense of the Hopi Indians
   (Prescott, 1968)

Standard Book Number: 8061–0870–3

Library of Congress Catalog Card Number: 69–16732

Copyright 1970 by the University of Oklahoma Press, Publishing Division of the University. Composed and printed at Norman, Oklahoma, U.S.A., by the University of Oklahoma Press. First edition.

For Max Brand's grandchildren

PROLOGUE

MAX BRAND was the best-known pen name of one
of the least-known giants of U.S. popular literature, Frederick
Faust. Faust created Dr. Kildare, Destry, and many other fictional
characters who have found favor with readers and viewers the
world over. Faust was published under 20 different names. He
produced an estimated thirty million words of fiction, the equivalent of 530 ordinary books. He was associated with more than 70
motion pictures. Stage, radio, and television shows based on his
work have been presented continually for many years. These
are resounding statements, but they merely outline the truth
about a man whose identity has been a mystery and whose desire
for anonymity sprang from deep inner sources.

Few men have reached so large an audience while remaining
so unknown.

Frederick Schiller Faust was born in Seattle, Washington, on
May 29, 1892, and grew up in poverty in the rural San Joaquin
Valley of California—the valley and foothills written about by
Mark Twain and Frank Norris and later by John Steinbeck and
William Saroyan. From childhood he was forced by bad health
and family indigence to rely on his own resources. An orphan at
thirteen, he made his living by manual labor. After attending
the University of California at Berkeley, where he became a
campus leader and outstanding literary figure, he had a series of
adventures best described as fabulous, culminating in New York
in 1917 when he suddenly became a successful poet and prose-
fiction writer.

From there the story reads sometimes like a fairy tale, sometimes like a tragedy. Hidden behind pseudonyms, Faust lived a life which tended to surpass those of his fictional characters: A villa in Florence . . . cruises to the Greek Islands . . . nearly disastrous heart trouble . . . a tragic love affair . . . transatlantic descents upon the U.S. to retool production lines for an almost unbelievable output of words . . . crushing debts . . . alcoholism.

To establish markets for his varied products, Faust divided himself into an increasing number of pen names and finally became twenty men, each a fictitious personality, while he strove to establish his real identity. Sometimes a single issue of a magazine would carry two or three stories or novels by him, each under a different name. As many as five U.S. book publishers, besides several more in Europe and elsewhere, were engaged in keeping his output moving. Hollywood once released seven of his films in a twelve-month period. Dr. Kildare television shows have been seen by millions in many parts of the world.

It would be next to impossible to measure Faust's impact on his audience. Twenty-five years after his death, his books are being published under various pseudonyms at the rate of approximately one a month. They sell more than a million copies a year.

This is the story of Frederick Faust. It is a story about a man who hid behind aliases, who endured tremendous suffering, who achieved gigantic successes which he held of no account, who loved at first sight, and whose search for self-realization was crowned by success in the last seconds of his existence—an ending such as he himself might have written.

CONTENTS

	Prologue	*page vii*
1.	A Boy and a Valley	3
2.	The University of California	15
3.	Wanderings	27
4.	Canada	34
5.	New York	39
6.	A Young Writer	48
7.	In Uniform at Last	55
8.	Western Novels	65
9.	A Touch of Death	76
10.	The Uphill Road	89
11.	England	103
12.	Florence	113
13.	Ireland and Italy	129
14.	U.S.A., 1929	134
15.	Destry Rides Again	142
16.	Editors and an Agent	153
17.	Ordeal by Writing	169
18.	Fictional Summits	176
19.	A Faustian Olympiad	185
20.	Two Women	193
21.	Dionysus in Hollywood	201
22.	Deepening Conflicts	217
23.	Farewell to New York	237
24.	Outward Bound	242
25.	Combat Correspondent	249
26.	The Stuff of Dreams	258

ix

Epilogue	263
A Faust Bibliography	273
Film, Radio, and Television Appendix	302
A Faust Filmography	305
Books About Faust	310
Author's Acknowledgments	311
Index	313

ILLUSTRATIONS

Frederick Faust.   *Frontispiece*
The *Occident* staff, 1915.   *Following page* 116
William Rose Benét.
Robert H. ("Bob") Davis.
Kiss or Kill, First Big Film for Faust.
Movie Based on Faust's First Novel, *The Untamed.*
Cover, *All-Story Weekly*, July 14, 1917.
Cover, *All-Story Weekly*, October 27, 1917.
Cover, *All-Story Weekly*, November 1, 1919.
Cover, *All-Story Weekly*, March 13, 1920.
Faust as a Young Father, 1923.
Playing Chess with Leonard Bacon.
Villa Negli Ulivi, Florence, Italy.
Swimming Pool, Villa Negli Ulivi.
Dorothy and Heinie Faust, 1929.
Faust's Study, Florence.
Aldous Huxley.

The Faust Family, 1933.   *Following page* 244
Faust with Dr. George W. ("Dixie") Fish.
Signatures on a Contract with MGM.
Carl Brandt.
Page from *Argosy*, August 24, 1935.
Internes Can't Take Money, First Dr. Kildare Picture.
Thomas B. Costain.
Cass Canfield.
James Stewart and Marlene Dietrich in *Destry Rides Again.*
Stars of *Dr. Kildare's Crisis*, 1940.

xi

Richard Aldington.

Dorothy Faust, 1941.

Last portrait, 1943.

Rita Hayworth and Gene Kelly in *Cover Girl*.

Decca Album Made from Broadway Musical of
    Destry Rides Again.

Richard Chamberlain and Raymond Massey in the
    Dr. Kildare TV Series.

MAX BRAND

The Big "Westerner"

1.

A BOY AND A VALLEY

ELIZABETH FAUST sat at a trestle table in the front room of the dilapidated California farmhouse darning her husband's socks. From time to time she glanced anxiously at her firstborn son, who lay reading on the cot that served as sofa. She was afraid he was mentally retarded. He just couldn't seem to master his school work.

The pale, thin, dark-haired boy looked dangerously frail to her. Only the year before he had been threatened with tuberculosis and she had skimped and saved to send him to a sanitarium in the mountains.

"Put down that book now, Frederick," she said gently, "it's time for your arithmetic."

"But I'm in the middle of a story!"

"What are you reading?"

"King Arthur."

"Again?"

"Now Elizabeth, don't be too hard on the boy," the father's deep theatrical voice interrupted.

In his easy chair in a corner surrounded by books, Gilbert Leander Faust seemed for a moment the man he wanted to be. Strong-featured, graying, he seemed accomplished, cultured, a man of the world. The book in his hand was Goethe's epic poem, *Hermann and Dorothea.* But the chair was threadbare, the floor had no rug, the table at which his wife sat, though covered with a bright red-and-white checkered cloth, consisted of three boards laid over two sawhorses.

"If you can put aside King Arthur a few minutes, son," he

continued, "there's an errand I wish you would run. It's getting late and there's not much kerosene in the house. Run up to the store and ask him to give us half a gallon on credit."

The boy turned cold inside. He had gone on this errand before, but he had never grown accustomed to the misery it caused him. Though only eight, he understood what was happening.

As he trudged up the road, an empty gallon can under his arm, Frederick was chilled by the March wind that came off the Sierra Nevada and swept down the San Joaquin Valley. He recalled the mountains where he had spent the previous summer as a patient. He knew that he had been touched, though faintly, with death. It had given him a special sense of identity.

He reached the store at the crossroad settlement of Collegeville, a few miles east of Stockton on the Mariposa Road, in a region he later described as "impoverished and despairing, where the black adobe soil turned to glue in winter and baked hard as rock in summer." The storekeeper, a cadaverous man who wore a green eyeshade, looked at him suspiciously as he entered and put the rusty can on the counter. Frederick made himself speak coolly through shame and fear. "A half gallon, please!"

"You haven't paid me for the last ten gallons. What do you think this is—the Salvation Army?"

"My father will pay you tomorrow."

"Always tomorrow. And where's your old man going to get the money tomorrow?" The storekeeper's voice rose in sarcasm. He winked at the loafers gathered around the stove.

"My father is working at a case."

"He's a case all right!"

"My father is a lawyer!"

Their laughter cut into the boy, but he stood his ground. Perhaps it was his courage that finally moved the storekeeper to credit him with the kerosene.

Walking home, Frederick sensed that he had served as respite from the pain and dreariness which he and his tormentors shared. Beyond his resentment and their cruelty he thought he saw a bitter truth. An equally bitter hatred was fanned. For the hundredth time he promised himself that some day he would lead a life of quality and splendor.

As he neared the darkened house he heard his father's voice raised in a solo from Wagner's opera *Tannhäuser*. The tones were stentorian, bombastic, absurd. The elder Faust was a passionate man of German extraction with considerable charm and a good deal of intellect, but with an unhappy talent for acting parts and giving them a false sentimentality. The boy loved his father but saw through him clearly. Sometimes he wished he could accept the aging pretender as he wished to be accepted—as a successful man of the world—instead of a failure on his last legs.

The father was a large man who had been an athlete in his youth and even now at sixty-one moved with a quick step and a snappy military swing to his arms. He had served in the Union Army during the Civil War, and had marched with Sherman to the sea, and up the Atlantic Coast to Washington, and along Pennsylvania Avenue in the first parade of the Grand Army of the Republic. Gilbert Leander Faust was singing in the darkness partly to remember better days and partly to forget them.

After the war, he had read for the law in Illinois, practiced, prospered, and come west where he invested heavily in the first Southern California land boom. When the boom turned into a bust, he lost nearly everything. Then he moved to Seattle and tried again. With two marriages behind him, he embarked on a third. He became a successful lumber mill operator and a bank director. But the lumber mill burned, uninsured, and bad investments followed. Now he was eking out a living as an itinerant lawyer, hawking about the small towns of the San Joaquin Valley, advising country people on their petty litigations, broken and beaten but refusing to admit defeat.

The boy's mother was nearly fifty. She was a tall, handsome woman whose gray eyes shone happily except when she was angry, and then they turned very dark. She was Irish, and had a rich sense of humor. She shared with the boy a knowledge of the

5

father's tragic pretensions and the family's decline. They were so poor that an older sister and a younger brother were continually staying with relatives, easing things at home and leaving sickly Frederick to the care of both parents.

The three of them ate a supper of bread and milk and cheese by the light of the kerosene he had brought. After supper the mother read aloud from Scott's *Ivanhoe*.

The novel's pages told of the adventures of a young man named Wilfred among knights and ladies and castles in an England of long ago. It seemed to Frederick a wonderful time to have lived. As she read, he forgot the San Joaquin Valley. The experience at the crossroad store grew dim. There was only his mother's steady, loving voice.

His mother died that same year. One night, not long after the funeral, he and his father were alone in the house and there was nothing for supper except a bottle of milk. His father skimmed off the cream and gave it to him, keeping the thin milk for himself.

"Now I'll tell you a story, son," the old man began. "I was marching with Sherman to the sea. The great Army of the West was on the move. Not far from Atlanta we came to a magnificent old southern mansion. It was one of the finest estates in all the South—broad lawns, a columned portico. It was a house as stately as a castle."

The boy looked at the dark, uncurtained window, but what he saw was his father riding beside General Sherman toward a shining white mansion.

"And in the stable was a chestnut stallion. He was the finest animal I ever laid eyes on. I couldn't resist the temptation to take that horse!"

The father said that he rode his stolen stallion for half a day, until his conscience began to hurt. Finally he turned around, rode back, and returned the horse to its stall.

"But why?"

"Because, son, I realized how much that beautiful animal must have meant to its owner!"

To escape a life that seemed unbearable, Frederick lived more and more in stories, told and printed. The first book he read by himself was Malory's *Morte d'Arthur*. By the time he was ten he knew that some day he was going to be a writer.

He was seldom with other children except to fight his way into position each time his father moved to a new town and he entered a new school. Literally "Faust" means "fist." He grew into his teens withdrawn, sensitive, gangling, awkward, feeling outcast, inferior. His face was scarred by schoolyard fights. His emotions were scarred even more deeply.

When he was thirteen his father died. Relatives came and took charge of the house, but when everyone else was in bed he stole downstairs. Holding a candle high, he looked at the face inside the open coffin. His father seemed to be quietly sleeping, peaceful at last.

As an orphan, Frederick made his home with relatives or friends of relatives, on valley farms or in small towns, working for his keep, fighting for his place, often hungry, and always lonely. He became filled with bitter hatreds, powerful resentments, giant ambitions. He filled his school notebooks with stories and poems that were more real to him than the world around him. Besides Malory, he read Dickens, Scott, Thackeray, Goethe, Schiller, Dumas, Hugo, Mark Twain, Poe. He often walked several miles to school along country roads between acres of wheat and barley. To pass the time he recited aloud the poetry of Keats, Shelley, Tennyson, Milton, and Shakespeare.

After school and during summer holidays he experienced directly the raw, often brutal life of valley farmhands.

"Let us say it is mid-June and light enough for our hay-baling crew to start to work at four in the morning," he wrote, years later, in a vivid record of what life was like for a San Joaquin Valley farm worker half a century ago. "The cook bangs on a tin pan at that terrible hour, and after a moment vague grunts and murmurs make answer, and then the boss (who sleeps with the cook and is a poisonous little bastard with the face of a she-goat and the habits of a he-goat) comes around and speaks cheerfully and announces that the day is already old. To the feeders and balerollers, being dignitaries, he is apologetic. The rest of us he is apt to kick out of our blankets. At fifteen minutes after four the beater rises in the box, and it's important to waste no time because the hay is heavy with dew now. Some of the men have started with slugs of whiskey and a false enthusiasm. Others simply accept misery, or hope to die soon."

The nature of the work and the conditions under which it was performed were hard. A large iron weight, called a beater, was lifted to the top of a scaffold by horse power and allowed to fall repeatedly into a box containing loose hay, mashing this hay into the form of a bale. The loose hay was fed into the box by hand, the wires were tied around the compressed bale by hand, the finished bale was rolled away by hand, and stacked by hand; and the men performing these and other labors worked at a desperate pace, almost a run, for sixteen hours a day for pay that might reach eighteen cents an hour.

"There is breakfast at six. Somebody already has knocked off a chunk of hide from his hand, and the crew sweats and stinks. At nine-thirty is morning lunch of prunes and bread (without butter) and two cups of boiling-hot, tar-black coffee; lunch at twelve. Beater drops again at one and the more tired members of the crew have to be dragged to their feet and wonder if God will get them through the really long part of the day. Lunch again at four or four-thirty, and work until sunset, though for several hours the sun has remained stuck in the sky and refused to budge. Then supper, and to bed in blankets laid on a shock of hay. A few dirty stories, a cigarette or pipe, and then sleep. And so for six days a week and then a good Saturday-night drunk for some, or others go miles and miles to a dance, and Sunday you lie around trying to sleep, except that the flies won't let you. Sunday is the worst day because your pains, of body and soul, overtake you."

The overwork strained his heart but this was not evident until later. For the present it simply intensified his desire to escape from the valley.

When he was sixteen, he left the region of big wheat ranches around Stockton and went south fifty miles to Modesto to go to high school. Attending high school was generally regarded as a privilege, and Modesto High had an excellent reputation. Its students were expected to prepare for college and to take all courses offered, except second-year French and mechanical drawing, which were optional.

For Faust the venture loomed as a first step in his escape, but at first there seemed to him nothing very appealing about Modesto. The dusty, raw, sunburned, farm community looked like dozens of others strung along the tracks of the Southern Pacific in the vast valley.

At a big frame house on Downey Avenue he met the distant relative he was to stay with, Thomas Downey, the high school principal. Downey welcomed him warmly. "I can pay my own way," Faust replied. He had found many hands lifted against him and was not sure whether Downey's would be.

Downey was in fact a genial person of great dignity, occasional sternness, and remarkable hospitality. In addition to their own children, three girls and a boy, he and his wife liked to take into their household not only relatives but any boy or girl who needed a helping hand. Their big house was a sort of youth hostel.

Downey casually outlined a year's course of reading in classical literature and history for Faust to do in his spare time if he cared to, and Faust completed it in three months and asked for more. Homer, Hesiod, Herodotus, Thucydides, Xenophon, the classic myths, Vergil, Livy, Dante, Gibbon, Rawlinson's *History of Ancient Egypt*—Faust could not get enough.

One day Downey said to William Williams, the high school science instructor, "There's a boy in your physics class who's got considerable talent in English and history, but I think we've got an obligation to teach him some science and math. Will you try?"

The next day when Williams called the roll, he took a hard look at the boy laboring under the appellation of Frederick Schiller Faust. He saw a lone wolf, somewhat older and taller than most of his classmates, disdainful, and apparently utterly bored by science and those who taught it. The day's lesson involved the laws of falling bodies formulated by Galileo. Williams determined to bring the rebel to terms.

"Faust, what can you tell us of the significance of Galileo?"

"He was born the same year as Shakespeare."

"What else can you say about Galileo?"

"Galileo risked life and reputation by publishing his scientific discoveries when he knew they would offend the church authorities, and he was placed under arrest by bigots who felt their tyranny threatened by his work."

So it went for most of the semester. Williams finally had to admit to Downey he couldn't make a scientist out of Faust. Downey replied, "I'm not surprised. I think he's going to make his mark as a writer some day, and your effort may help make him a well-rounded one."

During midnight conversations, Faust had shyly shown Downey poems and stories he had written. Downey had encouraged him to continue memorizing Shakespeare's poems and plays. This memorization eventually totaled more than 25,000 lines, a figure Downey liked to hold up as example to successive generations of students. Aeschylus was another favorite subject of their midnight talks, Faust apparently identifying strongly with the fatherless Orestes obliged to make his way alone in the world.

Faust was at first regarded by his classmates as different and strange. During his first days at Modesto High he accepted an invitation to box with a muscular bully who had the habit of trying to beat up any opponent. As his gloves were being laced on, Faust seemed like a lamb being prepared for the slaughter. However it soon became apparent that the lamb was able to butcher the butcher. While fighting his way up the pecking order at the eighteen different schools he had attended, Faust had developed not only a liking for personal combat but an effective technique.

Soon he was developing socially as well. He had moved out of Downey's house, in order to avoid the appearance of being dependent on a relative, and was living at a neighbor's. He paid for room and board by cleaning yards, running errands, or clerking in shops. He had become intimate with John Cooper, another fatherless boy, whose admiration had been roused by Faust's conquest of the school bully. As a first gesture toward friendship, Cooper issued a challenge to a boxing match.

"Faust was doing yard work and other chores for his board and room at Mrs. Purvis' place one block from my home," Cooper recalled in later years. "I worked at a stationery store after school and it seemed that 6:30 P.M. was the most favorable time for the bout. I ate dinner and appeared at the selected spot equidistant between our two houses. 'Have you eaten?' I asked Faust. 'No,' he replied, 'I would rather box any time.' Then followed the best fight I ever had. Neither of us guarded or clinched. Both stood and slugged until we could no longer hold up our hands. We quit without discussion. Tired as he was, Faust's eyes were gleaming. I got to the stationery store in time to vomit."

The two soon ranked among the town's leading troublemakers. They sorely tested Downey's patience by cutting classes and rafting, Huck Finn style, down the Tuolumne River, which gushed undammed out of the Yosemite region and past the city limits of Modesto. To prove their pugilistic mettle they picked fights with toughs at the saloons opposite the railroad depot. They proudly wore black eyes and contusions as badges of courage. To confound critics, including Downey—or to give further play to their expanding personalities—they founded and edited a high school literary magazine.

Faust seemed to be continually trying something new. For a while he lived in the home of a music teacher and developed an

11

interest in music. He rode borrowed horses, dashing at full gallop through the streets of Modesto. He talked with cowboys who had ridden in from the big ranches of the Coast Range to the west, and prospectors down for supplies from the Mother Lode country to the east. He joined younger boys in stealing rides on the backs of wagons piled high with grain sacks that went jingling toward the railroad station to the music of bells on the harnesses of six-horse teams, and he liked to talk with the hobos in the jungles along the Tuolumne River.

Trains connected Modesto to the world beyond the mountains. As they crashed and wailed through town their sound was a kind of music from the life of quality and splendor for which Faust hungered.

While dreaming of that life, he was exposed to a new kind of social reality. A railroad worker was labeled a red for advocating the eight-hour day. Two teachers reportedly lost their jobs for playing tennis on Sunday. A civic leader was known to keep a mistress. Conventional society appeared to Faust as largely hypocritical. It seemed organized along self-perpetuating lines designed to bar outsiders like himself from entering.

At times he identified strongly with outsiders such as the Mexican and Negro laborers and Portuguese dairy farmers. He felt a kinship with other local minorities, including the Jewish merchants at B. Weil & Son or D. G. Plato's, where he bought his blue jeans and work shirts. Being Irish and German, he felt at odds with a predominantly English world.

There were genteel youngsters in town, boys who did not have to fight and girls who were regarded as young ladies. But Faust saw little of them, though he thought about them a good deal, especially the girls. He dreamed of a girl he might marry some day who would be a mixture of Rowena of *Ivanhoe* and Guenevere and Iseult of *Morte d'Arthur*. He had had experiences with girls familiar to the hay-baling crews—sex was no mystery. But he felt terribly shy with so-called nice girls. He believed that none of them could ever love him because of his scarred face, old clothes, and lack of money, parents, and status.

Often as he walked home from school he saw a brown-haired girl walking along the other side of the street. She was Lena Schafer, daughter of a prominent department store owner. Though he frequently looked for her, he was too shy to speak to her.

In what appears to have been frustration over Lena or someone like her, Faust wrote a poem which was published in *The Sycamore*, the high school literary magazine.

Iseult is speaking to her lover:

> The harbour bar is not a mile away
> And see how grim above the forest swell
> The frowning walls of Castle Tintagel.
> Tristram, we must say farewell today,
> And think the past a vision if we may;
> And all the dreams we two have dreamed, 'twere well
> The Future by some magic could dispel;
> Perhaps grim Tintagel will banish dreams away.
> There is the wine my mother's hand prepared
> For Mark and me; let us toast oblivion,
> And tune the burden of our lives anew,
> That we may never let the past be bared.
> Drink, Tristram, drink. A health—a health to you.
> That memories may perish, one by one!

His first published prose fiction was in similarly romantic vein. It concerns a farm horse turned race horse. The farm horse defeats a heavy favorite at the wire.

Despite all handicaps, Faust was determined to win. The writing that was beginning to pour out of him in steadily increasing quantity fanned a tremendous desire. In what he imagined as the shining region toward the sea, he believed he would find fame, fortune, beauty, and love.

Downey loaned him fifty dollars. As an outstanding graduate

of Modesto High School—pre-eminent in liberal arts courses and quite competent in science, algebra, and calculus—Faust prepared to enter the University of California at Berkeley, as William Howard Taft entered his last year in the White House and the U.S. entered a period of profound change.

It was the beginning of a new era. In the fall of 1911, Faust rode the day train to Berkeley on a $1.90 fare.

2.

THE UNIVERSITY OF CALIFORNIA

Desperately lonely, I wandered about the streets of Berkeley, past the doors of the fraternity and sorority houses, watching the light pour out, wondering how people could be so happy."

The lonely freshman was pleased when he was invited to a fraternity rushing party. At luncheon he sat next to an important member, a leading campus figure. Somehow the subject of cello music came up. Instead of dismissing the cello and continuing with lighter subjects, Faust grew thoughtful. "The cello has even greater emotional power, I think, than the violin." He was suspected of having serious cultural tendencies and was not invited to join.

Rejected and angered, he decided to go his own way and found he was on a campus where he could do so without much difficulty. There was non-conformity at Berkeley then as later. In addition to native dissenters, a substantial number of professors and students came from other states and from foreign countries, and they tended to introduce varied patterns of thought and behavior. At the campus entrance at the end of Telegraph Avenue, soapbox orators advocated joining Pancho Villa's irregulars in revolutionary Mexico, or called attention to the radical views of a professor at nearby Stanford University named Thorstein Veblen. There was excited talk of Fabian socialism and of Bolshevik plots against the Tsar. Meanwhile the Berkeley faculty offered such stable names as Charles Mills Gayley, a noted authority on classical Greek and Roman literature and mythology; Arthur Ryder, a distinguished professor of Sanskrit; and Brailsford Robinson, a noted Australian biologist.

Escape to the country was possible by a short walk up Strawberry Canyon into the Berkeley hills. A trolley car ride and ferryboat trip would take you to San Francisco in about an hour.

Faust found a scantily furnished room in a back yard on Shattuck Avenue in Berkeley. It contained an iron bedstead and one shelf on which he placed his *Iliad* and J. B. Bury's *History of Greece*, both gifts from Thomas Downey. There was also a copy of *The Return of the Native* by Thomas Hardy, then considered an iconoclastic novelist, which Faust had purchased in admiration. A tiny mirror graced one wall. Under it was a dingy walnut dresser with a top of gray, stained marble and a large white chinaware washbasin and white pitcher. There was no plumbing; Faust used a bathroom in the rear of the main house. The premises were occupied by a Swedish wood-and-coal dealer who had three large, unattractive, and unmarried daughters.

Faust was soon distinguishing himself on campus, though not by scholarship. A traditional smoker was held in the gymnasium a week or two after the beginning of each fall term. It was given by sophomore men as a welcome to their freshman counterparts. Entertainment consisted chiefly of informal boxing matches between members of the two classes. Anyone could step into the ring. The lanky unknown who did so on behalf of the freshmen, on a particular September evening in 1911, did not look like a good bet. He seemed all arms, legs, and awkwardness and was greeted by catcalls and a few perfunctory cheers. The husky sophomore contender made his entrance amid a din of approval. But when the two squared off, the sophomore rooting section fell silent.

The freshman champion was revealed to have a sharp left and a devastating right cross. The two pounded each other for three rounds under the smoky lights. The referee tactfully declared a draw. Faust stepped down from the ring never to be obscure again. From that day forward he was "The tall guy with the

German name, Heinie Faust—the guy who fought at the smoker."

His classroom activities were distinguished in a different way. Leonard Bacon, youngest and newest member of the English department, just arrived from Yale, soon noticed the student who sat in the back of his English class, who appeared "as big as a Kodiak bear" and who regarded him with chilly unemotional eyes.

"As a matter of fact, Fred was not a very large man. I don't think he was over six feet three. But he gave the impression of being gigantic. And the cold look was deceptive, too. For he burned perpetually with enthusiasm or indignation."

As his first offering, Faust submitted a thousand-word paper on Thomas Hardy. Bacon found it a better piece of criticism than appeared in most literary monthlies.

Faust found in Bacon the kind of man he was looking for. Together they translated Grillparzer's romantic tragedy *König Ottokar* into blank verse, but it was rejected when submitted for publication to the English Club. The defeat cemented their friendship and initiated Faust's rebellion against literary establishments.

Bacon (who was one day to win the Pulitzer Prize for poetry) conducted a poetry-writing group after hours for the benefit of Faust and a few other students. Hazel Havermale, Helen Cornelius, Hildegarde Flanner (whose sister Janet was to become "Genêt," Paris correspondent of the *New Yorker* for more than forty years), Sidney Howard, John Schoolcraft, Roswell Ham, Deborah Dyer (later a *Fortune* editor), and others who later distinguished themselves in the writing world were members of the group.

The informal talks at Bacon's apartment on Piedmont Avenue were intellectual boxing matches. Faust excelled in them as he had in the ring. Out of the give and take developed a regular English course for which he collected fifteen promising students.

"He was the attractive force that held them together, and his written contributions came in an Amazonian flood," Bacon re-called. Bacon was deluged by thousands of lines, many of which indicated promise. But it was their volume that astounded him; he had never seen such production.

By Faust's sophomore year the dynamic rebel was merging into the campus scene. He had moved to more congenial quarters in a student rooming house, while continuing to support himself with the proceeds from odd jobs. He was studying the Greek and Latin classics in translation and involving himself deeply and permanently in the ancient myths, dedicating himself to the philosophy that literature must be lived as well as written, and seeing in myth the justification for what he considered his pagan-ism and his commitment to art.

He was also becoming deeply infected by athletic fever, es-pecially by the traditional rivalry between the University of California and Stanford. On the Wednesday night before the 1912 Stanford football game, twenty male sophomores gathered secretly in the eucalyptus grove behind the Greek Theater in the upper reaches of the Berkeley campus. Senior leaders outlined plans for a raid on the Stanford campus across the bay. The sopho-mores were directed to burn the pile of combustibles scheduled for ignition during the enemy's pre-big-game rally the following evening, paint statues blue and gold (the Berkeley colors), leave derisive marks everywhere possible, and return safely yielding no prisoners.

Under Faust's leadership it was done. No matter that Satur-day's game ended in a tie. Faust and his cohorts were considered to have won a great victory.

Some called him show-off and glory grabber, but he advanced in most student opinion to the status of campus leader. The fraternities that had denied him acceptance extended invitations. He had the pleasure of declining.

Despite honors and fame he was at times weak from hunger, half dead from lack of sleep. There were days when he had no money at all. For a while he worked in a laundry, as Jack London had done fifteen years earlier, under similar circumstances. Sometimes he subsisted on stale bread obtained from food stores at cut-rate prices. His one garment was an old blue-serge suit with holes. For a while he was leaving the Berkeley campus in mid-afternoon, crossing the bay, and working an eight-hour shift handling packages and freight at the American Express Company office in San Francisco, returning to Berkeley late at night, and settling down to reading and writing in the small morning hours. Black coffee, a superb constitution, and a strong will, plus such sleep as he could snatch in class, pulled him through. His grades suffered, but his reputation grew.

While still a sophomore he was elected to the editorial board of *The Occident*, the undergraduate literary magazine. Faust's friend Sidney Howard was also distinguishing himself as a writer. (Howard became a Pulitzer-Prize-winning dramatist, author of *They Knew What They Wanted*, and many other successful Broadway productions.) Collaborating with Howard, and publishing his own work in *The Occident*, Faust felt himself arrive.

He was elected to the English Club, a high-water mark of campus culture. Honor societies opened their doors to him. The university authorities loaned him money. Everywhere he turned he belonged. These were the men and women he had dreamed existed. "Suddenly I begin to drink with them, all the dark walls fall down, and I am in the midst of a glorious, shining, noble humanity."

From this time forward friendship and fellowship became a major part of his life. The regular dinner of the literary crowd took place at an Italian restaurant in San Francisco. It began with mussels and ended with zabaglione, washed down with "rough red wine of the country." Zola, Hardy, and Vachel Lindsay were discussed with ardor. Style, tone, diction, the propriety of a masculine or feminine ending on a line of poetry, were matters of grave import.

A quite different group appealed to Faust even more. It was called The Gun Club, though it had nothing to do with firearms.

It was composed of campus leaders—athletes, editors, managers, politicians—who shared an interest in power and success, as well as in wine, women, and song. Their meetings started at The Hofbrau Rathskeller in downtown Oakland, but sometimes ended on the Barbary Coast or at a sporting house in San Francisco, or perhaps at the Last Chance Saloon or the police station on the Oakland waterfront.

Stepping down from Homer or Dante, Faust declaimed Kipling or Robert Service to the gun clubbers with exemplary gusto:

> We must go, go, go . . . The Red Gods
> Are calling, we must go!

The rampages of the gunners up and down San Francisco's Market Street, often led by Faust, became legendary. Fabulous Faust, many were calling him, though some regarded him as an obnoxious egotist who did not know when to stop. His casual habit of enrolling in courses and dropping them if they bored him without bothering to notify the instruction office had turned administrative circles against him. He had gone so far as to make a standing offer to take anybody's final examination in any course for a fee of five dollars, a passing grade guaranteed; and he had made good on his offer more than once. He ghost-wrote essays with which others won prizes. His natural tendency was to disregard limits.

If one drink was good, two were better. Three drinks, and like the legendary Faust he felt the universe within his grasp. Though he disciplined himself with periodic dry spells, during which furious work replaced liquor, he became, in his own words "the most famous drunk on campus." This was a far-from-strategic position to be in at a time when the movement which led to the prohibition amendment to the U.S. Constitution was steadily gaining force.

Meanwhile his writing was becoming the talk of the campus. His comedy *Fools All* had been described by one reviewer as "some of the best blank verse which has appeared . . . a play which is not merely pentameter in prose, but real poetry and Mr. Faust has exhibited his customary skill in matters of sound and color ... there is about it a freedom from ugliness which bespeaks his power as a poet."

With George A. Smithson, instructor in English philology, he began work on a scholarly translation of *Beowulf* which was eventually submitted for publication. He had established personal relations with a number of faculty members and was supporting himself in part by reading English papers and coaching backward students.

His own writing was by now inundating *The Occident*. In volume and extent it set a record, totaling more than seventy-five pieces, seven of them appearing from one to three years after Faust left college. Included were lyric and narrative poems, literary criticism, prose fiction, and plays in verse and in prose. One of his best efforts was "College Sonnets," a series of twenty-one related lyrics written while he was still a junior and occupying no less than eleven pages in *The Occident* for September, 1915. There were many good passages and one sonnet of distinction that expressed what he called his devotion to the life of emotion as opposed to the life of reason.

> You who love not the stars, but one by one
> Catalogue meteors; you who are bold
> To search for dross where common men see gold;
> You who find ends for what God has begun
> Who analyze the heavens and test the sun,
> Makers of vast hypotheses, I hold
> More reverence for the child who forms a mold
> Ingeniously of dust—and breaks when done.
>
> Critics of nature, cautious searching men,
> You worshipers of reason I defy
> To circumscribe my minutes with your laws.
>
> So may an instinct lead me, now and then,
> To stand here quietly beneath the sky
> And feel its wonder, asking not the cause.

His 309-line narrative poem, *One of Cleopatra's Nights*, won the Cook Prize in a competition sponsored by the university and by Professor Albert Stanburrough Cook of Yale. It was Berkeley's top literary award. Judges included Professor Gayley, head of the Berkeley English department, and Professor Bliss Perry of Harvard.

Surprisingly, for one who was to become such a prolific writer of prose fiction, Faust published only one story while in college. It was a South Sea romance with racial overtones, titled *The House of Rulaki*. It appeared in *The Occident* for October, 1913, and was regarded by campus critics as good enough to have appeared in a general-circulation magazine of the period.

In addition to his work for *The Occident*, Faust was contributing historical material to *The University of California Chronicle*, a quarterly devoted to recording university activities, and had become an editor of *The Blue and Gold*, the university's yearbook. At the same time he was serving as associate editor of *The Pelican*, the campus humor magazine, and soon accepted the editorship simply because it paid a salary of $100 a month. As his senior year progressed, Faust had become a sort of one-man literary movement.

He had written and *The Occident* had published a one-act play titled *Brother John* in which the lady of a castle and a priest are desperately in love. The conflict brings on the medieval version of a psychosomatic illness. The lady takes to her bed. The priest visits her. A page looking through the keyhole sees Brother John first on his knees, then rising to his feet and breaking his cross to bits. By the standards of 1914, this was extremely bold.

As if all this weren't enough, under the pseudonym of "Little Bobbie" Faust was writing a column for the *Daily Californian*, the campus newspaper, in which he satirized faculty and administration dignitaries, sacred cows, sacred codes, and sorority row. He simultaneously attacked convention by means of jokes and editorials in the light-hearted *Pelican* and essays in the serious *Occident*, declaring in *The Pelican* some views on education that were to be characteristic of Berkeley undergraduates fifty years later.

In her sleep Pelly had a most fantastic dream, for she thought that she was in a new university where there were no lectures and where no one ever slept. In this strange place the classes were all small, and the number of professors was large in proportion with the student body, for a maxim of this queer university was that it is better to teach a few people well than to teach many ill.

In *The Occident* he announced:

In the list of "Sports of All Nations" the United States stands represented by "Moralizing and Reform." This pleasant occupation, long a favorite in the New England States, now ranks with baseball as our leading sport, but with this great advantage over the national pastime that it is limited to no season of the year. To the sour face of the Puritan all days, hot or cold, are alike.

This was not the kind of writing best calculated to endear a student to Benjamin Ide Wheeler, the dignified president of the university, or to the university's equally conservative and dignified board of regents—particularly when the author was an undergraduate whose drinking was a campus scandal. There were even rumbles from the legislature in Sacramento. A member demanded that appropriations for the university be held up until moral conditions on the campus could be investigated.

Having achieved dubious notoriety as well as real distinction, Faust now found love. He met a blonde sophomore at an English Club dance at the Hotel Oakland. It was love at first sight on both sides. He had arrived quite drunk but sobered immediately, danced with her once, talked to her briefly, and went home shouting to roommates that he had met the woman he was going to marry. Her name was Dorothy Schillig. She was three years younger than Faust, a recognized campus beauty, a member of a leading sorority, and as conventional and genteel a person as Faust was at times the opposite.

A whirlwind courtship followed. Dorothy was reprimanded by her housemother for staying out past the ten o'clock curfew. After three meetings there was a secret engagement; and at the Easter holidays, that spring of 1915, Faust accompanied her on the train part of the way to her home in Yuba City near Sacramento. Ironically, it was located in the very valley from which he was trying to escape.

There were immediate complications. Faust, the noted reprobate, was denied access to the Kappa Alpha Theta sorority house to see his beloved. He likewise was forbidden to enter Kappa Kappa Gamma, another fashionable sorority. All of this raised the Heinie-Dorothy love affair to Tristram-Iseult levels in the undergraduate imagination.

Pertinent as these developments may have been to Faust, they did not prevent President Wheeler from unofficially selecting him as the man least likely to succeed in the Class of 1915. (Wheeler was described by a classmate of Faust as, on the whole, liberal in his attitude toward students but quite willing, now and then, to select a student and make him a negative example to the rest of the university.)

When Wheeler's intentions toward Faust became known, friends rallied behind the unfortunate victim. George Smithson jeopardized his own career by championing Faust in a hectic meeting of the academic senate. He termed Faust "a man of unusual brilliance whose writings frequently showed signs of genius." The fact that the controversial figure's grades were of Phi Beta Kappa level in courses he had completed was cited. The eminent Henry Morse Stephens, professor of English literature, also supported Faust, as did other prominent faculty members.

When the day came for a conference between Wheeler and Faust, friends scoured the saloons and beer joints of Berkeley, Oakland, and San Francisco searching for the defendant. They found him at the Bank Exchange Saloon in San Francisco and pleaded with him to let reason govern and make some concessions to Wheeler.

"Reason is another name for cowardice," Faust retorted. "Why should I kowtow to that fathead?"

When he and Wheeler met, Faust simply said what he thought. Among his statements were, "Ideals are the bunk. Only action matters." Then he added the clincher, "Why should I worry about ideals as long as I can have ideas?"

Wheeler admitted privately that no other student had so shaken his composure. Coming from an educator of international reputation, who had recently been President Theodore Roosevelt's choice to represent the U.S. academic community in a year-long residency in Germany, this was a considerable statement. The shock was transmitted via Wheeler's commencement address delivered in the Greek Theater a few days later.

The open-air theater set against the hillside was the site from which Faust had departed to lead the successful raid on Stanford, where his plays had been presented, and where he had appeared as campus leader. On hand for the ceremonies and to receive honors were 1,200 members of the graduating class wearing traditional robes and mortarboards. The theater was nearly filled with families and friends. As President Wheeler mounted the rostrum and began to speak, he recognized a young man dressed in blue jeans sitting alone in the misty sun on the top row of seats. There Faust sat in solitary bitterness and heard his action philosophy described as "that of a man who would eventually slop along with eyes in the mud." Faust had been denied graduation on technical grounds of unexcused absence from classes. Actually the grounds were personal and moral.

"With all my heart," said Wheeler to the graduates—and to Faust—"I warn you against that which I name the frank 'opposite' of our life of ideals, namely the life which assumes to satisfy itself with 'action.' Life on this theory is a body of organs with functions. All this is the philosophy of the swine and the trough . . . ."

25

Wheeler and Faust in effect talked to one another across the heads of the crowd. Faust said later that a "fat-jowled reactionary had dragged his ideals through the mud." Secretly he was keenly hurt—nonetheless so because he recognized his own fault in what had happened. The dream of a promised land beyond the mountains had collapsed. With no money and no certain prospects, he was obliged to look for it elsewhere.

3.

WANDERINGS

FAILURE to graduate was a humiliation from which Faust suffered the rest of his life. It drove him to justify himself in the face of heavy odds, such as those represented by Wheeler and the authority of the university, or any other established order that might be arrayed against him. Meanwhile he was looking for a way out of the new valley he had created for himself, and in a rather fantastic humanitarian scheme he found one.

Lajpat Rai was an Indian nationalist who had a plan for recruiting young Americans for teaching in India's educational institutions and helping in the struggle for independence against the English. Rai had met Faust in the home of a faculty wife who brooded tenderly over Faust's wild campus doings and felt he needed understanding. Many women felt, and were to feel, sympathy of this kind for Faust. But he was deeply in love and he believed it to be love of a marrying kind. Yet he found it impossible to suggest immediate marriage to Dorothy while he was penniless and in a state of social disgrace. They may have discussed elopement, but by her standards elopement, too, was out of the question. Since marriage seemed beyond reach for the time being, Lajpat Rai and Indian nationalism looked like an interim solution.

Faust decided to go to India, make money, achieve status, come back, and marry Dorothy Schillig. Along the way he would write. He had written well enough to astonish the campus. He would write well enough to astonish the world. India became his promised land beyond the mountains.

Dorothy would finish college and be ready when her conquering hero returned. He broke the news of his immediate departure in a letter intended to make her feel that they were at last man and wife, living in a wonderful house in the country. "The house has a high-ceilinged wood-beamed living room and huge fireplace where a fire roars continually, and there is a large bay window through which—interrupting his writing of poetry—a guy watches a certain frau and two young kids come tramping in from the fields, their boots muddy."

The dream was in his mind and hers as he worked his way to Hawaii, a first step toward India. There he talked himself into a job as reporter on the Honolulu *Star-Bulletin*, traditionally a stepping-stone for globe-trotting newspapermen. On the day in August, 1915, when Faust walked into the *Bulletin* office, Riley Allen, the editor, happened to be in a tight spot. A tramp reporter had just quit without notice, leaving him with no sports writer and no coverage on the police beat.

"The job pays a grand salary of fifteen dollars a week and carries with it the handsome but unremunerative title of Sports Editor!" Faust wrote Dorothy.

His duties included covering such public functions as the seventy-seventh birthday party of the last of Hawaii's native rulers, Queen Liliuokalani. He claimed in a letter to Dorothy that he sympathized with the aged Queen: "She once led the islanders in revolt against American colonialism, which I translate into Benjamin Ide Wheelerism, and she was once defeated by American troops, as I have recently been defeated by the troops of orthodoxy." It was more of his life's special symbolism. "She has a rather kindly face of the old native type, a shiny tight black skin and a good-humored rather pathetic smile. At the reception, which was quite a formal affair, she sat in a big ebony chair with her kind old head resting against an Hawaiian cape of yellow feathers crossed with black. She wore a most incongruous dress—an elaborate black silk gown with shadow lace at the edges. And around her throat was a bright band of lavender. And such a crowd—partly curious and sneering howlis (as they call the white people) and partly wide-eyed natives all standing bare-headed under the palm trees listening to the Royal Hawaiian band playing gentle Hawaiian hymns on SLIDE TROM-BONES."

He also had some contact with the underworld: "I'm digging into a sordid prostitution scandal involving city politicians. It seems to bear out what Zola, Hardy and other naturalist writers depict in their novels."

Hawaii was rich grist for a writer's mill. Faust was living plots of stories he would someday write. He also gained valuable insight into areas of experience heretofore unknown, covering a society wedding and a political meeting, taking a twenty-mile hike up Mt. Tantalus, through the Nuuana Valley, and back to Honolulu, and interviewing such visiting celebrities as Paul S. Reinsch, U.S. Minister to China, formerly president of the University of Wisconsin.

In his spare time Faust was producing hundreds of lines of verse and writing passionately and paternally to Dorothy, advising her what to read. "Damn those French with their eternal insistence on the material facts of living and flesh. Consign Maupassant to the devil. Rather pick up your filthy old Rabelais. He is an out-and-out sort of fellow who calls a spade a spade. But no one's education is complete without reading him." The gargantuan appetites of the one-time Franciscan monk for obscenity, sex, food, drink, writing, and life apparently fitted Faust's notions perfectly.

More to Dorothy's tastes were the small intimacies he recalled in his letters to her, especially a certain night when they had walked to the house of friends in the Berkeley hills. "I wanted to draw my chair squarely in front of yours and watch the fire chase the shadows through your eyes—and how hungrily I looked at the curve of your throat—and how I watched the strange half smile of your mouth till I wanted to jump up and shout 'Madame, if you don't stop smiling I shall kiss you where you sit!' " He said he had written almost a whole scene for the last act of his new play simply by remembering some of the things that had happened between them that evening, and he quoted three pages of the play.

Their engagement had been announced in the *Daily Californian* and in the Berkeley and Oakland papers, so Sidney Howard wrote him. Their Tristram-Iseult-style love story had taken on added dimension—the lovers were even separated by water as in the original legend.

Before Faust could advance his romantic drama further, however, a decisive event occurred. As far back as the fall of 1914, immediately following the outbreak of World War I, there had been excited talk in Faust's circle of joining the British or French armies, going to Canada and enlisting, or joining one of the overseas ambulance units being formed in New York City. Faust, violently pro-Allied, had advocated American intervention. Then in 1915, just as he was about to leave college, Rupert Brooke, the young English poet, idol of poetry-minded youth on both sides of the Atlantic, had died while serving with the British Navy. Brooke, handsome, brilliant, romantic, had visited the Berkeley campus while returning from a trip to the South Seas and had read his poems to Bacon's poetry class.

Faust had been deeply moved, just as F. Scott Fitzgerald and others on the Princeton campus were moved by hearing Brooke. Brooke's tragic death in uniform now helped crystallize idealistic notions of patriotism and commitment in the minds of many young people. Each was apt to think of himself in terms of Brooke's:

> If I should die, think only this of me:
> That there's some corner of a foreign field
> That is forever England.

In Honolulu such thoughts culminated for Faust in the proposal by a group of Anglo-Americans to pay the traveling expenses of young men willing to go to Canada and enlist in the Canadian Army for overseas service in France.

Coincidentally, word came from Lajpat Rai releasing him from obligation to the Indian venture, and at the same time he heard that several members of the nationalist group he had been planning to join in India had been hanged by the British. It was a turning point. The offer of the Anglo-American citizens group provided a new future: free passage to adventure, achievement, and escape from routine in Honolulu.

All this had deeply personal implications. Faust wanted to vindicate his German name and origins against the forces of Kaiserism, and he also had long since committed himself to the dictum enunciated by Brooke that, "The best of all is to live poetry." Therefore Brooke's death in uniform had special meaning. Brooke had died, furthermore, in the very heartland of poetry, the Aegean Sea, while his vessel was steaming to take part in the Gallipoli campaign, near the Hellespont and ancient Troy, a region Faust hoped to visit and where he lived constantly in his imagination.

Though he went to war outwardly light-hearted and casual, inwardly he carried these fundamental commitments.

However, it was in slapstick vein that he wrote Dorothy, "Well, I'll soon be at the front, and I only hope that they give all recruits a change of drawers for the first battle."

She strongly opposed his enlistment. Was he truly thinking of their love? Why must *he* be the one to volunteer?

Nevertheless, off he went to Canada to enlist, taking 20,000 lines of an unfinished epic poem on the Tristram-Iseult theme. The offer of the Anglo-American group had failed to materialize, so he was obliged to pay his passage by stoking coal on a decrepit freighter that was dangerously overloaded, sadly in need of repair, and probably should not have been at sea at all.

Faust boarded her in company with a friend, George Winthrop Fish, a chunky, bullet-tough Berkeley classmate known as "Dixie" who had played quarterback on the university football team. Fish was thinking of becoming a doctor and would one day be the prototype for Doctor Kildare. Faust and the embryonic Kildare worked themselves into a state of desperation in the freighter's furnace room. The heat was nearly unbearable and the physical demands more formidable than any Faust had yet encountered. With their hands bleeding and their backs aching, escape became imperative.

In an autobiographical novel, *Harrigan*, Faust fictionalized this escape into a murderous contest of strength between himself in the person of Harrigan, common seaman aboard the "Mary Rogers," and McTee, the slave-driving ship's captain. In a titanic deckside fight, Harrigan and McTee battle for supremacy, surrounded by savage seamen who wait, wolflike, to follow the winner and devour—figuratively at least—the loser. Despite such cruel handicaps as hands cut to the bone from shoveling coal, Harrigan-Faust defeats McTee and escapes from slavery in the ship's hold.

In reality of fact, Faust escaped by revealing a knowledge of typing to a no-more-than-ordinarily brutal ship's captain in search of someone to do clerical work. But in the reality of imagination, Faust was the young god Zeus rebelling against the aging inept Cronus.

He continued to view experience largely in terms of myth. As if to confirm him in this instance, there was later an actual mutiny in which the crew attempted to seize control of the ship. The freighter turned out to be loaded with contraband ore. Fact began to surpass fiction.

In a narrative poem based on the Odysseus legend-myth, which he had written during his junior year in college and published in the *Occident*, Faust had announced that perilous adventure was more important to Odysseus-Faust than the security and immortality of any Circe's love. Now he was experiencing perilous adventure on the high seas, en route to involving himself in a war. When the other members of the freighter's crew—the Greek, the Negro, the Chinese, the Englishman—looked at him, it was with "a cold calculation," to see how much of a man he was. He felt himself able to look back unwaveringly. He had seen a similar appraising look in the eyes of the hay baling crews and in those of the night shift during the long hours of weary labor at the American Express Company in San Francisco. The look impressed itself on him permanently. It was, he sensed, the ancient glittering look with which Homer's characters had regarded each other in the *Iliad*, and it became an essential element in Faust's work and in his judgment of men.

For the moment, he remained topside doing clerical work while Fish continued to suffer the discomforts of the furnace room. Sometimes Fish would sneak up the companionway at midnight and the two of them would raid the food set out by the cook on a table in the dimly lit deckhouse for the benefit of officers at change of watch. Once the raiders were surprised in the act and were forced to hide under the table. With noses less than a yard from the captain's shoe laces, they spent a tense half-hour while the officers grumbled above their heads about the meagerness of the evening's repast.

Such escapades were brought to an end by a violent storm which left the ancient and overloaded freighter helpless, her rudder smashed. For five days she wallowed in sinking condition, raked by huge waves. All hands manned the pumps. Faust and Fish learned the virtues of prayer as the "Mary Rogers" "lurched forward in a long sickening slide that buried half the ship under the sea. A giant wave towered above the side and licked the wheelhouse away. Even that splintering crash was hardly audible above the yelling of the storm."

At last a tug came out eight hundred miles from Portland, Oregon, put a line aboard the helpless vessel, and towed her to Vancouver, British Columbia.

There Faust and Fish joined the Canadian Army.

4.

CANADA

I'VE GOT a soft job for you with the battalion saw-bones," Fish announced a few days after they had enlisted.

"I can stand a touch of soft life after that shipboard experience," Faust replied.

They were members of Company "C," 62nd Battalion, Canadian Expeditionary Forces, stationed at Hastings Park Barracks, Vancouver. The battalion doctor had taken a fancy to Fish, detected a medical interest, and hoped to keep him on his staff by placing Fish's pal in the more muscular part of medical work. Faust was given a job as stretcher-bearer. It was a far cry from heroic front-line duty, but as he rationalized fluently to his fiancée in California, "This means I will have no chance to pop away at the Deutschers but still will be able to help against them, and I guess a man is only a unit of value no matter where he serves, so long as he tries like a man to do a man's work." He hoped Dorothy would forgive him for enlisting. "Think of your wandering boy about to serve side by side with the Army that produced a Wellington and a Marlborough." Dorothy was beginning to wonder how far he would wander before their wedding day.

There were certain other wanderings he had not told her of. He was having a passionate affair with an army hospital nurse. It had given him a guilty feeling and made him wonder if he wanted to be tied to Dorothy. In a mood compounded of self-disgust and a desire for freedom, he wrote her an impulsive letter, hinting at the truth, reviewing the issue of his enlistment, and proposing they break off their engagement on grounds of incompatibility.

He immediately regretted the letter and haunted the post-office, dreading her reply. A thick envelope arrived. He opened it with a sick feeling, believing it contained all of his letters being returned. Instead, Dorothy asked him to forgive her selfishness for trying to interpose her love between him and his career.

Faust read the words through tears. "Of one thing I am certain," he wrote back fervently, "I was made to love only one woman and that woman was you."

He and Fish were now engaged in basic hospital training, but all the while Faust was producing serious poetry—thirty-eight poems sent to various magazines, thirty-eight poems sent back.

The two adventurers quickly became dissatisfied with hospital life. Nothing had lasting significance that did not lead to front-line combat, and the 62nd Battalion seemed stuck in Vancouver. Fish obtained an honorable discharge by buying his way out of the army (then a legal practice in Canada—fifteen dollars was a standard fee) in order to enlist in a volunteer ambulance unit being formed in New York. Faust, intending to follow, got involved in a series of complicated adventures.

He was unable or unwilling to obtain a discharge, though Fish had sent him money. Instead he decided to desert and head for the U.S. But he spent too much time saying a liquid farewell to friends in Vancouver before boarding the boat for Victoria, B.C., and Seattle, U.S.A. A policeman recognized him and telegraphed ahead to Victoria, where Faust found a reception committee composed of "large-sided detectives in formidable overcoats" awaiting him when the boat docked. He was placed under arrest and taken back to Vancouver.

Following ten days in jail he was given the choice of buying his discharge or spending two years in prison. He bought the discharge, but it left him completely without money, so he attempted to reenlist in order to keep moving toward the front, or at least eastward.

The military authorities were at first glad to see him again—casualties were high in France at the time—but they found themselves obliged to reject him on physical grounds. A too-conscientious doctor had discovered a slight disability, a varicocele. It was the result of an injury incurred as a boy while riding horseback.

The doctor's findings left Faust stranded in Vancouver with no prospects but the bleak snow-covered scenery of a February day. After several such days subsisting on a diet of bread and milk, and several more of straight water, he was somewhat thinner and considerably more desperate.

His only negotiable assets were youth and vigor. Again he tried to persuade the military to take him, and a deal was consummated whereby they admitted him to a military hospital to have an operation on the varicocele, thus making him fit for service.

From February 18 to March 2, 1916, Faust was hospitalized in Vancouver. Emerging fit for duty, he enlisted for overseas service in the American Battalion, known as the American Legion, of the Canadian Army, and on March 4 left Vancouver by troop train for points east.

At Toronto he caught up with the Legion, which was quartered in the machinery building of the Canadian National Exposition Grounds. Immediately he felt at home. This first American Legion had been formed at the instigation of the American Club of Toronto and consisted of 1,200 men, all volunteers. Included were soldiers of fortune, professional mercenaries, ex-convicts, sincere idealists, men escaping from their past, college boys out for adventure. They were known as "Americans who were not too proud to fight" and had become a celebrated sight parading along the main streets of Toronto on Sundays, many of them wearing U.S. Army, Navy, or Marine Corps uniforms under their Canadian greatcoats.

"We're fifty percent hoboes, fifty percent old U.S. Army men, and I reckon the terms are synonymous," Faust told Dorothy. "Anyway, it's a great aggregation of the unshaven. A group picture looks like an excerpt from the rogue's gallery. But I like the gang."

It was the broad slice of humanity that would later be his chief audience. He found that the best way to hold its interest during barracks bull sessions was to "lie back on your elbows and tell every lie you ever heard from your chest out. If you're interesting, no questions asked. If you're not interesting they go to sleep. It's a great test." So he perfected his narrative style.

Legion members found him scowling, tough, aloof, different. Though he joined the general good times, the singing and fish fries on the beach, he was always removed from those around him. He carried a sheaf of papers with him constantly and spent every spare moment writing. He worked hard at poetry, trying to finish the Tristram-Iseult epic before going overseas.

Faust was learning semaphore and Morse code and had been named gunner in an elite machine gun section commanded by Tracy Richardson, a veteran adventurer and soldier of fortune. Having committed himself to experiencing war, Faust found delay irksome, even though the Legion had moved on to Nova Scotia and a camp near Aldershot. Fish wrote from France that his ambulance unit was in action under fire. "Big air battle above our station today. Two German planes down, ten engaged. We are just behind the lines and are working twenty to thirty hours at a stretch. Where is Heinie?"

The scheduled sailing of the American Legion for Europe in the summer of 1916 had become an international issue. The prospect of an American unit fighting on the Allied side while the U.S. was still officially neutral became embarrassing to Washington. The departure of the Legion was postponed indefinitely.

Legionnaire reaction at most levels was bitter. Word circulated that enlisted personnel could go absent without leave and enlist in some unit not so entangled in red tape. Against this background, Faust decided to desert, make his way to New York, enroll in the ambulance service, and join Fish in the action in France.

It was comparatively easy to secure civilian clothes—black sateen shirt, blue overalls, and a cap—and carry them in a paper bag to some woods at the outskirts of camp. Hidden in the undergrowth, he stood looking down at his uniform in a heap on the ground. For a moment he felt like a traitor. Then once more he turned his back on conventional society. He began walking toward the U.S. border, a hundred miles away.

During the last week in July he walked across Nova Scotia and New Brunswick, traveling mostly at night, dodging the law. He knew that the penalty for a second desertion in wartime might be death. Luck favored him until he reached the Maine border, where he came to a guarded bridge. There seemed no way to cross without detection. Men of military age in civilian clothes were likely to be questioned by the armed sentry. But he waited until the sentry's back was turned, mingled with passers-by, and walked boldly across unchallenged.

Safe on American soil, he hiked south through the deep woods of the Maine back country, slept in barns or haystacks, worked for meals on isolated farms, cut wood, shocked hay. One day there was an eclipse of the sun and the solid Maine farmers with whom he was working said, "This is no time for us to be away from our families!" and they went home, leaving Faust alone in the fields until the sun shone again.

He reached the coast at Bangor and shipped as stoker on a cargo vessel bound for New York. Shoveling coal in the now familiar routine, he arrived in Manhattan in late August, 1916. France and the battlefield seemed almost within reach.

5.

NEW YORK

DURING his first night in New York, Faust slept in a seaman's home near the Bowery. The next morning he went to the Volunteer Ambulance Service on 40th Street, sure that he would be enrolled. Much to his astonishment, they refused him. The service was recruited largely from graduates of Harvard, Yale, and Princeton; typical candidates were gentlemanly Ivy Leaguers, though Ernest Hemingway got in. Faust, in blue jeans and black shirt, did not seem the right type.

Rejected once more, he went to the British Consulate and tried to enlist in the British Army, but there his German name was held against him. They even suggested he might be a spy, and he was practically thrown into the street.

Now thoroughly rebuffed and acutely short of money, Faust found a job as laborer in a subway construction project at Beekman and William streets and took a room at the Bowery YMCA. He had momentarily abandoned hope of getting to the front, when one evening he read a newspaper article by Will Irwin describing the work of American ambulances in France. It revived his determination. He went back to the office of the ambulance service.

"I was eloquent. They told me that I seemed like a STALWART YOUNG MAN with a lot of ENDURANCE which is what they call in the disgusting West GUTS. And I told them to cut out the BULL which they did by telling me that all I needed was a dozen strong letters of recommendation from notable people and a few volumes of incidentals. I said that sounded nice and started home for my typewriter. In five hours I had the letters

39

written—16 of them. Then I went to the corner and posted the junk and ate a hearty ten-cent meal of spoiled hamburger and damaged potatoes at Busy Jack's Lunch."

Among Faust's letters was one to Charles Seeger, professor of music at the University of California. Seeger replied, "I have decided that I cannot write the letter you desire, in the first place, because I do not know you well enough; in the second place, because I do not particularly approve of anyone's becoming 'Kannonenfleisch,' and thirdly, because I just lost my brother in the Somme offensive."

The brother was Alan Seeger whose "I Have a Rendezvous With Death" was to become a minor classic of war poetry.

When Faust's new approach to the ambulance service proved fruitless, he got a job handling freight in the basement of Wanamaker's department store. There he decided to mount a counteroffensive. He would break into the New York writing world here and now. He had planned to make such an attempt after the war, but since the war would not accept him, he decided to make it at once. It might be a shortcut to fame, money, Dorothy.

He made fruitless visits to several newspaper offices in search of employment, got in touch with Sidney Howard who was studying playwriting at Harvard, and they discussed collaborating in the writing of a theatrical pageant to be produced in Detroit; but none of this led to anything except living on a reduced budget.

For a time Faust lived in a room on East 115th Street in what is now Harlem. For several weeks he lived with Garnet Holme, an actor, in Holme's studio on Washington Square. Holme was an Englishman who had toured the United States with the Ben Greet Company, which played only Shakespeare and specialized in outdoor performances. Faust had met him at Berkeley. Faust also lived for a time in the apartment of a poor Jewish rabbi where he sublet a room. The apartment was located on the Lower East Side and gave a young writer insight into New York's lessprivileged Jewish community, a community he incorporated later into one of his frequently reprinted short stories, *Our Daily Bread*, also titled *The Thief*. After several months of such moving around, consciously or subconsciously gathering material he could use in writing, Faust returned to the Bowery YMCA.

His YMCA room was a tiny cubicle containing a bed, chair, table, and a rented typewriter. He often returned to it in the evening laden with volumes from the New York Public Library. His reading list included John Stuart Mill's *Liberty*, Nietzsche's *Thus Spake Zarathustra*, Spencer's *First Principles*, Darwin on evolution, Huxley on biology, Marx on capital, Kant, Cardinal Newman, Locke on human understanding, and Hume's theory of knowledge. As in college, he devoted most of the night to writing and reading. He greatly admired Balzac, identifying himself strongly with the French popular writer's struggles as a commercial hack, his soaring ambition, his vast generosity, his unlimited appetite for experience.

Giants and giantism preoccupied Faust. His forthright hero worship was apparently due in part to compensation for early deprivation, and partly due to natural inclination. Certainly a giant effort had been needed to overcome his handicaps. He said later that he wholly agreed with Nietzche that excellence could be developed only by a constant struggle against mediocrity, and for guidance he had chosen people who had excelled greatly.

One night in mid-November, 1916, Faust was having supper at Busy Jack's on Skid Row with a Berkeley friend, John Schoolcraft, who had entered graduate school at Yale. They were eating a fifteen-cent meal composed chiefly of beans. That morning Faust had mailed off his usual quota of poems to magazine editors. He was spending a substantial portion of his Wanamaker's earnings on stamps, envelopes, and typewriter paper, but most of his incoming mail was rejection slips.

During the afternoon he had visited the Metropolitan Museum of Art for the first time and selected a small painting by Memling as the object of his enthusiasm. He had also seen Greek antiquities and in particular a grave stele. The stele had given rise to the opening lines of a poem he hoped was good, and in the hustle and bustle of Busy Jack's he read it aloud:

> Along the gallery the dead endure
> In stone, cat-headed goddesses of Nile
> Or Roman busts in gloomy porphyry,
> Until I come to the radiant place
> Of Sostrate bending her lovely head . . .

People at nearby tables turned their heads. Poetry was not a regular item on the menu at Jack's, and the speaker's voice was unusually deep and resonant. Faust was wearing a secondhand suit for which he had paid three dollars. The coat was much too small and was bleached a light mouse color. The trousers ended far above his ankles. His shirt was the black sateen model acquired in Nova Scotia. He looked like a bum, and evidently sounded a little crazy, but he had a sense of being on the verge of success.

Following the supper and an economical walk with Schoolcraft through the New York streets in lieu of entertainment that might cost money, Faust returned to his room.

Not having anything else to read at the moment, he took a Gideon Bible from the dresser drawer. It was virtually his first encounter with Holy Writ. Almost the first words he focused on were, "Seek and ye shall find. Knock and it shall be opened to you."

The passage seemed to have been written especially for him. Two days later he received a letter from William Rose Benét, poet, critic, and assistant editor of the prestigious *Century Magazine.*

"I find that three of your poems," said Benét, " 'The Jester's Song,' 'In Our Humiliation,' and 'Golgotha,' were returned to you on November 10. In regard to the enclosed poems, we like the one about the rain, but we are sorry to say we cannot use either of them just now. Please keep trying us."

Faust was nearly overwhelmed at this first notice from an editor, especially one so highly placed.

A few days later Benét accepted a poem. Perhaps more to the point, he paid fifty dollars for it, a remarkable payment for poetry at any time. The poem dealt with the death of Faust's father. The father's tragic failure now helped his son toward success.

> They drew the blinds down, and the house was old
> With shadows, and so cold—
> Filled up with shuddery silence like held breath;
> And when I asked, they told
> Me only that the quietness was death.
>
> And afterward, with no one there to see,
> I got up quietly
> And stole along the hall in my bare feet
> Until it seemed to me
> That all the air grew sorrowful and sweet.
>
> There was an oblong box and at its base
> Grew lilies, in a vase
> As white as they. I thought them very tall
> In such a listening place,
> And they threw fearful shadows on the wall.
>
> And all at once I knew death is a thing
> That stoops down, whispering
> A dear, forgotten secret in your ear
> Such as the winds can sing,
> And then you sleep, and dream, and have no fear.

Cashing Benét's check, Faust hurried toward the Greenwich Village room occupied by his friend Garnet Holme, handing a dollar bill to a beggar en route.

"Holme, you bastard," exclaimed Faust with his usual unprofane profanity, "come help me celebrate! I've just sold a poem. Look!"

They went to the nearest bar. Good whiskey burned down Faust's throat for the first time in months. A cab took them in search of the best dinner in town. Faust decided it should be at the exclusive Plaza Hotel. By now he was uproariously drunk, and when they reached the Plaza they were refused admission. Holme dissuaded the tattered and reeling poet from all-out assault on liveried doorman and bellboys and led him away to the nearest lunch counter.

Faust's fifty dollars dwindled rapidly. It did not matter, because another miracle of good fortune soon occurred.

In anger and frustration while working in the subway, Faust had written a letter to the *New York Times* demanding to know whether a subterranean existence was the best that society could offer a young man who had spent four years in a good university. The letter attracted the attention of the mother of a college friend, Clemens Moffett. Mrs. Moffett was Mark Twain's sister. Her husband had been a member of the staff of the *New York Sun*, and she provided Faust with a letter of introduction to Robert H. Davis, chief executive of the multifarious Frank A. Munsey publishing interests, which included the *Sun* as well as other newspapers and a number of magazines.

Faust took the letter of introduction to Davis' office, high in the Munsey Building at 280 Broadway. Still elated by his success with Benét, he felt that no matter what confronted him he would be able to overcome it.

Robert Davis may not have been the greatest of American editors but he was among the most colorful. A westerner born in Nebraska, he had moved at an early age to Nevada and tasted the frontier. His breeziness and gusto, plus a vast store of anecdote, were drawn in part from life on the Comstock Lode, the fabulous mining region where Mark Twain had flourished a few years before him. Davis had followed in some of the footsteps of Mark Twain. His first job had been that of compositor on the *Carson Appeal*. He had been employed by the leading San Francisco newspapers and, coming to New York in 1896, had held important posts on the *Journal American*, Sunday *World*, and Sunday *News*. In 1905 he became associated with Frank Munsey, and for the rest of his life, with some interruptions, he worked with and for the Munsey interests.

Though now overseer of a host of pulp magazines (called pulp because they were printed on the unglazed newsprint known as "pulp")—such as *All-Story Weekly, Scrap Book, Railroad Man's Magazine, Woman, The Ocean, The Live Wire, The Cavalier*— Davis' interests went far beyond pulp. He was honorary president of the Stevenson Society, had bought some of Joseph Conrad's early output, and claimed to have helped Conrad rewrite *Victory*. He was among the first to detect talent in O. Henry, whom he persuaded to write introductions to articles in the *World* (and whom he had to dun furiously for copy, Henry being flagrantly lazy about production). Davis had helped bring about a revival of interest in the work of Samuel Butler, author of *The Way of All Flesh* and *Erewhon*. He had written and published several plays, as well as biographies of O. Henry and of Robert Prometheus Fitzsimmons, holder of the world's heavyweight boxing championship. Such writers as Upton Sinclair, Edgar Rice Burroughs, E. Phillips Oppenheim, Mary Roberts Rinehart, and John Buchan had appeared in his magazines. So it was no ordinary editor who faced Faust that morning.

"You're supposed to be able to write?" growled Davis when he had perused the letter of introduction, fixing Faust with an ever-present cigar and an arctic stare, "Well, let's see if you can."

Davis was as big around as a barrel and had a longish nose and small, twinkling eyes that were now frosty. He reserved his most negative moods for young men of supposed literary talent bearing letters of introduction from well-intentioned females.

"Here's a plot," Davis continued, handing out a sheet of paper he felt sure would rid him of his unwelcome visitor. "There's an empty room down the hall with a typewriter and a ream of paper in it. Go down there, if you like, and see if you can write a story. Third door on your right."

Faust read the plot: "Two young crooks, one male, one female, are converted to honesty by love and the kind deed of a man who is about to be robbed of the assay papers describing a certain mine." It was what Davis called "the old sure-fire regeneration stuff," popular with readers of a dozen Munsey-produced magazines.

Faust looked at the clock. It was a little before ten.

"Will you be here till five?" he asked.

"I may be here till midnight."

"Till five will do," said Faust coolly and walked out with the paper in hand.

At ten minutes before five Faust emerged from the room down the hall with his story. He had made the two young crooks members of the same underworld gang. He had put them unknown to each other in a hospital situation, the man an emergency patient with a gunshot wound in his head, the girl his night nurse. The hero's face and eyes were entirely bandaged. The heroine had no idea who he was, and he could not see her. He fell in love with her voice, touch, movements, presence. When the bandages came off there was an unraveling of more than gauze. In the end, love won and morals were regenerated. It all happened in six and a half hours of furious typing.

Davis was flabbergasted. At best he had expected a short work of unacceptable clumsiness. Instead he was handed a seventy-eight-hundred-word story, publishable then and still readable today. It was a feat of legerdemain, not quite believable.

"Where did you learn to write?" Davis asked.

"Third door on the right—down the hall," Faust replied.

It was nearly the truth. He had attempted little prose fiction before that moment. He certainly had published none since *The House of Rulaki* appeared in *The Occident* in 1913. Almost all his imaginative output had been poetry. As he saw Davis' astonishment, a small misgiving mingled with his satisfaction. Success had come almost too easily. The story had cost him little more than the time required to type it.

Davis had no misgiving. He bought the story for $78.00, a penny a word, and started a flood of prose fiction probably unequalled before or since. In the next twenty years Faust was to produce nearly thirty million publishable words.

Some claim that the foregoing account of Faust's first encounter with Davis is apocryphal to the extent that he took the plot home and worked a couple of days before submitting the story. Whatever the fact, the principle remains. The pent-up energies of an organism born to write were now set free. Faust was in promised land. The doors described in the scriptural passage he had read in the Gideon Bible had opened wide. At long last it seemed he had escaped from the valley from which he had been fleeing.

The Secret, the poem about his father, appeared in the *Century* for February, 1917. It was printed alone on two pages, set off by decorative art, and centrally located in the issue. *Convalescence*, the story about the two crooks, appeared in *All-Story Weekly*, a Davis-Munsey pulp magazine, in March. Both the story and the poem were signed Frederick Faust.

6.

A YOUNG WRITER

WITH the publication of his verse and prose, two heavens opened before Faust. The one he wanted most to enter was represented by Benét. The one he must enter if he were to eat regularly, marry, and do other things he considered a normal part of life was represented by Davis.

He had only fleeting illusions about supporting a wife and children by writing poetry. But with his new-found talent for producing salable prose fiction—a talent he regarded as a kind of trick—he saw that he might support himself while writing poetry, marry Dorothy, and establish a family.

He seems to have been by nature a family man. There were in addition the deep-seated needs for status and security which a family represented to him and which sprang from the tragic experiences of his childhood.

But would writing commercial prose debase his poetic talent, destroy his integrity? As far back as college he had decided that prose was inferior to poetry and that he would never try to write it seriously. He pondered the matter as he sat in his newly occupied but drearily furnished room behind an old brownstone front at 169 East 63rd Street. There was the example of Balzac who had begun much as he was beginning. Balzac had survived by producing what would later be called pulp fiction at the rate of a book a month, in order to write better later. Faust believed he could do the same, except that he would write poetry later. Davis had shown him the way to make money. He felt he could produce and sell, but he would remain a poet. Hadn't Goethe and others written prose while remaining primarily poets? Hadn't he earned his first professional writing money by means of poetry? He decided to enter both heavens at once. He would write both poetry and prose.

But Benét was already cautioning him, "Interesting to hear you are writing prose for Mr. Davis. Don't let him lure you away from better things, though!"

Benét was a perennial encourager of young writers and a defender of literary shrines against what he considered the philistinism represented by Davis. Benét liked to invite Faust and others, including his younger brother Stephen Vincent, already publishing verse though still at Yale, and his sister Laura, soon to produce her first volume of poetry, to the cottage at Port Washington, Long Island, for food, drink, and talk. There one might meet Philip Barry, the promising playwright; Henry Seidel Canby, the scholar and critic; or Sinclair Lewis, a publishing house employee with ambitions to become a writer. Benét had been a California resident while his father was commander of the U.S. Army arsenal at Benicia, not far from Berkeley, and he had been a close friend of Leonard Bacon, and possibly it was through Bacon that Benét first heard of Faust. In any event, Benét went out of his way to make the young writer from the West feel at home.

A second and third story appeared in *All-Story Weekly*, both signed Frederick Faust. For subsequent stories, Faust stopped signing his true name to his prose fiction, intending to reserve it for poetry. Meanwhile, with the help of the playwright Sophie Treadwell, wife of W. O. (Bill) McGeehan, a sports writer for the *New York Herald Tribune*, Faust had devised a pen name for his prose. Miss Treadwell advanced the theory that a good pen name should consist of two monosyllables with the same vowel sound in each. During a party at the McGeehans' apartment, the subject came up. In committee, Miss Treadwell leading, all present produced "Max Brand." The name contained the necessary vowel duplication and monosyllabic requirements. Someone remarked that it sounded Jewish. This was a time when to be Jewish was to be rejected in many circles, but it was also a time when such barriers were beginning to break down. Faust accepted the pseudonym and a drink confirmed the selection.

The name was then and later the source of some amusement and even embarrassment to the man concealed behind it. Faust often referred to himself jokingly as "The Jewish cowboy." If the term didn't fit his concept of Frederick Faust, tragic poet, at least he could laugh at it.

The most significant thing happening to him now was the inner conflict formalized by the decision to sign a false name to his prose and his true name to his poetry. Though he did not realize it, the two signatures spelled out a division that was to grow and grow. The overpowering fact of the moment, however, was success. A distinguished editor-poet and a prominent editor-publishing executive were bidding for his work.

He still had no accurate conception of the golden flood that lay ahead. After finishing a story his mind was a total blank, he said later, and he believed that he would never have another plot idea, never be able to write another word. But faced with a deadline, he was able to produce.

He spent his earnings lavishly. There were costly dinners at good restaurants, huge tips to waiters and hatcheck girls, debts paid off—including the fifty dollars to Thomas Downey back in California—and there were indiscriminate loans and gifts to friends in need. He roamed New York with the pockets of a new overcoat—the first he had ever owned—stuffed with paper money.

Women found Faust as attractive as ever. One, believing herself profoundly in love, wanted to have a child by him. The fact that she was already married did not seem to matter, at least to her. His amorous escapades began to parallel his other adventures. He told one friend of having to spend half a night in a closet when a girl's roommate came home unexpectedly. He did not tell Dorothy. Dorothy was the nice girl who did not need to know. He had long proclaimed adherence to what he called the European concept of sexual morality. Americans knew it better as the double standard: promiscuity for men, chastity for women —at least for so-called nice women.

Whatever the label, Faust continued to follow the practice. And he continued to sublimate experience in elaborate dreams, speculating to Dorothy about their ideal marriage in the not-too-distant future, now that he had rejected the idea of immediate enlistment and was becoming a successful writer.

At the same time he was being confronted by the realities of membership in a persecuted minority group. As the war progressed, feeling was rising sharply against Americans with German names or German blood. Faust had German blood and his name could hardly be more German.

Bob Davis talked to him about such things in fatherly fashion. He advised Faust to control his drinking, spending, and love affairs and to stop feeling guilty about his German blood. Davis had been married twenty years and had wanted children but had had none. In Faust he found a foster son. Davis urged him to meet the right girl and get married. Faust told him about Dorothy, and Davis decided to encourage the match.

When money began to come in regularly, Faust stabilized his living in the room on East 63rd Street, part of the dilapidated premises operated by a Mrs. Murphy, a widow fresh from Ireland. Almost every day she entered his room and stood with wash-reddened hands wrapped in her dirty apron, and worried aloud lest the young man ruin his health spending such long hours at the typewriter. Six, eight, ten hours at a time went by.

When Faust did leave his work it was not always for the best. Proximity to Third Avenue was good and bad. To the good was Joe's Restaurant, later called Original Joe's, where he could get a fish dinner for 25 cents, a pot-roast dinner for 35 cents, a chicken dinner—most sumptuous of all—for 45 cents. On the less good side—though it provided material for fiction—was a colorful saloon life with strong Irish flavor. Like other newspapermen and writers, Faust found this life particularly attractive and was continually short of money because of it.

Once in that winter of 1916–17, he spent his last bit of change on a loaf of bread and a jar of jam and carried them toward Garnet Holme's studio apartment. Crossing Washington Square, he slipped and dropped the jar. "Some day I'll show you where," he wrote Dorothy, "perhaps some of the stain is still there. I scraped up the jam, trying to keep the broken glass out of it, put the jam into the bag that had held the jar, and went on."

He and Dorothy were still engaged, or so he thought. However, she was less than beguiled by his periodic silences, gusts of sudden attention, tales of high adventure and important people—all three thousand miles away from her. She had left college and was living at home in Yuba City, quite ready for marriage.

Meanwhile the United States had broken diplomatic relations with Germany. On April 2, 1917, President Wilson stood before Congress in Washington, and—while Davis and Faust, in New York, plotted a new novel called *The Homecoming of Lazy Purdue*—Wilson asked for a declaration of war on Germany.

Faust was riding the elevated when he read the headlines. He said that passengers remained calm, brooding in the private worlds to which subway and elevated passengers normally retreat. No flags waved. No whistles blew. He inwardly reaffirmed a decision made the week before Wilson's congressional address. He would go to California, marry Dorothy, bring her to New York, establish her in an apartment, write furiously and put some money in the bank, then enlist in the U.S. Army. He felt himself entitled to a month or two of respite, having been rejected by enlistment offices so often.

In his haste he failed to keep Dorothy abreast of his thinking. When he arrived in California in mid-May, 1917, he found she had broken off their engagement and was about to marry a young lawyer approved by parents and friends.

The sequences building to a romantic climax in Yuba City read like a passage from one of Faust's later novels. They began with a letter from Faust to W. T. Dewart, business manager of the Munsey Company, written before Faust left New York.

"Please be kind enough to pay to Robert Davis, Trustee, all moneys due me for motion picture rights negotiated by the Frank A. Munsey Company, from this date and day, until I return from San Francisco, sometime in the month of June."

Next came a telegram from Davis to Faust, Faust on the Overland Limited speeding westward. "Picture contract closed. Two thousand on account. Balance sixty days. Advise as to your movements."

Next came a telegram from Faust—in Yuba City—to Davis. "Game is won. Nearly broke."

Next was a memo from Davis to Dewart. "On the first motion picture contract, Faust's share is $1200. Telegraph him $500 to Yuba City, California. Deposit to his account with the Frank A. Munsey Company, at 5% the sum of $500. Take up the tag standing against his name for railroad transportation from New York to San Francisco, in the sum of $114.50. Repay the cost of telegraphing $500 to Yuba City. Pay balance in check to R. H. Davis, Trustee."

Under such an onslaught, the young lawyer was forced to retire from the field. Having won the game and the girl, Faust retired to the Shattuck Hotel in Berkeley, while Dorothy made preparations for a hasty wedding.

"Four thousand words today," Faust wrote her from his hotel room on May 25 when he had finished typing his daily quota of fiction. He said he had had lunch at the University Club with Leonard Bacon, during which, he swore, he had partaken of no alcoholic beverages. He was abstaining "at least till after our marriage."

Revisiting the University of California campus, he found himself something of a celebrity. His work was still appearing in *The Occident*. A poem was scheduled for the coming September, and another was to appear as late as March, 1918. It was pleasing to return in triumph after having left in disgrace; but he stoutly resisted all temptations to celebrate unduly, and instead pointed out to Dorothy that only ninety-six hours remained before their marriage.

They were married on May 29, 1917, his twenty-fifth birthday, in the Schillig home on "B" Street, the Reverend Mark Rifenbark of the Episcopal Church officiating.

Dorothy's father, Lawrence Schillig, a conservative lawyer, had opposed the marriage initially and was not keen for it now. He foresaw a precarious existence for his daughter, married to a harum-scarum writer and former campus reprobate. His wife, Belle, however, had liked Faust from their first meeting. She saw something promising in the young man who had ridden out of the East on the Overland Limited and carried away a bride.

Yuba City was rudely shaken. So were other quarters. Friends who had known Faust in college and elsewhere, hearing of the unorthodox manner of his marriage, recalled his nickname, "Fabulous Faust." His legend was growing.

Dorothy had little idea what lay ahead. She scarcely knew the controversial figure she had married. His determination had made the marriage seem inevitable. But underlying was the fact that they had loved each other at first sight.

"I see in you my perfect woman," he informed her. "Guenevere, the queen; Sappho, the poetess; Aspasia, the mistress; and Mary Smith—healthy, wholesome mother, U.S.A.!"

Dorothy was nearly overwhelmed on several levels. She had been reared in strict Victorianism about sex, for example. Until she was in college, she had thought babies were born through the navel. She said later that all she knew about sex she had learned from Faust and that he "had been wonderful"—explaining it all to her and being very patient.

Aboard the Sunset Limited, bound for New Orleans, the newlyweds were supremely happy. When the boat from New Orleans docked in New York, Faust delivered the second installment of a new novel to Davis.

The wedding had been financed by the sale of motion picture rights in a story called *Fate's Honeymoon*.

7.

IN UNIFORM AT LAST

THE FAUSTS' first home was a high-ceilinged studio on Gramercy Park South, belonging to Jules Guerin, an artist and designer who had been consultant to the 1915 Panama-Pacific Exposition in San Francisco. The apartment had been leased to Winifred Rieber, herself an artist, wife of Professor Charles Rieber of the University of California philosophy department, and she had loaned it to the Fausts.

Though charming, the premises were too large for their needs, and the feeling of being in other people's quarters was uncomfortable. They quickly found a three-room apartment of their own at 49 East 10th Street, the property of a French-born woman who operated a tearoom in the basement. There were not enough chairs, but one of their first purchases was a player piano. They liked to set it on automatic and dance to "Alexander's Ragtime Band." Practicality was from the first a minor consideration.

Faust retained his bachelor quarters at Mrs. Murphy's on East 63rd Street. The bride's first visit to these earlier haunts was something of a shock. He had spoken of old-world charm, and Dorothy had expected a gracious room hung with chintz, carpeted with wine velvet, brass at the fireplace, perhaps a bit of antique silver winking here and there. The realities of stained and yellowing wallpaper, a cracked ceiling, a white iron bedstead, a dirty backyard, and of Mrs. Murphy herself were eye-openers. Then and later Faust said little about his painful childhood, ordeals in the valley or in Canada, or his struggles in New York. He wanted to forget them. "Human beings don't benefit from poverty and degradation," he replied summarily in response to Dorothy's questioning.

His room at Mrs. Murphy's became the first of several offices away from home. The distractions were minimal, those of his own household were compelling. For a writer dedicated to supporting a family at the rate of a penny a word, optimum working conditions were essential.

Faust's program for the future was enough to test the strongest mettle: establish himself in his market, accumulate a bank account and an earning rate sufficient to care for his wife and the child they wanted, and then enlist in the Army. He was under severe emotional pressures. Severest of all was Dorothy's unspoken pleading not to leave her and go off to war. She had decided to say little, but he well knew how she felt. Nevertheless he continued to regard enlistment as fulfillment of a personal commitment and as a patriotic duty.

Benét and his circle continued to encourage Faust's writing, but Davis had the greater influence. Davis was delighted as salable copy rolled in as if from a vending machine. Drop in a small idea; shake the hand; three days later the first installment of a book-length serial appeared and the second was clearly outlined. The copy was so clean it went straight to the printer. There was next to no overhead. It was machine-like production. It was in keeping with current business trends. But the assembling of raw materials, the production, the finishing of the product—all were done by one man.

Faust had taught himself to type swiftly and accurately, using the newspaperman's two-fingered hunt-and-peck method, both fists flying. His hands were stubby-fingered and splayed at the ends as if for better purchase or touch. He literally punched out words on the typewriter.

A second market opened. Down the hall from Davis' office in the many-corridored Munsey Building was a cubicle in which sat Robert Simpson, editor of *Argosy Magazine*, an earnest, sandy, very bald man, with pale blue eyes. Simpson, a Scot, had lived on the African Gold Coast, been a trader and traveler, and was something of a writer himself. He was eager to buy the historical romances which Faust was anxious to write and which Davis cared little for, though Davis had published one or two in order to keep the vending machine in production.

Argosy was a magazine of established reputation. It had been one of the first all-fiction magazines to appear in the U.S. and had published such writers as O. Henry, James Branch Cabell, William MacLeod Raine, Albert Payson Terhune, Frederick Van Rennsselaer Day, who wrote the "Nick Carter" stories, and P. G. Wodehouse.

Faust wrote a historical novel, *The Sword Lover*, which Simpson published as a serial in *Argosy* under the Max Brand pseudonym in November, 1917. It dealt with eighteenth-century England in the time of George III. It was limited in scope and depth but showed unmistakable power, imagery, conviction. No one expected it to be a masterpiece, least of all Faust. If it entertained and rang the cash register, that was enough.

Davis had no objection to his writers working for other Munsey editors such as Simpson, providing they did it under names other than those used in Davis' pet *All-Story Weekly*; but he thought that Faust had better start marketing his varied products in separate packages or the public would become confused when the same author offered them a historical romance one week and a contemporary underworld thriller the next.

A second pen name evolved—John Frederick. It was attached to a historical novel, *The Double Crown* (written in collaboration with Schoolcraft), which appeared in *Argosy* in 1918. Faust planned to make John Frederick his historical-fiction pen name, but the volume of his output and the demands of editors and publishers eventually obliged him to evolve several others as well.

He now realized that the only practical limit to his publication was the time it took him to type a story, serial, or book. He was in effect Aladdin and had been handed a magic lamp. All he needed to do was rub it and a magic future would unfold, a future that included that shining land beyond the mountains which he had dreamed of as a boy and as a young man. It included the writing of poetry and prose. No Faust of legend could have wished for more.

As Faust contemplated this future he foresaw many kinds of stories published in many kinds of magazines. He would sign them with many names, and no one would know who really had written them. Books would follow. So would films. And all the while his incognito would be protected and he would live the kind of life he wanted and become the kind of man he wanted to be.

At the end of nine months of writing Faust had earned $8,281, an astonishing sum for a beginning writer to make in three quarters of a year in those days.

Further evidence to support his vision of the future quickly appeared. It was a film based on his story, *The Adopted Son*, released by Metro Pictures Corporation on October 17, 1917. It starred the famous Francis X. Bushman and a prominent leading lady, Beverly Bayne. *Motion Picture News* reported that *The Adopted Son* was making a hit in most sections of the country. It was based on the *All-Story* novelette that Faust and Davis were plotting when President Wilson spoke to Congress in April: Lazy Purdue leaves Texas hurriedly as the result of a shooting affray and finds that the train he has jumped aboard has brought him to the Tennessee mountains and deposited him in the middle of a feud. The feud is finally settled when Purdue reveals himself to be a member of one of the warring families. By his marriage to the heroine, enemies are united and peace reigns.

Metro had bought the story several months in advance of publication. Two more films were in the making at two other studios.

Faust continued to spend extravagantly. He paid $1,500 for an Oriental rug, and bought Dorothy a silver coffee pot. They were like two children in wonderland.

He was, furthermore, working hard at something new and different, a novel about the American West; and he had sub-

mitted his long poem on the Tristram-Iseult theme to Henry
Seidel Canby, author, critic, and Yale professor. Canby conducted
classes in writing attended by such promising beginners as Archibald MacLeish, Britten Hadden and Henry Luce, who were to
become founders of *Time* magazine, Thornton Wilder, Stephen
Vincent Benét, Philip Barry, and others. Though Canby was an
academic, he had a strong sense for the kind of imaginative writing that could be published on the current popular market, and
neither he nor members of his clientele seem to have had any
objection to writing for money. Thornton Wilder recalled nearly
fifty years later the deep impression Faust's astonishing production of this period made on him. Benét appears to have been
equally impressed.

In submitting his Tristram-Iseult epic to Canby for criticism,
Faust hoped for recognition and publication of a major poetic
work. Canby, whom he had met through the Benéts, was kind but
firm. By way of post mortem, Faust commented, "Canby must
have damned near laughed himself to death. I don't know how it
is but I'm always turning loose a lot of junk about 'soul' and
'passion' and 'eyes' and 'lips', etc. Jesus, the Tristram is really a
hell of a mess. I thought there was something in it, and there is—
words. I've cut out six thousand lines and it's still crude. However, I'm going to try it on Putnam."

His natural optimism bore him up. He decided to show Canby,
William Rose Benét, and others that they were wrong, that he
could write both prose and poetry successfully. But first he would
keep his commitment to action.

With Bill McGeehan he was considering joining the much-
discussed Roosevelt Division. It was to be composed entirely of
volunteers and to be commanded by the former President. It
would go into action in France immediately. Faust realized
Roosevelt's charge with the Rough Riders in the Spanish-
American War wasn't going to be repeated in this war, but he
believed a similar dynamic spirit was necessary. He admired
Roosevelt's commitment to action and his vigorous attacks on

Kaiserism and disliked scholarly Wilson and his "sissified backing into war." He was bitterly disappointed when Wilson forbade formation of the Roosevelt Division.

By now—the winter of 1917–18—many of Faust's contemporaries were in service. Dixie Fish had joined the Air Corps and was engaged in aerial combat in France. Sidney Howard, John Schoolcraft, Archibald MacLeish, both Benéts, and Leonard Bacon were in uniform or in process of getting in. Faust's civilian clothes were beginning to bother him.

He laid firm plans to enlist immediately after the birth of the son, expected at any moment. He and Dorothy were so sure it was to be a boy that they christened him Jim and planned his career up until the time he became a classical scholar, all-American halfback, and budding epic poet.

Faust's own poetry got a boost meanwhile—and Canby's comments on *Tristram* a partial refutation—when the *Literary Digest*—the period's equivalent to *Time* or *Newsweek*—reprinted "The Secret." It appeared on *The Digest's* "Current Poetry Page" in company with verse by John Hall Wheelock and Sara Teasdale.

On the night before the baby arrived, the young couple took the subway to the circus in Madison Square Garden. Dorothy was enormous. Her coat hiked nearly up to her waist when she sat down. The subway passengers smiled. Faust assured her nobody would ever guess she was pregnant.

Next day Jim turned out to be Jane; but Faust put a brave face on the matter, named many of his fictional heroes Jim in years to come, bought cigars for Davis, and consoled Dorothy who feared she had disappointed him. It was she, however, who pronounced the definitive remark on the blessed event. "Dear, maybe a girl is better now, because a boy has to have his father with him all the time, and you must go to war before long."

On his twenty-sixth birthday, which was also his first wedding anniversary, Faust presented himself to his draft board. A kind of merry-go-round began again. The board rejected him because of a recurrence of the varicocele for which he had been operated on in Canada. It strained his credulity and patience to the limit. Fate seemed to intervene every time he took a step toward war, but his determination to enlist remained undiminished. He reached an agreement with the board whereby he would enter a hospital and be operated on at his own expense, and then they would accept him. Dorothy begged him not to go to such unheard of lengths but he was deaf to her entreaties.

While lying in a bed at Roosevelt Hospital recovering from the operation, Faust began writing a ballad based on the legend of St. Christopher. The words came well and before the sun went down he had done four stanzas. Eventually there were sixty-eight.

The poem's central idea is that though Christ may take pity on the weak, he weeps for the strong who like himself must assume the world's burdens. *The Ballad of St. Christopher* was published in *All-Story* in July, 1918, and later in the first book of Faust's collected poems.

While hospitalized he received a letter from the publishing house of Putnam forecasting a great sale for his first book, a western novel titled *The Untamed*. Then Macmillan, another publisher, wrote asking to look at some of his short verse. Four books were in prospect. He seemed about to reach his nearly superhuman goal of providing financial security for a family while publishing serious verse and remunerative prose fiction, and at the same time participating in a war.

During July, Faust recuperated from his operation, worked hard to finish a sequel to *The Untamed*, and completed some short verse. In August he presented himself to his draft board again. By September, 1918, he was in uniform. On September 18, a short poem for children, "My Heroes," appeared in *St. Nicholas Magazine*.

His draft board had promised him immediate shipment to the front line in France. Instead he found himself digging latrines in red Appalachian clay. He had been assigned to the Army Engineers at Camp Humphreys, Virginia (now Fort Belvoir), a few miles from Washington, D. C.

During September and October Faust struggled grimly against the red tape that had placed him in this Siberia instead of in combat. He cited the promises of his draft board and the operation at his own expense. No one listened. He was kept busy digging latrines, carrying boards, picking up cigarette butts. He lived in tents and barracks, learned close-order drill, was issued a rifle, which he loathed—he abhorred guns and shooting. But he learned the manual of arms and the trick of spinning the .30 caliber Springfield around his finger, and he picked up Army talk and attitudes which could be used in stories.

There were 40,000 men in the camp. Assigned to a work detail that seemed to take forever to load a pile of lumber onto a truck, he lost patience and, with the help of the Negro driver, finished the job in five minutes. He refused an opportunity to go to officer training school in favor of remaining an enlisted man. While on K.P. duty he noticed that it took seven men six hours to prepare enough string beans for one meal. Once he was marched out to the parade ground for immediate overseas shipment with a casualty company, without a chance to see Dorothy or the baby, but was marched back again when the shipment was canceled. When Dorothy informed him that she thought she was pregnant he told her to bring on the babies, he would support all of them and her too.

As he raged inwardly and outwardly at what seemed the Army's injustice, Faust felt himself sinking back into what he called the "undistinguished morass of humanity" from which he was trying to escape. "There was never one who came out of the dirty mob and hated his origins more than I do!" he wrote in one of his letters to Dorothy. Yet there were surprising compensations. A tentmate mistaken for a barber of Italian-American descent turned out to be a Russian-Jewish-American singer with a memorable voice. Under the influence of Faust's sympathetic listening, his tentmate "rose, paced the floor, and sang me an aria from *Pagliacci*." It was followed appropriately by a selection from Gounod's *Faust*.

Regular food and exercise kept Faust fit, and he impressed a doctor during a physical examination with his five-and-one-half-inch chest expansion. He tried to enlist the help of the post chaplain in getting a transfer to the combat infantry, but was himself enlisted to write orientation pamphlets about camp life. The chief compensation was free access to a typewriter after working hours. Until now, he had been writing his stories in pencil by candlelight in his tent.

Flu struck him down as he was desperately trying to finish a sequel to *The Untamed* at the rate of forty typewritten pages—12,000 words—per weekend. He entered the infirmary with a fever of 103, a victim of the influenza epidemic of 1918. He wrote Dorothy that her hands were the only cool things he could think of.

Their bank account showed a balance of eighteen dollars. Desperately Faust sat up in bed and, with head reeling, wrote a story about a man with a fever. Back came a check from Davis and a cheery note: "This is very convincing. You really sound like you have a fever yourself."

Visiting New York on convalescent leave, the invalid suffered a relapse and was barely able to drag himself back to camp—to find people dying right and left. He dreaded lest what was happening around him happen to Dorothy or the baby, with him far away and helpless to assist, and he felt bitterly frustrated at having to sit all day Sunday writing a pretty love story in the midst of tragedy.

By November 11, 1918, Faust had at last succeeded in enlisting the help of a friendly major at post headquarters in securing a transfer to the infantry, when the Armistice was declared. He reached New York in time to see employees of the street department sweeping up the waste paper after the celebration.

"I take my hat off to the fellows who got into action in this war," he told Dorothy, "and shall always be humble in their presence. Camp Humphreys, Virginia! What a legacy to hand down to my children!" Even his sister Pauline, he pointed out with chagrin, had succeeded in getting overseas. She had served as an Army nurse in a hospital in Scotland.

Despite his many efforts to become involved, he felt he had failed himself, his country, and the cause of freedom by not getting into combat. In the context of the times, failure to get overseas left him vulnerable, he believed, to charges of shirking and cowardice. It denied him an authenticity he craved, and it kept him from identifying fully with the protagonists of the heroic literature he admired.

He said later on numerous occasions that a man's chief business was fighting of one kind or another and that to die in battle was the best kind of death.

8.

WESTERN NOVELS

Faust was discharged soon after the Armistice and his life quickly took on new patterns. The publication of *The Untamed*, first as an *All-Story* serial beginning in December, 1918, and a few months later in book form, represented a milestone in his writing career because it set his course decidedly toward western stories. Yet the first book had simply reeled off his fingertips along with a variety of shorter prose.

The Untamed is about a larger-than-life hero and the wrath of that hero. Its setting is in some indefinite locality in the Far West at some indefinite time. A young man named Dan Barry, who is partly Faust and partly Homer's Achilles, confronts certain problems, such as a beautiful girl, an ungovernable temper, an invincible ability to kill people when roused to anger, and an uncertainty about the future. Barry is trying to come to grips with himself. He is torn between adventurous freedom (war, action) and love (Dorothy, baby), between civilized society (the here, the now) and unresolved possibilities that lie out yonder where the wild geese call (the possibilities of poetry). Faust felt such forces stirring in himself and was trying to reconcile them, and these forces included a sense for the values he associated with Homer and they also included his murderous attitude toward the Germans which was comparable to Achilles' attitude toward the Trojans.

Myth though it was, *The Untamed*, like true myth, was symbolically true. It was nearly as close as Faust came to the serious fiction he swore never to write.

The novel is also notable for what it did to a native American art form, the western story. In the first paragraphs, classic mythology enters saddle-leather fiction. "Over the shoulder of a hill came a whistling which might have been attributed to the wind, had not this day been deathly calm. It was fit music for such a scene, for it seemed neither of heaven nor earth, but the soul of the great god Pan come back to earth to charm those nameless rocks with his wild, sweet piping." Before the book and its successors were done, Faust had introduced most of the Olympian hierarchy, not to mention Norse gods, Celtic master-spirits, and Arthurian heroes.

Gods and heroes became a trademark of his prose fiction, particularly of his westerns, but they are also found in much of his non-western material.

Faust linked his work to mythology by means of simile, metaphor, and a poetic tone. Zeus, Cuchulain, Odysseus, King Arthur, Helen, Andromache, Aphrodite, Morgan le Fay, Pan, are not present literally but their spirit pervades. Earthly men and women are likened to them and earthly atmosphere to their atmospheres.

Part of his reason for doing so, Faust said, was to achieve classical values of remoteness and timelessness such as Homer achieved in *The Iliad* and Shakespeare in *Hamlet* and other plays. He believed these values enabled an author to use his material more freely and with greater effect.

Sometimes as in *The Untamed* he used mythical and legendary plots. In his novel *Pillar Mountain* (published in 1928) he used the Theseus myth to tell the story of a son who grows up strong enough to move a huge rock, under which an illustrious father has placed the symbols of power—in this case a rifle and a pistol. In *The Garden of Eden* (first published in 1926 in England) there are strong elements of the Odysseus legend-myth. The Oedipal search for a father occurs repeatedly, as in *Trailin'* (1920). The list could be extended to scores of novels and stories.

Perhaps more important than background effect of gods and heroes and borrowing from classical myths was the larger-than-life quality Faust imparted to his major characters and the timelessness he gave his settings. His eminent predecessors in the western field, such as Owen Wister and Zane Grey, had taken pains to fill their work with circumstantial detail. Their characters were often based on actual people. Their settings were frequently historical. Wister's Wyoming was actual Wyoming. Grey claimed to have based all his western heroes on one man, Buffalo Jones, the so-called "Last of the Plainsmen," a genuine frontiersman and buffalo hunter turned preservationist who introduced Grey to the West.

Faust's procedure was just the opposite. His characters existed only in his imagination. His setting was a never-never land. He used a minimum of actual circumstance, partly because it was natural for him to do so, partly because intensive research and personal western experience did not interest him, but chiefly because he was a natural tale teller and wanted to free his work from everyday reality. He had few conscious thoughts about writing myth. The result flowed naturally from his interests and methods.

Thus Whistling Dan Barry and Kate Cumberland of *The Untamed* move in heightened dimensions in a Far West that never was but is clearly recognizable. We are not told whether the story takes place north or south of the Union Pacific tracks or east or west of the Staked Plain. We are not told the time. Such details are immaterial. We know where we are imaginatively, mythologically.

Faust introduced old world myth into the new world West. This—with his poetic approach—is his unique contribution to the western story.

Supporting this contribution, as in *The Untamed*, was a unified vision of experience which made the western part of world literature as it never had been before. Men in chaps and women in gingham were united with gods and goddesses in situations nearly as old as mankind.

A still further contribution took the form of a fast-moving style that was lucid and lyric and focused on action and more action.

Its tempo reflected contemporary tensions which Faust himself had experienced:

The bullet shattered the glass lamp. Thick darkness blotted the room. Instantly thereafter a blow, a groan, and the fall of a body; then a confused clamor.
"He's here!"
"Give up that gun, damn you!"
"You got the wrong man!"
"I'm Bill Flynn!"
"Guard the door!"
"Lights, for God's sake!"
"Help!"

Critics are divided in their opinion of Faust's effect on the western story. Some think he degraded the western and that his influence begins with *The Untamed*. They say he fancified and distorted the genre and is largely responsible for discrediting it as serious literature. This may be true. Certainly he moved the western away from the historical West. In his hands on a good day, however, the American Myth can be seen in the making, as king-sized heroes move in pursuit of queen-sized heroines, on a landscape of mythological dimensions, all of it elevated by a distinctive epic tone.

The critics that say Faust put the western where it belongs, in the realm of myth, may be right.

The Untamed has sold about a million copies in hardcover and soft, has been made into a motion picture twice; and as this is being written, preparations are in progress for a third filming. Originally Tom Mix played the starring role.

But Faust belittled the book. "Daily I thank God in three languages that I write under a pen name," he told Dorothy.

No matter. *The Untamed* was so popular that readers demanded a sequel, and then another. These sequels (*The Night Horseman, The Seventh Man*) appeared first in magazines and then in book form, and thus whether he liked it or not Faust got double—sometimes triple—income from much that he wrote, because *The Night Horseman* like its predecessor was eventually filmed (and is about to be filmed again).

When Faust finally killed Barry off in *The Seventh Man*, there was such a protest from readers that he decided to produce a sequel and wrote *Dan Barry's Daughter* before finally stopping the series.

So Faust became in effect the prisoner of a market and of an audience he had created almost against his will. Yet he lived by the money his popular fiction made him. That money, he thought, bought him time in which to write poetry.

There is a further aspect of *The Untamed* that makes it of special interest. As has been pointed out by C. D. Cuthbert and several other students of Faust's work, Dan Barry is a character of almost other-worldly—and sometimes unsavory—attributes, and his intimates are not humans but a black wolf-dog and a black horse named Satan, both of supernatural powers. In the classical Faust legend—current since the sixteenth century and with which Frederick Faust was thoroughly familiar—Faust is accompanied to hell by a remarkable black dog and performing horse that are regarded as evil spirits.

Significantly, *The Untamed* was written at the prompting of Bob Davis. Davis was aware of the rising popularity of the western story and wanted to exploit a good thing. Zane Grey had shown what could be done. In company with Jack London, Grey was famous as the first American to earn a million dollars by writing. Faust had demonstrated a financial potential similar to Grey's and a greater literary versatility.

Davis regarded his protégé much as the farmer in the fable regarded the goose who laid the golden eggs. The time would come—and there had been an inkling of it at their first meeting—when Faust would regard Davis as the Mephistopheles who had persuaded him, as the legendary Mephistopheles once persuaded the legendary Faust, to sell his soul for riches and power.

In these postwar years, however, Faust had plenty of company

among young writers seeking money with one hand while grop-
ing for serious art with the other. Hemingway had been sending
his manuscripts to the best-selling Owen Wister for criticism.
Hemingway had tried and failed to publish in *Argosy*. Both
Benéts had taken jobs writing advertising copy, as had Sherwood
Anderson, J. P. Marquand, Scott Fitzgerald, and Philip Barry.
Many of them were vainly attempting to break into the popular
fiction market Faust had succeeded in entering.

It might be remembered that foundation grants and similar
financial aids for creative writing were almost nonexistent, and
that colleges and universities looked far less kindly on writers
than in later years. The would-be authors had to furnish their
own cash, and it is interesting to note that from such efforts came
most of the best writing so far produced in the United States in
the twentieth century.

Davis' influence was synonymous with cash and success and
Faust needed both. Davis was fully aware of Faust's tendency to
place stories in settings beyond the bounds of accepted reality.
(Faust had written two pieces of fantasy, *Devil Ritter* and *That
Receding Brow*, simply because he felt like it); and the impresario
now decided that if his rising star took a trip into the Southwest,
where he could observe life on a large cattle ranch at first hand, it
would restrain a tendency toward the fantastic and increase a
tendency toward profitable western subject matter. "Get yourself solidly tied down in corral dust and horse manure, son!"
Davis advised.

Few things could have appealed to Faust less. He had no illusions about farm and ranch life. He was busy escaping the very
environment that Davis wished him to return to. But dependence
on Davis' cash register proved overwhelming. Enhancing Davis'
influence was the continuing sale of motion picture rights to
Faust's work. *Lawless Love*, based on an *All-Story* novelette
Above the Law, had been released by the Fox studios in August,
1918, as Faust was entering Camp Humphreys. It starred Jewel
Carmen, Henry Woodward, and Edward Hearn, three well-

known names. In September, while the author was wielding pick and shovel in red Appalachian clay, Universal had released *Kiss or Kill*, starring Priscilla Dean, a major attraction of the day, and Herbert Rawlinson. It was the first big hit based on Faust's work. Exhibitor comment on the underworld thriller ran as follows: "Great picture. Priscilla Dean has pinned her hair back and we now put our official o.k. on her as a star . . . Excellent production with big drawing powers."

Faust was deeply engrossed elsewhere. As consolation for traveling westward, he had taken along a volume of Sophocles' plays, his own poetry and notebooks, and a typewriter. Winifred Rieber and Mrs. John L. Howard (Sidney's mother, a strong admirer of the Fausts—she had an apartment opposite Carnegie Hall and frequently entertained them there) had promised to keep a helpful eye on Dorothy and the baby, who now occupied an apartment at 110 Morningside Drive.

When he stepped off the train in El Paso one wintry day in February, 1919, Faust was armed with a letter of introduction to the owners of a nearby cattle ranch. He was scheduled to live at ranch headquarters, ride range, conduct interviews with the cowboys, and make notes. It was the approved way for western writers to proceed.

Proceeding only as far as the ranch house, he pleaded a heavy case of literary inspiration and managed to remain in his room most of the time. He was busy completing a historical novel he was ghost writing for Bob Simpson, editor of *Argosy*; in reading *Oedipus Rex*; and in writing poetry. "I did a hundred and twenty-five pages on Simpson's novel before getting off the train," he told Dorothy, "and want to add a four-thousand-word scenario of the rest of the book and to finish a close study of Sophocles."

Corral dust was not entirely avoided. "This ranch life is worse than being in the Army," he complained. "Stinking cowpunchers, rides in all sorts of weather—and all the stuff that hundreds have done before me—and which in reality is so discouraging."

A climax came when he camped out in the mountains for three

nights with two veteran trappers, Nick and Alec. The two had roamed the wild places for sixty years, had shot and been shot at by Indians; but they bored Faust with their incessant wrangling and successfully kept him not only from Sophocles but also from finishing Simpson's novel. He was glad to get away.

The editors of *Argosy* eventually felt obliged to present the experience in somewhat different light. Needing promotional material on Faust, they reported that Nick and Alec had loved one another with a perfect devotion, "and the tales which they told in the evenings by the campfire making sixty years of Western history breathe and repainting mountains and deserts, have never been out of the mind of Max Brand. . . . Brand has been a traveler for a great many years, from the Pacific Islands to the deserts of North Africa, but when he searches for stories, he most often goes back to that shanty in Texas, and the voices of the two old men pour in upon his mind."

The image of a western writer was thus established. It mattered little that Faust seldom saw and never took seriously such publicity. Similarly he seldom saw his fan mail. Editors and agents were asked to handle mail and publicity. Press interviews and photographs were taboo. The identity of Frederick Faust was to be hidden. Max Brand could grow as others pleased, under certain restrictions. Thus the figure of the writer of western stories grew large, while the figure of the poet remained small and indistinct.

The trip to the Southwest carried Faust on to California. He stopped in Santa Barbara and visited Leonard Bacon, who was staying at the Caroline Hazard residence adjacent to the old mission. Bacon was about to leave the University of California and devote full time to writing. Looking out over Mission Canyon toward the Santa Ynez Mountains, they discussed classic Greece, and Faust wrote a poem suggested by a jacaranda tree blooming in the Hazard garden. Then he argued with Bacon that serious poetry could be written only on antique themes, while Bacon maintained that he was completely wrong.

From the train that carried him east, Faust fired a final friendly broadside in verse, a parody of Bacon's use of anapest meter, and mailed it in Chicago.

While he was en route, Douglas Fairbanks purchased one of his stories for film use.

With a new western novel, *Trailin'*, almost ready for publication, Faust arrived back in New York to find Davis in trouble and himself in danger of losing his writing market. Working for Frank Munsey was proving difficult for Davis. He was a veteran newspaperman who loved the craft and had a weak stomach for Munsey's technique of terminating the lives of newspapers without notice. Few employees knew of these impending deaths until word came from the head office stating that that day's issue would be the last. On one such occasion Davis is reported to have actually vomited. In addition to such human weaknesses, Davis had a habit of buying a story he liked whether he could use it immediately or not. Thus he tied up thousands of Munsey dollars in manuscripts to be published at some indefinite date. When Munsey found out, he ordered Davis to stop buying stories.

Davis quit the Munsey Company and set up shop as literary agent, representing Faust and a few others—at the very moment when the postwar economic depression struck. Near-panic swept the popular fiction market. Even the buoyant Davis started to lose his confidence and his health. Faust rallied to support "the Chief," who had so strongly supported him in time of need. He went to Davis' bedside and cheered the ailing impresario with talk of future successes against the enemy.

Partly because of such encouragement, Davis' eclipse was short lived. He patched up relations with Munsey, who by now had swallowed or killed off all newspapers within reach; and then Davis began writing a series of columns for the *Sun*, "Bob Davis Recalls," "Bob Davis Reveals," establishing a wide readership and gaining considerable prominence as a colorful personality and author of travel books, but gradually fading from the scene as editor and agent.

He and his star writer parted company while remaining friends. Faust developed contacts already established elsewhere, and Frank Blackwell, editor of Street and Smith's *Western Story*, was soon able to exult, "How did I get hold of Faust? Bob Davis was over-bought. Munsey found it out, told Bob he'd have to shut off buying for as long as six months, and use up some of the stuff in the safe. Faust, always in need of money, no matter how much he made, came to me with a story. I bought it. He was mine, and mine only from there on."

Faust was not entirely Blackwell's from there on but he did begin to write prolifically for the Street and Smith publishing syndicate, publishers not only of *Western Story* but of *Ainslee's Magazine, Popular Magazine, Smith's Magazine, New Story & All Around, Top Notch Magazine, Women Stories & Live Stories, Tip Top Magazine & Wide Awake, Detective Story Magazine, Picture Play, Thrill Book, Love Story Magazine, Film Stories, Sea Stories, Excitement & College Stories, Sport Story*, to name a representative cross section.

A number of famous writers had written for Street and Smith. They included Rudyard Kipling, Theodore Dreiser, A. Conan Doyle, O. Henry, George Bernard Shaw, Jack London, H. G. Wells, Zane Grey, and Mary Roberts Rinehart.

Western Story Magazine had developed out of a venerable dime novel publication called *The New Buffalo Bill Weekly*. The first issue of *Western Story* appeared in July, 1919, as a semi-monthly selling for ten cents. In October, 1920, it began appearing weekly —a measure of the surging popularity of westerns. U.S. readers seemed suddenly to have gone mad with interest in their recent frontier past. Perhaps the war, perhaps the closing of the frontier, perhaps the realization that a new age had irrevocably dawned had something to do with it.

Faust used a new name, George Owen Baxter, for his first appearance in *Western Story*. It was attached to an action-packed thriller titled *Jerry Peyton's Notched Inheritance*, which appeared in the November 25, 1920, issue.

Popular writers appearing with Faust in *Western Story* now and later included Emerson Hough, Albert Payson Terhune, Hugh B. Cave, Ernest Haycox, W. C. Tuttle, Courtney Riley Cooper, Peter B. Kyne, Stewart Edward White, and many more.

9.

A TOUCH OF DEATH

THE new relationship with Blackwell and *Western Story* proved even more profitable for Faust than the old one with Davis. Blackwell lacked the inventiveness of Davis but had a keen grasp of what readers wanted. He also paid more, up to five cents a word eventually. For a writer who felt able to produce two million words a year with his left hand, while reserving his right hand for poetry, five cents a word was significant. It equalled an annual income of one hundred thousand dollars.

Faust needed money. A son, John, had been born eighteen months after Jane. Dorothy's health was failing. The summer of 1920 spent in Santa Barbara had not entirely restored it. There were other compelling reasons why a once-hungry orphan boy needed cash. Not the least of these was the sense of having it.

Blackwell summarily informed him that there were only two kinds of plots, "pursuit and capture," and "delayed revelation," and that "delayed revelation" was merely a variant of "pursuit and capture." "In the delayed revelation situation," Blackwell added, "the opening of the story should take place a little farther along in the course of action." That was all you needed to know—except how to write.

Blackwell reiterated something Faust already knew: that the best income from magazine writing was in the form of serials that could be continued in installments from issue to issue. Each installment of a serial should be something of a unit and should involve the theme of pursuit and capture or some variation of it.

In the early days of his relationship with Davis, Faust had

traveled downtown to the historic building at the northeast corner of Broadway and Chambers Street, the home of the *Sun.* When Munsey bought the building he had added two stories to the original five, and Davis' office windows had overlooked City Hall Park, a gathering place for immigrants and sightseers entranced by the skyscraping aspects of The Great City. There had been a breezy, cheerful atmosphere about Davis' office. By contrast, there was a grim mechanical air about the gloomy fortress-like building occupied by Street and Smith, at 78-79 Seventh Avenue. Cordial relations with Blackwell failed to change the climate. The premises resembled an early-model assembly plant —or prison. It was a dour square of red brick with industrial windows and a steam elevator operated by a man who looked like a trusty, and Faust could not help but shrivel inwardly every time he visited it.

From this prison-factory issued a deluge of reading matter that inundated the U.S. for more than two generations. Half-million circulations were large for those days. As *Western Story*'s weekly circulation approached this figure, Blackwell and Faust were doing most of the circulation building. It can almost be said that the western story boom of the twenties and early thirties *was* Faust—and Blackwell. Faust's first offering had appeared shortly after Harding was elected President of the United States; his last was printed on January 29, 1938, when Hitler had already marched into the Rhineland. During the eighteen intervening years there was scarcely a week that did not see a contribution by Faust, and frequently two or three contributions appeared in the same issue under various names.

Readers who waxed enthusiastic over George Owen Baxter would write letters of complaint about David Manning, at the same time praising Max Brand, belittling Hugh Owen, or preferring Evin Evan, Peter Dawson (not to be confused with a non-Faust Peter Dawson), John Frederick, (pressed into service as a western as well as a historical pen name), Nicholas Silver, Peter

Henry Morland, George Challis, or Martin Dexter, all of these being pseudonyms for Frederick Faust. He had had to subdivide himself even within his western field.

Readers never detected the subterfuge. "Last week you gave us a novel by George Owen Baxter," ran a sample comment, "continued stories by John Frederick and Max Brand, and advertised a story by Peter Henry Morland in the coming week. This is a number worth binding in leather. I read western stories in 'high-hat' magazines, but I have yet to find stories that stand in the same class as any of these writers I have mentioned."

Another reader wrote, labeling David Manning's *Golden Coyote* stories the bunk, and said, "Max Brand is able to portray life in the raw. In other words, he bares the soul of a man, shows the savage that is in him, and that still lies in most of us. Max Brand is better than good."

Later when Faust used the same subterfuge in "high-hat" magazines, readers were equally mystified.

He cared little for the notice his popular fiction was attracting, but he liked the sense of achievement and the challenge of playing the game. "I may as well warn you," he told a friend contemplating breaking into the market, "that this is the sort of yarn Blackwell laps up: A Western tale of action, without Mexicans, without women whose virtue is endangered, and concerning anything from sheepherding to lumber or mining or trapping, but preferably something about the Old Western Ranch House and a taint of cow dung early in the story. Action, action, action, is the thing." Faust added a bit of his own philosophy. "People who read Western fiction don't read sad things. The sadness of poverty and the sadness of life don't appeal to the horny-handed sons of toil. They have enough grimness stuffed down their throats every day and they want to read about millionaires and social butterflies, and the other 'wild free open souls.' My God! My God! Nevertheless it's the truth. The ones who want the bitter junk in stories are those who eat strawberries and cream every day of their lives."

His own natural optimism undiminished, he was functioning as a sort of literary relief agency and lonely-hearts advisor to a host of would-be writers. A typical case had followed him to New York after his Texas trip. The man was a historian and brought a fund of knowledge of the West, a secretary, very little money, and the supreme conviction that Max Brand was the one man who could make him a success—writing fiction. Each morning Faust helped the ex-historian plan the day's work. Each evening he read what had been written. Often he rewrote the entire product. And he naturally helped when financial crisis threatened. He was repaid in part by local color furnished free, and this particular venture turned out fairly well because the historian later had some success in Hollywood doing scripts for motion pictures, but the case was an exception. Most went down the drain dragging a substantial slice of Faust's energy and money with them.

Perhaps his ego was rewarded or his sense of power extended, but the results horrified Dorothy and his editors.

Editors began to shudder at word of his newest discovery. "If your potential genius is on the Coast, don't have him come to New York. If he's in New York, don't have him call on me," Blackwell would proclaim. "Business is slipping. It's a bad time of year."

Such croakings meant nothing to Faust. He seemed to some observers to be developing delusions of grandeur, or a friendship-potential beyond the grasp of mortal men.

Introducing a former classmate, Kenneth Perkins, to Davis, Faust announced grandiloquently, "You published O. Henry's stuff and you showed Conrad how to rewrite *Victory*, but here is a find that will cinch your fame as a discoverer of great writers. He was born in India. If you want a new Kipling, look no further."

Perkins recalled how Faust went over every one of his stories, literally word for word. "The stories were magnificent, Heinie said. They were far above anything else ever published, or that ever would be published. I would have to start over again with simpler plots. Actually it was Heinie who started over again."

Davis finally bought and Perkins was launched. Such generosity made Faust friends, but it was a constant drain on his time and strength. At the same time he was literally overflowing with his own work.

By November, 1920, he had seen the publication in ten months of 5 book-length magazine serials, 3 novelettes, and 5 short stories. Seven additional serials and 2 novels were sold or in process of completion; and *The Night Horseman* was out and selling well. *The Seventh Man* was in progress.

In one thirteen-day period in October he had set a personal record, perhaps a world's record, by turning out two long serials and a novelette—190,000 publishable words, three complete books—in thirteen days, or the equivalent of a book every four and one-third days. He accomplished this massive production in his downtown office at 5 Columbus Circle, in a triangular building completely engulfed by noise. Two busy streets were immediately at hand and three more were not far away. Part of his technique was to drown out such noise with the noise of his typewriter. Also the sense of being part of the busy stir and bustle of the city was stimulating to him.

Equally stimulating was the smashing success of the motion picture version of *The Untamed*. It had opened on Sunday, August 22, at the Capitol Theatre in New York, starring Tom Mix and Pauline Starke, and was doing a "tremendous business," according to *Motion Picture News*. "It is quite an upward step," the *News* announced, "from riding a bronc behind a herd of steers for 'steen a month and chuck to the position of movie star of sufficient importance to command stellar place on the program of the world's largest theatre . . . . When a Mix film goes into the Capitol it is to be taken as proof that the ex-cowpuncher has arrived." William Fox had been releasing Mix films for first runs in Fox circuit theaters throughout the country, but this was the first time he had attempted a New York opening.

By providing Mix and Fox with *The Untamed,* Faust helped usher in the heyday of the western film as well as of the western story.

Almost overlooked in the excitement over *The Untamed,* Faust's *Fate's Honeymoon* story was released at year's end by J. Parker Read, Jr. and Associated Producers as *A Thousand To One,* starring Hobart Bosworth and Ethel Grey Terry. Though its ingredients were in many respects more significant than those of *The Untamed,* the story failed to come alive on the screen and the production got mediocre reception despite the considerable reputations of Bosworth and Miss Terry. The story told how a physically strong but morally weak man left civilization behind and found his true self in the wilderness, returned, and won back his wife, very much as Faust had won back Dorothy in climactic days at Yuba City after his wild wanderings.

The real Dorothy had suffered a nervous breakdown. The birth of children eighteen months apart had been a severe strain. Living with Faust was an even greater ordeal. Their relationship grew troubled, though he remained emotionally and physically loyal to her and to his announced commitment to "all the world of men, and one woman." It was a revision of his once loudly announced double standard. Nevertheless, following Dorothy's curative sojourn with friends at Stockbridge, Massachusetts, a temporary separation in the form of a long-desired trip to Europe for Faust seemed indicated. It would be a working trip; and he planned to keep her and the children well supplied with cash and household help in a new apartment at 438 West 116th Street, near the Columbia University campus.

He sailed in late March, 1921, in company with Dixie Fish, now a New York medical student. For Fish the trip was to be a respite from intensive study and a revisit to wartime haunts. For Faust it was to be—in addition to the separation from Dorothy— satisfaction of a continuing hunger to enlarge his experience. He particularly wanted to do research on the French Revolution, which seemed to him a turning point in human history as well as an almost endless source of historical fiction. A further reason was the plan he and Dorothy had evolved for living in Europe some day. He would make a reconnaissance now.

The reunited adventurers were part of the rising tide of Americans visiting or living in Europe, and especially Paris, in these postwar years.

By early April Faust was writing enthusiastically about his first visit to the Louvre Museum. "Venus is ideally placed, though rather gloomily . . . . The first glimpse is lovely. Midway you notice the very pronounced and deep modeling of the chin and mouth, which seems too much. Also she seems to be leaning too much to one side in an uncomfortable attitude. Close up she is more wonderful than ever. I noticed that from the rear and to the left the curve of the back—the opposite side, of course—is exquisite."

Next he described the façade of the Madeleine for Dorothy's benefit. "The time was between twilight and night and the sky was a delicate blue-green, very dull, and all the pediment was a shadow, and all the base. Just the columns and a hint of the rest. The pediment seemed out of proportion, why I don't know. But the whole effect was so beautiful it came as a shock."

The Boulevard des Italiens delighted him, "full of bustle day and night and so lined with street cafes that it makes you happy in spite of yourself." There he met fellow expatriate Sidney Howard, "looking very Parisian with his cane and his swagger and his chin even higher than usual." After studying playwriting under George Pierce Baker at Harvard, Howard had done wartime service with the U.S. Air Corps and was now a member of the editorial staff of *Life*.

Howard took Faust and Fish up to Montmartre. They had dinner in a small café near the summit, well off the tourist track, at a cost of eighty-five cents each, while hungry children begged for scraps of food, and afterwards walked on down to the Café de la Paix and sat until after midnight drinking beer and watching the crowd.

All at once there was a sound of yelling and a strange procession appeared. "It was composed of half-naked and garishly painted men and women, many of them quite drunk, all en route to the annual artists' ball, yelling, singing and dancing on tables and on the sidewalk." Faust was astonished at what seemed the indecent exposure and outlandish conduct of the procession but noticed that few Parisians paid any attention. "It was the sort of thing that would have landed you in jail in our country."

At the Hotel de Berne, he tried to sleep alone on a hard bed, professing a vast homesickness for the wife and children he had absented himself from. He was holding himself to his regular production schedule: twenty typewritten pages daily. Beginning as near 7:00 A.M. as possible, he was usually through by 10:00 or 11:00. The rest of the day was free for research and sightseeing.

Howard had directed him to the Carnavalet Museum, which he found to be a charming old house begun in 1544, where the great letter-writer Madame de Sévigné had lived. The historical collection held little of interest for him, however, and he concentrated his researches at the Invalides and Louvre.

Through Howard, Faust encountered Stephen Benét, who was writing a novel and courting his wife-to-be, Rosemary Carr of Chicago. Faust also met the Douglas Moores and the Dick Myerses, the latter already modestly famous hosts whose Paris apartment door was open to many kinds of people. Ellen Semple, later Philip Barry's wife, was in town, as were Edna St. Vincent Millay, Scott Fitzgerald, and Edmund Wilson. Gertrude Stein, who had attended high school in Oakland, California, a few years before Faust's attendance in Modesto, was also present. Hemingway and his wife arrived a few months later.

Howard left for a walking tour of Switzerland and northern Italy, planning to meet Fish later in Spain, while Faust remained in Paris to work. His pile of notes about the French Revolution was growing. He had met an American film producer who was in Paris preparing to make a picture about the Revolution and had arranged to attend rehearsals so that he could observe authentic costuming firsthand, "if only they start work before I leave." He had planned a three-month stay. Nearly two had passed.

It was the Louvre that finally held his attention. He said that he went back to Leonardo's "Madonna of the Rocks" like a child to candy. "I stood in front of it today, for a long time, and felt a queer sad happiness bubbling up and overflowing like water in a well. Color is for the first time coming to mean something to me."

He informed Dorothy they must plan a lifetime of study, beginning with residence in the south of France or in Italy. He commended Rembrandt to her attention and asked that she send him the newspaper accounts of the Dempsey-Carpentier championship fight which had taken place in Jersey City on July 2.

Dorothy's letters did not conceal her bitterness at his long absence and seemingly unreasonable demands. His protestations of love and homesickness were not enough to take his place. Financial troubles complicated their relationship. Expected payments failed to materialize, and she was obliged to telephone Davis and beg for cash.

Faust's plans for returning in early July were disrupted when Fish was called home by the death of his father, Faust loaning his own ticket money when his friend was caught short of funds. The postwar economic depression was becoming acute. To add irritation to anxiety, that summer both in Paris and New York was unusually hot, the temperature hanging above 90. Faust thrashed in his bed through torrid nights, seldom sleeping more than three hours, but continued to pound out the daily prose.

Anger and frustration only served to increase his production. By July 10 he had mailed, since arriving in Paris just four months before, two novelettes and one serial of about 100,000 words, all together worth, he estimated, $3,000. He was planning to finish a serial for *Country Gentleman*—a magazine sometimes described as the rural version of *The Saturday Evening Post*—before he reached New York. He banked heavily on two manuscripts placed in Davis' hands before leaving, one of them an unusual western, *The Garden of Eden*, which he priced at $4,000 (the equivalent of about $20,000 by mid-century values).

A chance encounter with a former University of California student working on the Paris edition of *The New York Herald* led to a revealing confession on Faust's part: "Sometimes when I talk to this boy and see his real goodness and his doubt of himself I feel how bad I really am. I am not a good man. I do not love goodness. There is the end. One should love goodness for itself. I cannot. There is another thing, the great illusion, the sweet and pure and uplifting and terrible power of beauty." And he passed on to a detailed discussion of Fra Angelico's "Coronation of the Virgin," declaring it the finest bit of color in the Italian Primitives Room at the Louvre.

He decided to put aside the *Country Gentleman* serial in favor of a potboiler for Blackwell so that he could land in New York with $2,000 worth of manuscript under his arm, which would make his total earnings for the French holiday $5,000.

Dorothy wrote in panicky terms of a vanished bank account, intolerable heat, and the children ill with a mysterious fever.

The first real holiday in Faust's life was turning into a nightmare. "I am simply sick that I cannot be away from home one month while making $20,000 a year," he declared. His income for 1921 would in fact be nearer $40,000. "For four years I've prostituted everything decent in me—defiled my mind and soul to make money—and at the end of four years I have to cringe and quake in order to get a *two months vacation*! Jesus, Jesus, Jesus is there any justice in the world?"

On July 31 cabled funds finally arrived from Davis. On August 17 Faust reached New York on the "America," hollow eyed and thin, $2,000 worth of manuscripts under his arm, prepared to hammer out forty pages a day for an indefinite period.

The French experience completed his rupture with Davis and sealed his union with Blackwell. As he prepared to work himself out of the depression of finances and spirit, he had a feeling that he would never be able "to do one thing well," as long as he lived

—and this at the moment when his production was reaching astronomical proportions.

In 1921 he was to publish 9 serials equivalent to 9 books, 15 novelettes equivalent to at least 5 books, while Putnam brought out his fourth successful novel, *The Seventh Man*. There had been further sales to Hollywood. Before he boarded the boat for Europe, Universal had released *Tiger True*, based on an *Argosy-All Story* serial, starring Frank Mayo, Fritzi Brunette, and Eleanor Hancock. In June, Fox had released *Children of the Night*, "a series of remarkable adventures in the New York social and criminal worlds," as *Motion Picture World* described it, starring William Russell and Ruth Renick, and also based on an *All-Story* serial. In September the remarkable run of Faust films had continued with *The Night Horseman*, produced by Fox, presenting Tom Mix and May Hopkins in a film sequel to *The Untamed*.

Also in September and also from Fox came *Shame*, based on a novel *Clung*, starring John Gilbert and Anna May Wong. It brought racial problems to the screen in the form of a western hero who believes himself to be of Chinese ancestry in a Caucasian world. Some reviewers called *Shame* old hat. Most recognized it as unusually interesting. Exhibitors reported good houses. Next in what grew to be a record sequence came *Trailin'*, released in December by Fox and starring Tom Mix, Eva Novak, and Carol Holloway. Mix was described by reviewers as at his best, and box office reaction followed suit. At the very end of 1921 came *His Back Against the Wall*, produced by Samuel Goldwyn, starring Raymond Hatton and Virginia Valli. It was based on a *Western Story* novel by "John Frederick." *Motion Picture World* hailed it as "a conspicuous picture." Jeremy Dice, the hero, or anti-hero, is born a coward, continues a coward, and ends a coward. He is redeemed by a moment of self-forgetfulness in which he becomes a hero.

In the twelve months since the release of *A Thousand to One* by J. Parker Read, Jr., seven Faust films had reached the screen.

All had been produced by major studios and all had featured major players.

Partly because of prodigious exertions, partly because of frustrations generated by his Paris trip, partly because of demands on his time and energy imposed by multifarious friendships, dependents, and literary discoveries, Faust's health finally gave way.

The attack came without warning during a quiet moment late one afternoon in November, 1921. Faust and Dorothy were in their newly occupied apartment at 340 West 86th Street—a fashionable address reflecting a new affluence. His sister Pauline, who was employed at a Boston hospital, happened to be visiting them. He was preparing the customary prohibition cocktail of orange juice and gin, when his heart began beating wildly. He was seized with dizziness and began gasping for breath.

Dorothy, terrified, helped him lie down on the sofa. He was very pale. "I think it's my heart," he said. He felt a tightness in his chest, he said later, as if he were being strait-jacketed. She thought he was dying. Putting a pillow under his head, she rushed to the telephone and called the doctor.

There was no acute pain, such as is associated with coronary occlusion or angina pectoris, just the terrific pounding, a severe feeling of constriction, and a shortness of breath. Pauline tried to find his pulse, but there was none.

The children's pediatrician, the only doctor Dorothy was able to reach in the emergency, arrived to find her 29-year-old husband struggling for breath, his heart beating wildly, or totally lapsing. An injection of digitalis slowed the rate but did not stop the irregular beat or the lapses.

The pediatrician did his best to sound reassuring. He could not help, however, adopting the funereal demeanor then usually evoked by heart cases. Heart ailments were considered almost a guarantee of death or permanent invalidism.

A specialist, a distinguished cardiologist of the type that wore striped trousers and long-tailed coat, was equally funereal when he arrived the next day and pronounced a diagnosis.

He said Faust's trouble was fibrillation, or "fluttering," of the heart. The central pulse mechanism had broken down. Separate sections of the heart—separate bundles of muscular fibers—had taken on a beat of their own. Faust had in effect two or three "hearts" but at any moment might have none, if the muscular action became too diffuse, or the heart rate too rapid. Every fiber of heart muscle has in itself the potential for rhythmic beating. Normally all beat in unison. In Faust's case, the fibers of the auricles were beating separately from those of the rest of the heart.

Fibrillation, now recognized as not necessarily fatal, was then a little-understood condition widely regarded as disastrous. Then as later it was sometimes associated with heart disease, sometimes with external causes, such as tension.

"If you live a quiet life," the specialist announced, "avoid strenuous activity—avoid smoking, drinking, and excitement—you may live for quite some time."

For a person geared to live as tensely and abundantly as Faust was geared, it sounded like a sentence of death. He pressed for more information.

"Your heart muscle was probably weakened by infection accompanying your attack of flu at Camp Humphreys. The basis for the weakening was probably the years of overwork and overstrain in your boyhood when you were shooting up to six feet three and working the long hours on the hay-baling crews."

The valley that Faust had struggled to escape from suddenly became an ever-present physical as well as mental threat. Like a character in one of his plots, he had run from death—and was carrying it with him all the time.

10.

THE UPHILL ROAD

THOUGH both doctors had prescribed complete rest in bed for at least three weeks, on the third day after his attack Faust was sitting up in a chair and pounding his typewriter. He felt instinctively that his best chance to survive was to be on his feet, moving around, and doing something useful. He had no idea that he was demonstrating behavior that would later be standard treatment for heart patients. A further compelling reason for his action was necessity. Despite high earnings, there was little money in the bank.

At night he suffered from suffocation nightmares in which he was buried alive under loads of coal or earth and from which he would wake gasping and reaching out in the dark for Dorothy. He asked her to buy him a stethoscope and lay listening to his faltering heart, grim-faced and withdrawn. The heart sounded, he said later, like a gasoline engine running out of gas—*put-put, put-put-put*, then a long silence. Then a *put*.

Though haunted by the fear of dropping dead on the sidewalk if he went outdoors, or of dying in the back seat of a taxi if he went downtown, he visited the well-known heart specialists, Evan Evans and Robert Halsey. Evans was head of internal medicine at Roosevelt Hospital. Halsey had an international reputation.

They offered little encouragement. Evans warned him to live a life of moderation or be dead within a year. Halsey found his heart rate 155 and the pulse at the wrist 120 per minute, a deficit of 35. Blood pressure was a normal 125 systolic. Blood pressure is not necessarily affected by fibrillation, Halsey explained. He added that the difference of 35 between the heart rate and the pulse at the wrist was due to the rapid rate, which permitted the heart a very short filling time, resulting in 35 beats "so ineffective as not to be felt at the wrist." Fluoroscope and electrocardiogram, however, showed the presence of auricular fibrillation. He told Faust to go to bed, take digitalis daily, and lose 10 to 15 of his 204 pounds. Faust obeyed. After two days of digitalis, his heart rate, though still irregular, was 80 with a pulse of 72 per minute. Within a month of dieting, he had lost 10 pounds.

But the Halsey-Evans treatment seemed tedious and a mere stop-gap. He wanted a cure. Friends told him of a sanitarium at Lakewood, New Jersey, where cardiacs had found help. It was situated in a quiet countryside surrounded by pines. At Lakewood the doctors confirmed the instinctive treatment he had already begun. "Your heart is a muscle," they informed him. "Like other muscles, it needs regular exercise."

Faust took daily walks and light setting-up exercises. For a joke he let fellow patients listen to his heart. He was so convincing in belittling his ailment that then and later most people believed there was little or nothing wrong.

Back at the apartment, the temptations to talk, drink, work, live, were overpowering, and a new attack sent him crashing to the edge of death.

His pulse count rose to a near-catastrophic 200. The pounding seemed almost enough to break his chest open. He lay gray and shaking, sweat breaking out all over his body.

There seemed a gigantic irony about his condition. He had wanted to be great-hearted. Now he had not one but two or three hearts as the pulses beat in the separate fibers. He seemed condemned to suffer his image of himself in a way that he had never dreamed. Dante, a poet he admired, had put people in hell suffering the reality and not the dreams that they had embodied on earth. Forces almost too bitter to contemplate seemed at work.

Friends coming to cheer him only made him feel worse. Howard, Fish, Davis, Bill Benét, Winifred Rieber, Garnet Holme, Schoolcraft visited him, but they all had their lives to lead. Confronted with the inescapable fact of invalidism, Faust got out his stethoscope again and lay listening. For several days after the near-fatal attack he remained in a state of deep depression. Then he put away the stethoscope, got out of bed, and went with Dixie Fish to a prizefight at Madison Square Garden. As they watched two inept heavyweights fumble at each other, Faust became disgusted and angry and felt steadily better. All at once he felt himself larger than his illness. He would live, on his own terms.

His program was enormous before his attack. It now became gigantic. He set himself a schedule of daily walks and exercises and resumed the calisthenics learned at Lakewood. He determined to (1) challenge his heart daily to do a little more, (2) make all the money he could so that Dorothy and the children would have some financial security if he died, (3) produce all the poetry possible, (4) enjoy life as though every minute were his last.

In a few weeks he was writing at nearly the record rate established before his initial attack. A third and fourth attack felled him but he learned how to recover, what to guard against. "I'm taking only one drink at a time!" he wrote Bacon. He resumed smoking cigarettes and worked prodigiously.

Acute auricular fibrillation wasn't supposed to be treated in this fashion. Halsey and Evans made notes for articles they would write for professional journals. Thus, in addition to almost everything else, Faust wrote medical history.

Eleven serials, equivalent to 11 books, saw magazine publication in 1922, the year following his heart attack, as did 30 novelettes. McCann published the hardback, *The Gray Charteris*, which Faust had ghost-written for Bob Simpson. Chelsea House, another book publisher, prepared the first of many Faust titles they would issue, *Donnegan*. Putnam brought out a volume of poetry and announced a new western, *Alcatraz*. And in Hollywood, Fox released on August 20 a smash hit called *Just Tony*, starring Tom Mix's famous horse, who had recently been the guest of President and Mrs. Warren Harding during a lawn and garden party at the White House. *Just Tony* was hailed as the first major film with a horse as its star. Tom Mix and Claire Adams played supporting roles. The picture actually had a serious message. It centered on Tony's resentment of human brutality and his positive response to those who loved him. It wasn't a message, however, that Faust could take seriously when he evaluated his own work.

He was grappling with a large new poem on a theme from the Arthurian legends, his favorite subject matter. Recent publication by Edwin Arlington Robinson of a long poem, *Lancelot*, based on Arthurian material, had encouraged Faust's belief that modern poetry could be written successfully on ancient themes. He had chosen the legend of Balin, the knight errant who loves the fair lady Nerys, "and for her sake has rooted up a vow and foresworn a quest." It was, again, a theme which reflected the conflict between love of Dorothy and love of perilous adventure. But he was as unsure and tense about his poetry as he was confident and relaxed about his prose. "I have submitted my long-labored-on volume of verse to Putnam," he told Sidney Howard, "and I cringe to think what may happen."

Somewhat to his astonishment, Putnam accepted the volume. William Rose Benét, writing in the *Literary Review*, had this to say about *The Village Street* by Frederick Faust when it appeared in June, 1922. "The poet's technique, in his shorter poems, is not perfected, his touch is not altogether certain. Yet it is something to discover a modern writer so sensitive to the effectiveness of simplicity and clarity. . . . the qualities that promise here are delicacy of touch in the shorter poems, and distinctive narrative power in the longer."

Writing in the *New York Times*, Richard Le Gallienne commented, "The only fault to be found with Mr. Faust's poems is their lack of rhythmic vitality. They bring us charming pictures, and striking lines on occasion, and they are endowed with genuine poetic feeling."

The volume contained among other selections a song written

for Dorothy and the unborn baby in the fall of 1917 when war
hovered and Faust had not yet enlisted. It began:

> When the almond trees are sweet
> With blossoms pale as foam,
> We'll walk together to the church
> And walk together home.

And there were such lines as these from the title poem:

> Wait for the time between the day and night
> When up and down the street
> The pavements have grown soft with yellow light,
> And garden airs are sweet.
>
> Wait for a wind that moves so lazily
> It hardly lifts the scent
> Of honeysuckle or acacia tree
> With golden blossoms bent.
>
> Wait till the red geraniums on the wall
> Are dim beneath the blue
> Of the steep shadow, and the elm trees tall
> Take on a dusky hue.

The valley spoke in the poems; they were quite appropriately
dedicated to Thomas Downey. The escape from the valley spoke
too, in such poems as "Balin," exemplifying Faust's use of
Arthurian legends as, among other things, scaling ladders against
psychic walls that hemmed him in:

> Furiously they spurred;
> Above their heads the clotted turf was tossing;
> They leaned into the wind, yet nothing followed,
> Naught in the valley lived except dumb cattle
> Lifting their heads to watch the fugitives.
> Sweeter than tidings of the hawthorn bloom
> That blew upon the wind, the warrior breathed
> Perfume of mystery and adventure strange.

"Balin" exemplified an unfortunate tendency toward conscious poeticizing and inflated diction. Yet there were passages of romantic beauty:

> He saw the lady's hanging sleeves of blue
> That cupped the wind, her veil a blowing mist,
> The hooded hawk that wavered on her arm,
> And his heart leaped before he saw her face:
> Her beauty went before her like the breath
> Of unseen gardens walking through the night.

Applicable to Dorothy were lines from "To A Lady":

> I heard her first
> When first I heard your voice, I turned in haste
> Looking for her, and only saw your face.

Applicable to Faust himself and his new acceptances, following his heart attack, was "The Last Venture," which began

> He has stepped lightly on the long road out
> The grey road, old with dust,
> The stern road, never-ending as our doubt,
> For he was strong in trust.

Read today, *The Village Street* may give the same impression it gave Benét and Le Gallienne, of delicacy, perception, and promise. It announced no mastery. Some of the verse had a strong imitative quality. Some was original and good. It was, like Faust himself, unfinished work.

The book passed largely unnoticed—a not-uncommon fate for first volumes of verse. It did not make any money—few volumes of poetry do—but in the year of its publication, Faust earned more than $60,000 from his prose. He published some 1,500,000 words in 6 different magazines (*Western Story, Argosy-All Story, Ace-High, Country Gentleman, Detective Story, Short Story*) under 6 different pen names (Max Brand, John Frederick, David Manning, George Owen Baxter, Nicholas Silver, Peter Dawson); he established himself in a completely new field of writing by publishing 8 short detective novels; and he saw Hollywood make its twelfth film from his work.

Nevertheless he felt himself a terrible failure. His hopes for *The Village Street* had been too high. He felt that writing popular fiction had corrupted his artistic integrity. Perhaps Benét had been right from the beginning. What good was gold if you lost your soul?

There was some consolation in the fact that in November *The Literary Digest* reprinted his "Song" from *The Village Street* on its Current Poetry Page in company with verse by the recognized poets Angela Morgan and Witter Bynner.

Faust looked toward Italy and poetry. He and Dorothy had decided to move to Florence as soon as arrangements could be made. He hired a tutor and began studying Greek so he could read Homer in the original. Living in Florence he would be at the heartland of art and near the fountainhead of poetry, Greece, and would be reasonably near the cardiologists in Vienna, Amsterdam, and London, considered the world's finest. He would also be free of the excitement and social pressure of New York which he found a menace to health and time consuming.

As a first step toward peace, quiet, and Europe, the Fausts moved their household to Katonah in Westchester County, an hour's drive into the country from New York. The new residence, formerly the property of the playwright Clyde Fitch, was a two-story, white-painted frame house in a pastoral setting of pasture and apple orchard. As for peace and quiet, a chance visitor might have thought it the training camp for a heavyweight contender. White bull terriers, symbols of combat, overran the yard. Here was the woodpile where Faust did his chopping. There was the lane where he did his roadwork. In good weather a punching bag hung from a tree limb. Dumbbells lay everywhere. Sudden strain was bad for the heart, but regular exercise was a necessity. He had come to believe in the virtues of sweat with a faith that bordered on the religious.

Visitors entering the Katonah household at this period received unforgettable impressions. One recalled hearing Faust yell at Dorothy, "Cry, damn you, cry!", with tears of emotion streaming down his face as he stalked the living room declaiming Desdemona's final lines from *Othello*, holding the book in one hand while tearing at his hair with the other. Dorothy had mastered the art of letting a tear glisten in the eye and not fall, but he wanted a commitment equal to his own. Despite his great personal charm, there were moments when some observers thought him mentally disturbed. Others said that he lived in a make-believe world.

Guests were often obliged to participate in reading aloud, each taking a part in *Hamlet, Lear, Love's Labour's Lost,* or perhaps the prologue to the *Canterbury Tales.* "Jesus Christ, listen to how this beautiful son of a bitch Chaucer says it, will you?" the host might exclaim in the language of the hay-baling crews.

To the unsympathetic, Faust seemed at times boorish and overbearing. But many found him an understanding and inspiring friend who drew them out and made them feel important. Not a few left his house in the small morning hours, filled with his lavish hospitality and equally lavish enthusiasm, clutching an armful of books he had thrust upon them, believing themselves for the moment on familiar terms with the giants of literature whose works they were about to read. "There is a giant asleep in every man," Faust liked to proclaim. "When that giant wakes, miracles can happen!"

Dorothy presided over a household that threatened to turn at any moment into a madhouse. Filipino servants fought with knives in the kitchen, reflecting the tensions of the parlor, while upstairs in the quieter sectors the children were being reared in the genteel tradition by an English governess. Faust was incapable of living peacefully.

If he visited New York as he insisted on doing, Dorothy never knew whom to expect for dinner—a distinguished editor, a drunken cab driver delighted at the huge fare and the several drinks collected en route, a young and impoverished poet of great potential, or just her inebriated husband whose next tottering step might be his last.

She was obliged to devote herself more to husband than to children. Only the presence of the governess enabled her to be the necessary nurse, companion, secretary, servant, and mate to Faust. She administered the daily digitalis, recorded his pulse rate, accompanied him on walks, called the doctor when necessary, collected and filed the carbons of the stories that milled off the typewriter, bought the household supplies and the books, paper, pencils, erasers, envelopes, and carbon paper that kept the machine running.

She read proof to make sure he didn't kill the deputy on page forty and revive him on page one hundred and forty, and acted as general bouncing board for Faust's ideas.

In addition to long hours of talk, reading aloud had become a major function. Schoolcraft recalled how, during their first winter in New York, the Fausts had read—often with him or some other friend participating—all of Aeschylus in translation, all of Sophocles, some of Euripides, some of Aristophanes, most of Chaucer, all of Spenser's *Faerie Queen*, and five Shakespeare plays. Reading aloud now included background for western and historical fiction, as well as for poetry, animal and sport stories, and Arctic and South Sea fiction. Silent reading included popular magazines, daily newspapers (with special attention to comics and sports pages), and a broad selection of current books.

Dorothy often read aloud merely to put him to sleep after lunch or some time between midnight and morning. His insomnia, complicated by heart trouble, had become chronic. But her reading voice soothed and quieted him. When his crippled, overstimulated body fell asleep beside her, she knew how essential she was. But the strain gradually wore down her reserves.

Dorothy's problem became how to preserve herself as well as her husband. He insisted on trying to mold her into his ideal woman. She was to study Greek, the piano, sing, dance, take horseback riding lessons, excel at canoeing, tennis, golf. At one point he suggested they learn to fly. Yet he considered femininity and old-world charm essential. They had a decisive scene one day in New York while riding the open-air roof of a Fifth Avenue bus. She flatly refused to study Greek or Latin. In a fury he got off and left her. Immediately overcome by remorse, he dashed into a flower shop, snatched the largest gardenia, flung down a bill, commandeered a cab, overtook the bus, and presented the flower with humble contrition to a weeping Dorothy.

They kissed and made up, while passengers gaped. But she did not study Greek and Latin.

Being married to Faust was like being married to a nuclear reactor that might explode at any moment. On more than one occasion Dr. Halsey came out to Katonah to help the local doctor keep him alive. Halsey was professor of medicine at the New York Post-Graduate School and Hospital, Columbia University, and a founder of the American Heart Association and later its president. He seems to have taken more than usual interest in Faust's case, and incorporated it into articles he published in the *Journal of the American Medical Association* and elsewhere.

Faust continued to live dangerously if not suicidally, but the work poured out. In 1923 he published approximately 1.1 million words; in 1924, 1.4 million. Three hardback novels appeared in 1923, four in 1924. In 1923 Hollywood released three films based on his work. They were westerns, starring Dustin Farnum in *Three Who Paid*; Farnum's brother William in *The Gun Fighter*; and Tony, Tom Mix, Betty Jewel, and James Mason in *Mile-A-Minute Romeo*.

Despite enforced abstinence from social life, Faust and Dorothy were seeing a good deal of Sidney Howard and his wife, the former actress Claire Eames, as well as of the Stephen Benéts and the Richard Myerses. At a chance meeting in a Greenwich Village café, Faust was able to tell Mary Austin how much he admired her *Land of Little Rain*. He kept in touch with Bill Benét, now engaged with Henry Canby in founding the *Saturday Review of*

Literature; and there were constant renewals of contact with Bob and Madge Davis and the editors at Putnam, Macmillan, Dodd-Mead, *Argosy, Western Story*, and elsewhere. He continued to see the composer Frederic Geiger and his wife, who had befriended him during lonely bachelor days in New York, when Geiger had been setting Shakespeare songs to music.

Dixie Fish was interning at Roosevelt Hospital. Often he invited Faust to the hospital to watch operations, or took him on visits to charity cases and even to patients of questionable standing with the police and courts. Faust later incorporated these experiences into the Doctor Kildare stories, novels, and films. Acquaintance with a New York police official, Edward P. Mulrooney, led to first-hand knowledge of police methods and problems, valuable knowledge for a writer of detective and crime fiction. Acquaintance with businessmen such as Edward Streeter, author of the wartime best seller *Dere Mable* and a later success, *Father of the Bride*, and with such bankers as Robert A. Lovett, who was eventually to serve three presidents at cabinet level, led Faust to knowledge of top business and financial circles.

His contacts were touching practically all walks of life; but they were more helpful to a popular prose writer needing input for rapidly produced stories and novels than to a poet needing solitude for contemplation and careful work.

Faust had taken a quick trip alone to England and the Continent in the summer of 1923 to visit heart specialists and reconfirm the plan for living in Europe. Now he was putting what he considered his best work into a three-act dramatic tragedy in blank verse on the Paolo-Francesca love story from Dante's *Divine Comedy*. He had become deeply ashamed of his popular prose and film credits, avoiding discussion of such subjects whenever possible, or belittling them. He insisted on thinking of himself as a poet. When his children asked him what he was doing at the typewriter he told them he was making shoes. For years they believed that shoes were made on a machine called a typewriter.

There had been good promise in *The Village Street* and sufficient recognition to provide encouragement, but time was slipping by and he was publishing no verse at all. Adding to inner conflicts was the problematical state of his sister, who had become trouble-prone and largely dependent on him for support, and the early death of his brother, Thomas Carlyle Faust, and Tom's wife and two children. There was rumor of infanticide and suicide. At times it seemed there was a blight upon the Faust name, and he was struggling to keep a light burning in a sea of darkness.

His fiction and films of this period bore such titles as *Champion of Lost Causes* and *Against All Odds*. Charles Jones and Dolores Rousse played in *Against All Odds*, released by Fox on July 27, 1924, and classed as a "big" attraction in a number of theaters. Edmund Lowe and Barbara Bedford were featured in *Champion of Lost Causes* (1925), a mystery melodrama which *Motion Picture News* described as a starring vehicle for Lowe "well done with an eye to entertainment values."

Yet Faust was his own best mystery melodrama—a virtual Perils of Pauline serial, continued from day to day. The day often ended in a cliffhanger. Dorothy said that what cracked her nerves permanently was the time when she and Faust were motoring through New England, he at the wheel. They started to descend a steep grade with a railroad crossing at the bottom and suddenly found that a train was coming and the car had no brakes. There was only one thing to do. Faust beat the train to the crossing.

Through all of this his fibrillating heart bore up, sometimes haunting his nightmares like the telltale heart in Poe's horror story. Nevertheless he was progressing on his own terms. He could play nine holes of golf, two sets of tennis.

Life at Katonah settled down to an only mildly desperate whirl, as the sporting world readied itself for the first Dempsey-Tunney fight, and Anita Loos' *Gentlemen Prefer Blondes* became a best seller. In 1925, Sidney Howard won the Pulitzer Prize for his play, *They Knew What They Wanted*, Bacon produced a book-length epic poem, Hemingway was writing *The Sun Also Rises*, and Fitzgerald had published *The Great Gatsby*. Jimmy Walker was running for mayor of New York, the New York of Ring Lardner, Damon Runyon, Paul Gallico, Ziegfeld's Follies, the hip-pocket flask, and the rising stock market. In 1925, Faust poured 1.2 million words onto the popular literary market, including seven novels; and he made sixteen sales to motion picture companies, while finishing his three-act drama in blank verse and making plans for an epic poem. The amounts paid for the motion picture rights were relatively small by later standards, ranging from $500 to $3,750, but they totaled $34,450 for the year.

Saving proved an excruciating ordeal to a natural spendthrift, but Faust put $10,000 in the Irving Trust Company and obligated himself to additional amounts, so that Dorothy and the children would have something to live on if he dropped dead.

His literary affairs were being handled by the Service for Authors Agency at 33 West 42nd Street, though he was contemplating changes. The controlling factors in the final decision to go to Europe were improved health and finances, as well as the continued advice of doctors and Dorothy that the slower pace of European living would be better for him. Katonah had not proved a rest haven, and the prevailing U.S. intellectual and artistic climate did not seem sympathetic. A debunking type of realism had gone hand in hand with rising incomes. Sinclair Lewis' *Main Street* had set a pattern. Lewis' Main Street in Sauk Centre might have been "J" Street, Modesto, for Faust, but Faust's reactions to smalltown experience were quite different from Lewis'. He continued to sublimate them in the pursuit of what he believed to be beauty, and his millions of published words took the form of romantic idealism laced with only such negative realism as he found essential. The boyhood scars on his face had healed but not the inward scars. He still envisioned a life of quality and splendor. To the early vision had been added, he said later, the values expressed by Leonardo's "Madonna of the Rocks," Sappho's poetic fragments, Balzac's bitterly humane comedies, the mighty laughter of Rabelais, and the work and personality of Aeschylus. It was a vision of a community of kindred spirits devoted to age-old traditions of beauty and the arts.

Beyond the sea he hoped to find them, and he hoped they would find him.

Still hidden by his growing number of pen names, and financed by perhaps the most phenomenal literary production on record, he moved his household, his dreams, and his bad heart to Europe in the summer of 1925.

11.

ENGLAND

HE went first to London so that he could undergo treatment by Sir Thomas Lewis, widely regarded as the world's leading heart specialist. Halsey had provided an introduction. The patient entered a nursing home operated by Lewis near London, while his family remained in a London hotel. Treatment consisted of regular doses of quinidine, a drug which later became standard medication for arrythmic hearts, plus enforced quiet and rest. The regimen quickly became impossible to a patient of Faust's emotional dynamics, and he soon abandoned the nursing home, though he showed his appreciation by financially supporting a bed in it for several years afterward.

Deciding he needed a respite from doctors and hospitals, he hired a Rolls-Royce "touring car" and driver and he, Dorothy, the children, and the governess toured the island that was the home of so many of Faust's literary heroes.

They motored with the top down, the children riding on jump seats facing Dorothy and the governess who sat on the rear seat. Faust stationed himself in front with the driver. The two men discussed automobile engines, football, cricket, and the drawbacks of warm ale. Hair flying and shirt collar open so that his chest and throat could be exposed to the fresh air, Faust temporarily overcame the chronic feeling of suffocation from which he suffered.

Luggage was strapped to the running boards on each side. A typewriter and a specially built typewriter stand that could be adjusted to convenient height were in the trunk at the rear of the car. Every morning Faust produced approximately twenty pages of popular fiction in whatever hotel room he happened to occupy. In the afternoon they drove on.

The governess, Miss Grace Lamont, known as "Monty," proved a helpful guide. She was a native of the Isle of Skye and before coming to the U.S., she had been a governess in several English households including that of Kenneth Clark, the art critic. She was well informed, widely traveled, and her personal roots went as deep into English-Scottish life as did Faust's imaginative roots.

After visiting Winchester in the King Arthur country, the party stopped at Torquay on the Devon coast, where Faust inspected the ruins of Tintagel Castle, the central scene of the Tristram-Iseult story. He walked beside the sea over which, so the legend said, King Arthur had been borne by faeries in a magic boat to an island named Avalon far in the west. Faust began to feel that the dreams he had had a quarter of a century before, while walking on valley roads, were coming true. It made him feel that other dreams might be realized. He was working with new freedom, he found less need to drink, and his health was better.

As they turned north toward Stratford and the Shakespeare country, he felt a keen excitement. The thousands of Shakespeare's lines he had memorized as a boy, plus many readings and rereadings of the plays, had become deeply a part of him, and there were personal identifications with the bard himself. Shakespeare had begun life in obscurity in rural Stratford, a kind of Modesto of its time. Shakespeare had seen his father fall from success to failure and public humiliation. He himself had left his hometown in disgrace, or at least in obscurity, and had returned in middle age with status, money, and honors, to settle down and live the life of a country gentleman.

Shakespeare would probably have owned a Rolls-Royce, had one been available in 1612.

The parallels were close enough to be amusing as well as moving.

Each morning as Faust worked in his inn room, the children

worked in theirs, taught their lessons by Monty Lamont. Regularly included was a Shakespeare song to be memorized and recited to their father during the after-supper social and reading hour. "Full fathom five thy father lies/ Of his bones are coral made . . . ." Faust's particular favorite among the songs was the aspiring, "Hark, hark! the lark at heaven's gate sings . . . ." His favorite Shakespearean prose was the passage from *Hamlet* beginning, "What a piece of work is a man!" He was putting final touches on his dramatic tragedy on the Paolo-Francesca theme, finishing the latest western novel, and longing like the legendary Faust for a universal power that would enable him to transcend limits he keenly felt.

From Stratford, they drove northward through the Lake District where Wordsworth, Coleridge, Southey, and other poets had lived. Pausing near Melrose Abbey in the Scottish Lowlands where Sir Walter Scott had flourished, Faust read aloud from *Rob Roy* and *Lay of the Last Minstrel*. The region was rich in atmosphere for the historical novels he planned to write. Mary, Queen of Scots, had crossed the Solway on her flight to England as described in Froude's *History of England from the Fall of Wolsey to the Defeat of the Spanish Armada*, which Faust was also reading aloud as they traveled.

They visited Dumfries, once the home of Robert Burns, bought a black and white cocker spaniel for the children at Dundee, and went on into the highlands and the scenes of Stevenson's *Kidnapped*. On Thursday, August 20, 1925, Faust wrote to Basil Blackwell's bookstore at Oxford in England for a copy of Berner's *Froissart* and a copy of *Racehorses in Training*.

While they were staying at Portree, a cable arrived from his editor Frank Blackwell in New York saying *Western Story* was buying two serials. They drove on and spent the night at the Station Hotel in Inverness. Next day Faust finished a western novelette, *The Range-Finder*, mailed it to New York, and moved on to Edinburgh for the night. On August 24, they traveled to Carlisle via Glasgow, and the next day were back in London, staying at The Vanderbilt and finding that friends from Berkeley days, the Clair Torreys and Leonard Bacons, had arrived before them.

They spent the evening of August 28 with the Bacons (she was the former Martha Stringham, daughter of a University of California professor), and were introduced to Dr. and Mrs. H. G. Baynes. Baynes, a psychologist and psychiatrist, was known as Carl Jung's leading English disciple. He was a noted scholar with a Cambridge background and was later the author of several books on psychological and mythological subjects, including a psychoanalytical study of Germany under Hitler. Bacon had been taking psychiatric treatment from Baynes and it soon led to similar treatment for Faust.

On Monday, August 31, Faust began recording the number of typewritten pages he produced each day. The entry for that day was 31, perhaps deliberately intended to match the day of the month. On Tuesday, the entry was 26. On Wednesday his output dropped to 19, but he crowded in a game of golf at East Croydon. (On Tuesday he had found time for dentistry and a visit to a fashionable tailor as well as for the 26 pages.) On Thursday his page production dropped to 15, but he bought a new typewriter, a Woodstock, submitting his veteran Corona in trade, and he motored with Dorothy to Stoke Poges, visited New York friends, the Charles Willards, and was back in London by 6:30 P.M. On Saturday he did 12 pages and played golf at Addington.

On Sunday, while Dorothy visited the children and Monty at Copped Hall, Totteridge, where they were staying in a former manor house turned boarding house and school, he produced 18 pages. On Monday, he did 15. On Tuesday he did 30 and mailed a novelette to Frank Blackwell. Almost daily, he was seeing doctors, tailors, shirtmakers, and friends, and finding time for golf and chess games. Yet he had fallen into a mood of deep despondency about his writing and himself.

He had crossed the Atlantic with high hopes of finding new

answers. Instead he seemed to be finding the same old ones, and they seemed to lead back to himself.

T. F. Cotton, a new physician, had provided no solution to heart problems.

Depressing Faust further was the failure of "Rimini," his dramatic tragedy in blank verse. He had taken the typescript to his English literary representative, A. M. Heath, in hopes of finding a publisher, but it had been coolly received. Leonard Bacon put his finger on the root of the trouble. "Your manner is exactly the manner that Mr. Shakespeare would have adopted in treating the same subject," he told Faust in firm fashion.

Faust seemed unable to realize that successful contemporary poetry had as a rule to be written in contemporary language influenced by relevant contemporary issues.

Bacon's phrase "in the manner of" haunted him. Was he an imitation poet? Had he in fact exchanged his artistic integrity for money and become incapable of producing good verse?

"Verse has been the God of my worship and verse has been shabbily served by me," he confessed to Schoolcraft. "Christ tells his followers to leave everything and follow him, and I have often thought that one could transcribe the idea and phrase it in this fashion: 'Leave the whole world and follow your higher self, if you can be sure what your higher self is.' " He said he had met a London doctor who had abandoned a lucrative practice and reduced his living to a tiny house in the suburbs, so that he could devote his life to research. "That man had content. Jesus, what pure happiness he lived in. I felt like a worm while I talked to him."

There is no evidence that Faust considered his enjoyment of material comforts a compensation for earlier deprivations or later invalidism, but perhaps this should be read into the argument. Similarly there is no evidence that he blamed his family, his friendships, and his other distractive interests for his failure to produce the poetry he wanted to produce. He blamed himself

—and continued to find life and its enjoyment on the whole more important than art.

In distress, he decided to try the then quite new treatment of psychoanalysis, which Bacon had been undergoing with Baynes. A few days later he reported to Bacon: "Baynes is so damned keen that he gets a man's drift before a sentence is half spoken. I think he is going to untie some of the knots in the rusty old machine that serves me in place of brain."

But after two interviews Faust wasn't so sure. "What ugly business this psychological stuff is. It is like becoming conscious of one's digestive process. 'Now the starches are being turned to sugar; now the fats are being made easily assimilable,' and still, in the back of my head, there is a feeling that everything that lends an emphasis to self-consciousness is bound to be bad."

Shortly thereafter he believed he saw through to the truth.

"The word 'disciple' gives the game away. These birds start with science and wind up with religion. They try to remove the outer shell from everything and get the insides of a man and his ideas, but you can't remove the outside shell. It's a part of us, thank Jesus. If we are rooted in dirt, we don't know it, and Nature doesn't mean that we should know it. But these psychoanalysts— at least the Jung school—wrap themselves in mystery and get to writing stuff that sounds like a prophetic book from the Bible."

He said he had begun his treatment with the feeling that he was "a terrible nut" who needed a doctor and was ending by feeling that he ought to take his doctor by the hand and lead him out into the fresh air.

"I never felt so normal in my whole damned life as I did after talking to Baynes for twenty hours, off and on."

Faust may have been describing Baynes' subtle method of treating a difficult case. They played golf together, and Baynes gave him a book of ancient Assyrian poems. Faust bought a Rolls-Royce touring car for £1,350 (about $6,750), hammered out fifteen to twenty-five pages a day—some days hitting as high as fifty-two—and took Dorothy to see Charlie Chaplin in *The Gold*

Rush. Baynes asked to read "Rimini" and *The Village Street*, liking the latter particularly.

"I wasn't really analyzed," Faust claimed. "It took Baynes twenty hours just to get me 'prepared,' so you can see that I constitute a problem."

Having consulted the disciple, Faust moved on to the master.

"I met Jung the other day. He is a healthy guy and he smokes a pipe like a German—I mean, smacking his lips. He told me what Baynes couldn't find out in twenty hours—that all I needed was to stop kidding myself and live a simple life and find out what made an automobile run instead of just sitting in the front seat and pushing pedals. There is nothing more depressing than to think that you are sick and not be able to interest a doctor in your case. However, I had a pretty good talk with Jung after that. We shook hands on the idea that degeneracy in music starts with Beethoven and flowers in Wagner, that Michelangelo is a rotter, too, that Goethe is nine-tenths dishonest, and that the three artists are Bach, Rembrandt, and Shakespeare."

Jung let Faust do most of the talking, then delivered effective advice.

"He told me, in short, that the only way to be honest in writing was to search my own mind, because no outsider could put his finger on what was bunk in me and what was real."

Once more the answers led back to himself.

During what must have been a major personal crisis, Faust appears to have met no English literary people at all. He might have benefited by meeting one in particular who lived not far away. Robert Graves was struggling to come to grips with himself, his poetry, and a wife and three children at nearby Islip. Graves was soon to begin writing historical novels such as *I, Claudius* which earned him money and fame while his reputation as a poet continued to grow.

Faust and Graves had a number of personal characteristics in common. They were of similar blood (Irish and German) and interests (poetry, mythology, and classical literature) and age—

Faust being two years older. Both could tell time to within a few minutes' accuracy without the aid of a clock, and neither could carry or wear a watch without disrupting or stopping its operation, apparently because of their natural electro-chemical potential. When Graves' historical novels began appearing in later years, Faust read them with keen interest, while producing similar money-making efforts himself, for almost exactly the same reasons.

In October, he crossed to France with his family, the new Rolls, and a driver. After staying briefly at Saint Jean de Luz and at Paris, where he worked steadily between sightseeing jaunts, they motored south to winter at Menton on the French Riviera near the Italian border. Left behind were Baynes, Lewis, all such incubuses, and a new life began to unfold.

Faust acquired a deep tan in the Mediterranean sun, taught himself Italian so he could read Dante in the original, and taught his children English history by reading nightly from Froude or from Green's four-volume *Short History of the English People.* He worked furiously on verse in the morning, prose in the afternoon, and played golf three times a week on the superb course at Mount Agel, a half-mile high, with the Alps on one side and the Mediterranean on the other.

Sometimes he drove the Rolls at suicidally high speeds on the Grande Corniche.

Robert Benchley, Scott Fitzgerald, Archibald MacLeish, and other writers were at nearby Antibes, Nice, and Cannes, and there were many parties, but the Fausts seem to have participated infrequently if at all, and there is no evidence that he met any celebrities. He was deeply engaged in his personal survival game.

"I've never been busier or happier. If I live another ten years, I may write something worthwhile," he wrote Sidney Howard. Meanwhile, from the villa at Menton to the reading public in the U.S., *Trouble Trail*, *The Border Bandit*, and *Comanche* went galloping off. Faust was implementing an example which James Fenimore Cooper, often called the father of the western story, had set a century before while traveling and living with his family in grand style in Europe. Faust was to carry the example to extraordinary heights.

In addition to *Western Story Magazine,* his fiction was now appearing in *Far West Illustrated, Country Gentleman,* and *Collier's.* It was also in *Detective Fiction Weekly, Detective Story Magazine,* and *Short Stories.* As for books, in 1926 Chelsea House published 6 Faust novels (*Blackie and Red, The Brute, Train's Trust, Ronicky Doone, Ronicky Doone's Treasure, The Whispering Outlaw*); Bobbs-Merrill 2 (*The Splendid Rascal* and *Monsieur*); Putnam 2 (*Fire Brain* and *The White Wolf*); and in England, Hodder and Stoughton brought out 5 (*Harrigan, The Stranger at the Gate, Luck, Black Jack, Fate's Honeymoon*), in addition to announcing Faust's most unusual western, *The Garden of Eden,* for a grand total of 16 novels, that one year. Four of the titles issued in England had never appeared in book form in the U.S.

The Garden of Eden deserves special mention. It is probably unique among westerns. Not a fist is clenched or a shot fired throughout the entire book. The tale begins in characteristic Faust style as a racetrack tout from the eastern U.S. arrives in a western town, where he is struck by the appearance of a certain gray horse. The tout serves as major catalyst in what follows. Learning more about the origin of the impressive horse from a girl named Ruth, he makes his way into the mountains, where there is a hidden valley that is the home of a strain of some truly fabulous grays and some comparably fabulous people. The people are mostly the aged Negro retainers of a surprising young man named David Eden. Eden, another alias for Faust, has the delusion that he can live within himself and his secret valley, cut off from the world. The Negroes and the girl Ruth set him straight. Ruth and David agree in the end to face the world beyond the mountains.

Faust had never given up his own dream of self-realization beyond the mountains, and he felt he could face the world now.

In the spring the family crossed the Alps to Florence and leased the Villa Pazzi, a historic manor located in the Arcetri district high in the hills on the south side of the Arno River, overlooking the dome of the cathedral and the city where the Renaissance was born.

The location would have pleased William Williams, Faust's science teacher at Modesto High School. A few yards up the lane was the house where Galileo had lived while studying the stars.

12.

FLORENCE

"THREE lines of verse, twenty-eight pages of prose. A perfectly beautiful day," Faust wrote from his new home on July 26, 1926.

The blue sky above the Apennines and the shining city below were part of a great promise.

Mussolini's Fascism, though a latent menace, was hardly apparent. Florence lived timelessly apart from such temporal phenomena. It was the Florence of D. H. Lawrence, Norman Douglas, Aldous Huxley, Bernard Berenson, dean of art experts, and other notables; but it was outwardly a quiet place. Some thought it very dull. It was quite different from glamorous Paris or worldly Rome. Its 200,000 inhabitants, conscious of a special heritage, existed in a kind of honored decadence along the banks of the Arno, turning out during the day to make a little *movimento* in the bars and restaurants of the Via Tornabuoni or the Lungarno, or the Piazza Cavour, to laugh, gossip, shrug, and enjoy themselves as Italians have been doing through the ages, but shutting themselves away in their houses at night. By nine o'clock almost no one was about. Even the horses and carriages of the Piazza Signoria, that served the tourists, had gone to their stables.

Such retiring qualities were also true of the century-old foreign colony that once numbered Elizabeth Barrett and Robert Browning and Henry James among its members. This quiet life suited Faust. He had come to work. What was required, he knew, if he were to write an important poem, was the deepest kind of self-searching, the deepest kind of penetration through his many aliases to his true self. His mind fastened upon the myth of the god of poetry, Dionysus, descending to the underworld to find his mother and the truth about his own personality. Under the olive trees in the villa of the madmen—Pazzi literally means mad—Faust grappled with this theme.

The Pazzi Villa stands today as it did then behind a stone wall, a barred gate, a porter's lodge, and a bit of *podere*, or small Italian-style farm of grapevines and olive trees and patches of wheat, on the upper reaches of a narrow lane that winds from the Piazzale Michelangelo toward the hilltop of the Arcetri. It is a pleasant hillside with a mellow atmosphere in which lurks an element of ancient violence. Leonardo and Michelangelo walked here as boys. Dante knew it, and so did Boccaccio and Petrarch. On the flagstones of the courtyard where Faust worked out of doors in good weather, men of the Pazzi family had once stood, daggers dripping blood, after stabbing Giulano de Medici to death in the cathedral.

Here if anywhere the many-faceted spirit of the Renaissance should surround a man. No other city contained as much of the world's great art as Florence. Greece, which had inspired Florence, lay just across the water, a step eastward. It was the atmosphere for which Faust had longed.

But he must hurry. He had published no poetry since *The Village Street* in 1922. He was thirty-four years old. Each year might be the last.

At the same time that he began the major poetic effort of his life, he began an unusual piece of work in prose. It grew out of the prolonged visit of an old friend, Chandler Barton, who was sinking into alcoholism and was largely dependent on Faust for support. Barton had once had a small talent for writing, and to keep this talent alive and to keep its owner occupied while he lived at Villa Pazzi, Faust helped him develop the concept of a three-way dialogue between Jesus, Judas, and Pilate. When Barton proved unequal to the task of writing the work, Faust wrote it himself.

It begins:

> In the evening Pontius Pilate liked to dine in a small remote courtyard of his palace on Mt. Zion. Darkness and the quiet beauty of the garden were all that made life tolerable in this city of the Jews. As he reclined there, even the three ugly towers of David which rose over the palace took on a shadowy, foreboding charm, and looking across the Xystus towards Mt. Moriah, at the great Roman bridge, and at King Herod's Grecian palace, the governor could almost dream that he was back at his Sicilian villa.

Pilate hears an uproar in the city below, summons an attendant, and inquires the cause. He is told that the people are being disturbed by a villager who calls himself the son of God.

Pilate recalls the Nazarene he attempted to question earlier that day and who was sent to prison. He orders the man brought before him.

When Jesus appears, Pilate upbraids him for not answering him when questioned that morning.

> "You were not then disposed to listen."
> "But will you speak now? The mob howls for your blood. Let me place an accuser before you and let you justify your life if you can, with this added assurance: that I believe that you may be an honest man."

Judas is brought. He accuses Jesus of trying to destroy humanism and freedom of thought. This has been the reason for the betrayal.

The remainder of the work is a three-way dialogue in which Judas is given the role of poet and humanist, Pilate that of moderator and cultured man of the world, and Jesus is the Jesus of the gospels.

The manuscript is titled "Some Doubted." But as dawn breaks over the city, Pilate and Judas are persuaded—not by Jesus' doctrines but by Jesus the man.

"I have the remedy. [says Judas, turning to Pilate] In your prison is a man named Barabbas, a condemned murderer. Release him to the mob in place of this just man."

"Some Doubted" did not find a publisher. A Christianized Plato could scarcely have done justice to the dialogue Faust attempted. Yet for all his brashness a reader feels compelled to turn the pages. Had he been equipped with the temperament and finances to spend years instead of weeks on the work, he might have produced a masterpiece instead of a 247-page typewritten manuscript.

"Some Doubted" was one of Faust's rare prose failures. It was primarily metaphysics, not fiction. To be successful, he had to dream.

After a year, he gave his Florentine sojourn greater permanence by moving from the Villa Pazzi to a more cheerful and homelike residence on the north slope of the Arno near the suburb of Fiesole. The new villa was one of a group owned by a wealthy Englishman, Arthur Acton, descendant of an eminent family. Each villa in the Acton group was surrounded by several acres of grounds and gardens. Four were the traditional Florentine combination of grandeur and grace. Acton's own, called "La Pietra," was and remains a rather celebrated bit of architecture and has been duplicated as far away as the Dillingham residence in Honolulu. Other villas in the group were the "Sassetti," occupied by the Peace Hazards of Peace Dale, Rhode Island; the "Natalia," occupied by Lady Eaton, a Canadian whose household staff included her personal dentist; and the "Emilia," occupied at various times by various tenants, including the Leonard Bacons.

Faust's eye had been taken by the fifth villa. It was hardly a villa at all when he first saw it. It was a remodeled farmhouse combined with a deconsecrated thirteenth-century chapel, situated in a *podere* of seven acres. Genuine *contadini* from nearby cottages

The *Occident* staff, University of California, 1915. Faust is standing, center; Sidney Howard is seated at right. (*Blue and Gold.*)

William Rose Benét, assistant editor of *The Century Magazine* and later co-founder of the *Saturday Review*, was the first to buy Faust's poetry. (*Saturday Review*.)

As editorial director for the Munsey magazine interests, Robert H. ("Bob") Davis launched Faust on his career as a writer of prose fiction. (Wide World Photos.)

Kiss or Kill, 1918, was the first big film hit based on Faust's work. (Reproduced from *Motion Picture News*.)

In 1920, Faust's first novel, *The Untamed*, launched Tom Mix and his horse Tony as motion-picture superstars in a gala opening on Broadway, New York City. (*Motion Picture News*, Twentieth-Century Fox Film Corp., Academy of Motion Picture Arts and Sciences Library.)

Cover of *All-Story Weekly* for July 14, 1917.
(Reproduced from *All-Story Weekly*.)

Cover of *All-Story Weekly* for October 27, 1917.
(Reproduced from *All-Story Weekly*.)

10¢ PER COPY SATURDAY NOV. 1 BY THE YEAR $4.00

ALL-STORY WEEKLY

DOUGLAS FAIRBANKS

As He Will Appear *in the* Film Version *of the* Great Western Story

TRAILIN'!
By Max Brand
Author of "The Untamed," *etc.*

Cover of *All-Story Weekly* for November 1, 1919. Faust's success in the popular writing and popular film markets was simultaneous. However, something went wrong when Douglas Fairbanks was advertised in a Faust-based film that later featured Tom Mix instead of Fairbanks. (Reproduced from *All-Story Weekly*.)

Cover of *All-Story Weekly* for March 13, 1920.
(Reproduced from *All-Story Weekly*.)

Faust as a young father, with Jane and John, 1923.

Playing chess with Leonard Bacon (right) at the Villa Pazzi, Florence.

The lane leading from the tennis court up through the *podere* to the
Villa Negli Ulivi, Florence.

Florence: the swimming pool and dressing rooms, Villa Negli Ulivi. A portion of Arthur Acton's villa is visible at right.

Dorothy and Heinie Faust in Florence, 1929.

Florence: Faust's study.

Aldous Huxley as Faust knew him in Florence and Hollywood. (Wide World Photos.)

worked on the farming land that surrounded the house and gardens on three sides. White oxen pulling primitive plows and carts moved with slow dignity among the olive trees. Now and then a barefoot baritone, pruning a grapevine, broke into a chorus from Verdi. It was what foreign visitors liked to call "the real Florence."

Before taking occupancy, Faust enlarged and redecorated the house at his own expense. He hired architects, pored over plans, and poured out money as though he were a Medici.

The finished structure contained the spacious living room he had long imagined. Its dimensions were approximately twenty by forty feet, and there was a floor of dark red tile. Its walls were lined with bookshelves and tapestries, and it had a high ceiling, giant beams, a huge fireplace, and the large window through which he had once imagined himself watching a wife and two children come trudging in from the farm while he worked at his poetry.

Above the living room was a master bedroom, and above that, his study. The whole addition was crowned by an observation tower with a flat roof accessible only by an outside staircase.

Upwards of $15,000 went into the creation of a dream house Faust never owned. Like most of his dreams it was supersize, twenty-two rooms in all. "We'll call it Villa Negli Ulivi," he told Dorothy, "the house among the olive trees."

In the Villa Negli Ulivi he and Dorothy began a life that was indeed a little out of this world. Each morning at eight-thirty he was served breakfast in bed, taking his digitalis with his orange juice. Then he climbed to the study in the newly constructed tower from which he could see Giotto's tower and the dome of the cathedral in the city below.

His study had nearly the same dimensions as the living room. It was big-windowed, tile-floored, and its walls were lined with books. Summer or winter Faust opened the glass doors to the balconies to give himself all the air possible. In winter he lit the fire he found ready-laid in the fireplace and, if the weather was very cold, he put on a heavy dressing gown for added warmth. Then he got immediately to work on his poetry.

He sat in a straight-backed wooden chair and wrote at a massive antique table of dark oak, a genuine Renaissance piece from a Benedictine monastery. He worked laboriously, using a quill pen on extra-long, extra-heavy sheets of plain white paper. If he produced three lines of verse that satisfied him, it was a good morning. If he produced six, he was more than happy with four hours' work.

Under no circumstances was he interrupted. At about one o'clock he came downstairs to relax before lunch. If the weather was good he walked in the garden, a glass of vermouth in hand, discussing horticulture and the construction of beds and walks with the head gardener, perhaps pruning a hibiscus or hydrangea himself. He was especially fond of the huge azaleas of many colors that grew in large terra cotta pots.

Often Dorothy accompanied him. They inspected the American Beauty roses in the special section of the garden which he had created for her and called her rose garden. It contained more than a dozen varieties displayed on trellises and arbors. Then they examined the Ampelopsis vine which he had planted against the south wall of the new addition and which was rapidly covering the entire side of the house.

If the weather was fair but not too hot, lunch was served on the front terrace overlooking *podere* and city. In hot weather it was served under the grape arbor on the secluded back terrace; or, if the weather were inclement, in the deconsecrated chapel that had become the villa's formal dining room. The walls contained low niches which had once housed sacred statuary. Faust's two Newfoundland dogs, Big Boy and Billy, sat in them during meals. The dogs were well disciplined and kept their seats unless invited to descend.

Table service was under the direction of the first butler, Elia, who also acted as general manager of the entire household and grounds staff. There were ten servants in all, including two butlers, two maids, one cook, one cook's helper, one chauffeur, and three gardeners.

The meals reflected Faust's hunger for excellence and desire for amplitude. They included best soups, tastiest *pastas*, finest sauces, thickest steaks, costliest French and Italian wines, and were capped with rare cheese, choice apples, and coffee royal. After ceremoniously mixing the salad dressing himself, he ate rapidly and little, almost wolfing his food, talking, expounding, gesticulating. A meal with him was more like a bout than a repast. It was an exhausting experience, organized around the principle that time is precious and life tremendously worth investigating.

After lunch he lay down for a nap on a day-bed in his tower study. Dorothy read aloud until he fell asleep. She continued reading lest he wake, her soft voice striking a relaxed pitch that she had learned to maintain for hours at a time. This was his best moment for sleeping. At night, nightmares, ideas, loneliness, insomnia of various kinds kept him awake.

He rested till three, then worked hard at his prose till five or later. Instead of going to the massive antique table as in the morning, he sat relaxed in a comfortable easy chair with the Underwood typewriter on its special stand between his knees. With scarcely a moment's hesitation he attacked it with both hands. He might begin: "Old Tom Baldwin came home between the daylight and the dark, and when his mustang scuffed the deep sand outside the corral gate, he dismounted, sliding slowly out of the saddle, putting his feet gingerly, one at a time, upon the ground."

Or he might begin: "When I was in Paris, Olympe Arouet wrote to me: 'Dear Paul, now you are in France, but May is still cold in Paris. Do come into the summer and visit us. Besides, I have a need to see you. That is a need very much. Will you come?' I had probably not seen Olympe more than six times altogether, but these were spread through ten years, and, since I had been a Christian name to her father, I suppose she had inherited the fashion of using it. Jean Arouet had been an entomologist, and in his torture chambers, which he called his 'studies,' I had seen a praying mantis clamp a cricket in its hinged jaws and turn its pointed little face to me as if inviting my attention before it began to eat. Jean Arouet was proud to claim that blood of Voltaire ran in his veins but, making a good modern transition, where Voltaire had plagued little humans in the name of Man, Jean Arouet speared insects in the name of Science."

Or he might begin: "Honesty is accepted as the best policy, but it turned out the worst policy for Bill Ranger, who was famous for his integrity and as a 'dog puncher' from Dawson to the Arctic Ocean."

Or: "Caterina, Countess Sforza-Riario, high lady and mistress of the rich, strong town of Forli, was tall, well made, slenderly strong, and as beautiful as she was wise. She used to say that there was only one gift that God had specially denied her, and that was a pair of hands that had the strength of a man in them."

By approximately five o'clock, he had pounded out the twenty pages he had set himself.

Then he changed to tennis clothes, took his racket and walked down the lane, bordered by the cypress trees he had planted, to the court at the bottom of the garden in the little valley occupied by the *podere*. Often the children accompanied him and acted as ball retrievers.

The court, which he had built at his own expense, was of a red clay that gleamed warmly among the olives and cypresses. It was cared for by an old retainer named Giuseppe who raked, watered, rolled it with a heavy iron roller, and relined it daily in preparation for the afternoon's game.

Leonard Bacon, coming from the Villa Emilia across the valley, frequently met Faust for a game of singles. Often with Bacon was his daughter Martha, who would grow up to be a poet and novelist. Others in the group might be Bill Yarrow, painter of the Princeton murals, or Dick Blow, husband of a promising young writer named Marya Mannes; or perhaps Piero Amici-Grossi, of an ancient Florentine family, and his American-born wife, the former Jesse McBride of New York.

Faust could now safely play two sets of singles or three of doubles. He leaned into the ball hard. It produced the sweat and challenge to the heart that he believed his system must have.

If the day were hot, the guests might swim in the nearby pool after the game. Faust had built the pool, in the shape and size of a small lake, and added a dressing room on the shore. Like the other improvements to his dream-house establishment, they remained the property of his landlord.

He did not swim himself. He found it hard on his heart. Also he disliked the steep climb back up the slope to the villa. Therefore when tennis was finished he summoned the butler, who roared down the lane on a motorcycle. Faust mounted the seat at the rear of the cycle, racket in hand, and the two shot up the slope, while the oxen in the nearby fields stared and the peasants exchanged glances.

Before changing clothes for dinner there was usually time for several bottles of beer, some talk, perhaps a game of chess or ping-pong; and sometimes Faust worked at his typewriter again before dinner at eight-fifteen. Whether there were guests or not, he put on a dinner jacket and Dorothy a long dress.

If guests were present there was a cocktail or two, exactly what the doctors had warned against. Such consumption of alcohol, plus what he would have at dinner, added to what he had already had at lunch and after tennis, was more than enough for a well man, let alone a condemned cardiac. But fortified by his understanding with his heart and his daily sweats, Faust thumbed his nose at the doctors and enjoyed his cocktail, while discoursing upon Henri Cochet's tennis-court coverage in comparison to his own—and with part of his mind moving Dionysus to the decisive crossing of the River Styx in his epic poem of the god in the underworld.

He would digress to comment on the flower arrangements— often composed of giant camellias—achieved by Elia prior to chauffering Faust on the motorcycle, and might make mental note that *Bandit's Honor*, the western novel being completed, should be published under the David Manning rather than the Max Brand pseudonym.

Guests at dinner might be the Kenneth Clarks, or the Frank Chapmans—she Gladys Swarthout, the opera and motion picture star; or Josephine and Leo Dietrichstein, he a once-noted actor now retired; or Janet Flanner of the *New Yorker*, now thoroughly expatriated and living in Paris; or Mrs. John L. Howard, Sidney's mother and a veteran European traveler; or Edward P. Mulrooney, risen to police commissioner of New York City. Or they might include a visiting writer such as Margaret Culkin Banning, or a publisher such as Cass Canfield, president of the Harper firm. Notables seem to have appeared naturally in the course of events. Faust avoided fashionable society. Most of his guests were distinguished in no way but as friends.

At dinner conversation ruled. All present including children and governess must have an opinion and be able to defend it. The atmosphere was that of a game. Jane might be dispatched to bring down a volume of the English Dictionary from the tower study in order to define the etymology of "palindrome." John might be called upon to fetch Jomini's *Art of War* from the living room bookcase so that all could see exactly what Marlborough's dispositions were at the battle of Malplaquet. It was a moment for enjoyment and growth, spiced with food and wine, while the tall white-gloved Elia replaced one plate with another, and the arched ceiling of the onetime chapel glowed with the light from huge candles that stood in five-foot-high wooden holders in the corners.

After dinner came the reading aloud in the living room. Everyone participated. If it was a play, each read a part; if a novel, discussion periods were interspersed between Faust's or Dorothy's solo reading.

Before the children went to bed at ten, Faust concerned himself directly with their education. The fact that they attended

Miss Barry's American School, a Florentine institution of many years' standing, was not enough, in his opinion. They were required to memorize and recite lines of poetry selected by him. He quizzed them on Greek and Roman history, Alexander Hamilton's fiscal policies, and the implications of the nebula in Andromeda. They were also required to memorize the Gettysburg Address. Every Fourth of July he read to them aloud from the Constitution or from some work of the founding fathers. He was a patriotic expatriate.

"A boy must know classical and modern humanities, Greek, Latin, and French languages, basic science and economics, and be able to box and kick a football," he proclaimed. Dorothy begged him not to be so hard on the children. She lacked energy and knew what it was to be weak and to be driven. But Faust was preoccupied by the necessity for strength. "We ask for our children virtue, for ourselves strength," reads one of his notebook entries. "Strength is never contemptible." He had so much of it that he could not understand the lack of it in others.

If a boy could know a bit about Mongolia, Basutoland, judo, the ocean floor, and the Arctic, and of course poetry, it would help.

A girl should substitute music, dancing, and fencing for the football and boxing gloves. A girl should be sheltered, a boy exposed. John was sent away to school in England at age eight. Jane was kept at home and reared like Miranda in *The Tempest*.

"Shakespeare is great. Homer is great. Aeschylus is great. Sophocles is semi-great," Faust informed his children with dictatorial enthusiasm, "But no gentleman would read Euripides." He actually made this statement in the presence of a cultured Englishman who ran from the room clutching his head in both hands and crying out, "Faust, you are a desperate man!"

The children remembered their father as a well-intentioned tyrant who disciplined them with a bare hand at times and always worked them nearly to death. They did not think of themselves as rich or especially privileged but as struggling through seemingly endless days, beginning at 6:30 A.M. with "bodily exercises" and ending at 10:00 P.M. with exhaustion.

Should guests be present after dinner, the talk and reading might continue for many hours. Some of those seeing Faust at these moments likened him to a Medici prince, dominating the room, whole, tall, commandingly generous, heightening others as well as himself. He seemed to have the power of giving the best that was in him.

"Good conversations die out but they have life somewhere," he insisted. "They are the food of the Deity, perhaps."

A friend, describing an evening at the villa, said, "I seemed to see a halo about the heads of the five of us, an electric manifestation of some sort of vital communion."

Julia Marlowe and Edward Southern, a leading team of Shakespearian actors, came to dinner and read *Hamlet* afterwards, Faust liking them and approving their rendition of the Queen's Closet Scene in Act III; and Miss Marlowe, wearing long green gloves, returned later to read *Romeo and Juliet* to the children.

Nor were the evenings always serious. There were masquerade parties at which the butlers released a hundred balloons and everyone came wearing masques. Faust could be frivolous on a grand scale.

Many visitors came to the villa among the olives. Sometimes they stayed as much as six months, enjoying the hospitality and generosity, totally deceived by Faust's Medicean style into believing that the whole thing was done by a kind of magic and that time, money, and courtesy were endless.

He might rage and groan privately to Dorothy; but he knew that he liked the grand gesture, the gigantic effect, and the sometimes congenial company. Like that other ex-poor-boy Balzac, he worked best in luxurious surroundings, pressed for time, deeply in debt, and continually on the verge of exhaustion.

As respite Faust periodically indulged in wild parties with a group of male friends at the Hotel Baglioni, opposite the Florence railroad station. The festivities sometimes lasted all night, or even all next day, while Faust's chauffeur waited patiently outside in the Rolls-Royce, and Dorothy and the children at home despaired of his life. Sometimes heart attacks followed these indulgences, throwing his work behind schedule, increasing indebtedness, and building other destructive tensions. After each attack Faust regularly swore off alcohol and might keep his vow as long as two or three months, during which intensive work compensated for the lapse.

When he and Dorothy were alone after the children and guests had gone to bed, they often went to the music room, adjacent to the living room, put *Alexander's Ragtime Band* or *Three O'Clock in the Morning* on the Victrola, and danced for an hour or two.

Then they climbed the stairs to his tower study. There she read proof, sorted the originals and carbon copies of manuscripts, while he typed notes or plots or added final pages to a story that must be mailed in the morning in order to catch the fast boat to New York from Genoa or Le Havre. Editors were waiting.

In the days before the transatlantic air mail, Dorothy kept track of steamship schedules and would specify vessel and sailing date in her own handwriting on the outside of manuscript envelopes, so that the editors could receive them before deadline time.

Thus she helped maintain the grand illusion, or the unbelievable achievement, whichever it was. She said later that she did not know which it was. She never wholly wanted to live in a fabulous manner that kept them constantly in debt, created mountainous problems and daily tensions from which there appeared no escape; but Faust insisted that next week, next month all would be well—the manuscript he had in his typewriter would take care of everything.

So they worked on into the small morning hours, discussing plot, character, the three lines of poetry that in his opinion constituted his day's best effort. Dorothy listened carefully to every word, sometimes doubting the value of the poetry but hesitating to say so, not sure of herself and not wanting to hurt him.

At three, she read him to sleep in their bedroom on the second floor. It was a king-sized room that had twin beds with painted, Venetian headboards. Between the beds was a small table, piled high with books. On it was a two-stemmed reading lamp, one light for her, one for him. Very likely some element of his mother's reading entered into these bedtime readings by Dorothy. He perhaps needed a subconscious reminder of a lost peace in order to obtain peace now.

Among the books might be novels by contemporaries such as Hemingway, whom he admired, or by John Dos Passos whom he disliked. Other volumes might deal with astronomy, religion, or the life of the ant. There were travel books such as the rare *Michaux's Travels Through Ohio, Kentucky and Tennessee,* and there was a compendium on famous pirates. He continued to absorb information and ideas by his own special type of osmosis.

Drawings by Rembrandt looked down from the walls. There was a Venetian desk for Dorothy. On it or on a chair near the beds was a tray containing two or three bottles of cold beer and a dish of fresh fruit. Sometimes the dish contained fresh tomatoes which Faust munched happily, spicing them with salt and chasing them with beer, until he fell asleep. Later he woke, turned on his bedside light, and read to himself and made notes.

In all he had slept perhaps three hours, when Elia woke him at eight-thirty bringing his orange juice and digitalis.

Faust became a Florentine legend at a time when others were establishing such legends. At the Villa Mirenda across the Arno in the suburb of Scandicci, D. H. Lawrence was writing *Lady Chatterly's Lover* and having it published downtown in Florence by Giuseppe Orioli. Bernard Berenson was living in the almost sacrosanct Villa I Tatti, not far from the Fausts, now and then receiving a close friend or distinguished visitor. Faust passed through the portals of I Tatti under the guidance of Kenneth Clark and made the acquaintance of Berenson, but appears never to have met Lawrence.

Except for heart attacks, he was never sick and never missed a day of work. He had no vacations. During frequent motor trips throughout Italy, and to Spain and other parts of Europe, he took his typewriter with him and worked every day as he had worked during the first family tour of England.

Weeks and months now turned into years that were the happiest and most productive of his life. He continued to publish between one and two million words of prose fiction annually, while developing the poem he believed to be his best work.

He was, also, making film history. Rudolph Valentino had purchased *The Bronze Collar*, a novel set in Spanish California, but had died before a film could be produced. Tom Mix and Clara Bow had starred in *The Best Bad Man*, based on an offbeat western, *Señor Jingle Bells*, and Clara had gone on to much greater stardom as the "It" girl of the 1920's. *The Flying Horseman*, based on a *Country Gentleman* serial, *Dark Rosaleen*, was described by *Moving Picture World* as "an exceptionally good western for both kiddies and grown-ups." It starred Buck Jones and Gladys McConnell.

Richard Talmadge, Barbara Bedford, and Stuart Holmes starred in *The Cavalier*, based on *The Black Rider*. It was a talking picture and it opened in style at the special-run Embassy Theatre on Broadway in New York and ran for ten days at a whopping $1.50 per seat.

By 1928, Faust stories had helped Francis X. Bushman, Priscilla Dean, Jewel Carmen, Hobart Bosworth, Tom Mix (and Tony), John Gilbert, Anna May Wong, William and Dustin Farnum, Edmund Lowe, possibly Douglas Fairbanks, Sr. (there appears no record of what Fairbanks did with the Faust story he bought), and certainly many others to stardom and super-stardom in addition to Talmadge and Bow, Jones and McConnell, and Bedford.

To come were George O'Brien, Sally Eilers, George Brent, Zasu Pitts, Andy Devine, Humphrey Bogart, Marlene Dietrich, James Stewart, Joel McCrea, Barbara Stanwyck, Lew Ayres, Lionel Barrymore, Laraine Day, Rita Hayworth, Alan Ladd,

Andy Griffith, Dolores Grey, Richard Chamberlain, Raymond Massey, and many more. It was a not inconsiderable contribution to the life and culture of the twenties, thirties, forties, fifties, sixties, and perhaps other eras, but Faust knew or guessed little of this.

He was debating what to have Charon, the mythical ferryman of souls, say to Dionysus when the two met in his epic poem at the brink of the River Styx.

13.

IRELAND AND ITALY

DOROTHY had been pregnant before they moved into the Villa Negli Ulivi. They had spent the summer of 1927 together in Ireland, leaving the children with Monty Lamont at Pover'uomo, a village on the Ligurian seacoast an hour's drive from Florence. Their Irish honeymoon, as Faust called the trip, was a visit to another of his imaginary homes.

The Uriels, his mother's people, were Welsh-Irish. They linked him, he believed, with Celtic bardic lore. Lady Charlotte Guest's collection of medieval Welsh tales, *The Mabinogion*, was a treasured volume of his library. The medieval romances in which Welsh-Irish elements predominated were major sources of his own writing. King Arthur was, after all, a Celtic hero.

Faust read contemporary Irish writers such as Shaw, Yeats, and Synge with approval, and admired the early Joyce. The Irish were emerging from a centuries-old subjection to the English. Like Faust, his mother's people seemed to have found themselves.

Perhaps it was infectious enthusiasm that led him to a sojourn at a model village created by the Earl of Dunraven not far from Dublin. The area was rich in another element he found exciting —horses, the tall, long-legged big-boned Irish hunters that regularly won steeplechases in England and elsewhere and were renowned as the world's best jumpers.

In the role of a modern or model Irishman, Faust was schooling a green hunter over a jump when his horse suddenly bolted, entangling his left foot in one of the wings of the jump, and breaking his leg near the ankle. After first aid in the field he was put on the train and taken to Dublin. There an ambulance provided by the Dublin fire department carried him across town to a hospital, where a crusty surgeon who boasted he had "set more limbs of more equestrian gentlemen than any other doctor in Ireland," set the break in high-handed fashion without benefit of anesthesia.

The break was poorly set and remained painful the rest of Faust's life. But his heart, so he wrote Dr. Halsey in New York, "though as foolish as ever in rhythm, is so much stronger through exercise that I can stand a fall from a horse and a broken leg without it failing."

Back in Italy, he spent a good bit of the autumn of '27 on crutches, superintending the final remodeling and redecorating of the villa. As the birth of their "Irish baby" became imminent, Dorothy went from Florence to London. Halsey had recommended an English obstetrician. Faust remained at Villa Negli Ulivi with the children and Monty, and wrote Dorothy at 27 Welbeck Street, where she and her mother had taken a flat, "Did you cable Frank Blackwell to merely advance three thousand, or to pay Fidelitas the three thousand we owe? In the former case, of course, I can't pay the book bill." In addition to book purchases, he asked her to take care of a special allowance of $370 for his sister Pauline.

He was accumulating what he called a library suitable for a civilized man in the twentieth century. Volumes he particularly valued were bound in morocco, pigskin, or calf—for example, the facsimile of the 1632 edition of Shakespeare, and the facsimile of the 1532 collection of Chaucer's work. He had purchased George Baker's 1797 translation of Titus Livius' *History of Rome* in six volumes and the entire Loeb classical library as well as Milman's *History of Latin Christianity* and *History of the Jews.* All of the major English, French, German, Italian, Spanish, Russian, and other European classics were represented; and his volumes on the American West were running into dozens, including Bayard Taylor's works, Horace Greeley's *An Overland Journey from*

New York to San Francisco in the Summer of 1859, and the complete histories of Bancroft.

There were scores of books on the Middle Ages, and the villa's shelves groaned under the works of the Renaissance. Leather bindings were often worked with gold. One invoice from Zaehnsdorf, his London bookbinder, ran to more than $10,000.

Faust's letters to Dorothy continued but he remained in Florence. His good intentions about joining her became entangled and finally lost in a maze of unforeseen circumstances. An invitation not made seriously but immediately accepted had obliged him, he believed, to take a tour of central Italy in company with English friends, the Herbert Dursts. They traveled with Faust's car and driver, visiting the monastery at Cassino and stopping at Sulmona, where the poet Ovid was born. At Terni he was typing in his room near midnight when a telegram from London announced the caesarian birth of his daughter Judith, three weeks prematurely.

Faust rushed back to the villa, but instead of continuing to London he regaled Dorothy with reasons why he could not. He was finishing a serial that must be completed to pay current bills. The children had the measles. Workmen were completing the decorating of the master bedroom. He and Elia were supervising the construction of walks and flower beds, so that he was obliged to spend as much as a third of each day in the garden.

Dorothy arranged a $1,500 advance from Blackwell, in New York, to pay London expenses and get herself, her baby, and her mother back to Florence.

It was becoming axiomatic that when they were separated he got into trouble and so did she.

"I notice that you have sent for a fifteen hundred dollar advance," Faust noted huffily. "Of course that's quite all right. Today I finish another complete serial, then start a series of novelettes, which I have planned to the last detail, so that they will be swift and easy. At this rate, we cannot long lack money, can we?"

From Dorothy's point of view, he was simply failing her one more time; yet from his, the aggravations of the moment were extreme. Improvements to the villa had cost more than expected. The London obstetrician had charged 168 guineas instead of the expected 125. With a grandiloquence that reminded him of his own shortcomings, Pauline had written from Seattle, his birthplace, that she needed $2,500 "to become a real estate dealer," plus additional funds so that she could "be properly dressed while acting as voluntary assistant to our woman mayor."

The return of wife and baby soothed things momentarily. Faust took Dorothy to Vienna on what was for him a working holiday; and they summered with the children and Monty at Camaldoli, a resort in the Apennines not far from Florence; and during the autumn they worked together at landscaping the villa's grounds.

Arthur Acton, their landlord, had allowed them the use of land immediately north of the tennis court for the construction of the swimming pool, and now spoke of buying acreage to the south so they could plant a grove of olives. They would become orchardists, husbanding the sacred tree once blessed by Athena. They would press the oil in their own presses and make their wine in their own vineyards.

Acton came calling with his wife, a former Chicago heiress, and two sons, Harold and William; and Harold remained to talk about poetry with Faust, Faust finding him "intelligent, gentle, and manly" and "trying to support himself without financial help from his father" while working at verse. The young Acton later became known as the author of *Memoirs of an Aesthete*, *The Last Medici*, and other books. Eventually he was to give his father's villa, as well as Faust's, to New York University, to be used as an international center for scholars and students.

Faust was pouring prose fiction into *Western Story* for quick financial return. At five cents a word, he was earning more than $75,000 a year from this source alone. In all, Blackwell was to buy 307 stories from him—perhaps more than any other editor ever bought from an author—while paying Faust reportedly the highest rates ever paid in the history of "pulp" publishing.

But suddenly *Western Story* rejected two serials and a novelette. Even one dropped stitch in Faust's tense fabric of production was a serious matter. Three loomed like disaster. Perhaps he had been abroad too long and was getting out of touch with his market. After an absence of four years, he decided to revisit the U.S. As usual his plans grew larger until they included a transcontinental auto tour in the company of Bob Davis, who was at the height of his fame as author and columnist.

"We'll really see the West this time!" Davis promised.

14.

U.S.A., 1929

IN January, 1929, Faust landed in New York to find his novel *Mistral* appearing serially in *The American Weekly*, a Sunday newspaper supplement of wide circulation.

His first order of business was a visit to the editorial rooms of *Western Story*. "I met Blackwell at three o'clock," he wrote to Dorothy in Florence, "and we talked until seven. Never were so many words shed. They fell like leaves." Faust said Blackwell's secretaries looked at the two of them as if they were watching two men drown and could do nothing about it.

He described Blackwell as a lonely little man unhappy with his work and hungry for a sympathetic ear.

Blackwell said that the reason for the refusal of Faust's three stories was a lack of adherence to the Blackwellian principles of pursuit and capture and delayed revelation. There also had been a tendency to develop character at the expense of action. However, no further problem in the purchasing of production was anticipated. "He will take everything we can provide," Faust assured Dorothy.

Dorothy was urging him to return to the villa, but he said that what he called his raid on the gold of the United States could not possibly be concluded so soon, so she must come to him. He was determined to secure old markets and open new ones. "There is no end to prosperity, here. Travel will soon be largely by air. The great business enterprises are taking in as partners the whole nation, as long as it has a penny to invest. There is more blood circulating in the arteries of America than in all the rest of the world."

With the 1929 market crash still six months away, the United States was at the height of its 1920's prosperity. Faust quickly produced enough revenue to pay Dorothy's transatlantic fare. A friendly Munsey editor went so far as to raise a purchase price from $2,500 to $2,750, "the extra 250 being a kind of grace note." Yet Faust found New York depressing. "People take me aside and ask me with hungry eyes how life is in Florence. In pity I talk down to them. I don't tell them how little I pay for rent [the entire villa and grounds cost him $3,000 a year], or how much room we have, or how wonderful our servants are. Partly because I don't want to boast, and partly because it makes them writhe like something underfoot. They *are* underfoot. New York has them down and walks on their faces. They look thin, weak, nervous, and hurried. They don't meet your eyes."

He did not tell his friends that it cost $2,000 a year just to heat his palatial villa.

Dorothy joined him early in March and they stayed a week at the Plaza Hotel, where he had once been denied admission. Then she left by train to visit her parents in California; and he and Davis began their cross-country tour in a new Willys-Knight four-door touring car purchased by Faust.

"We started out in style from in front of the *Sun*, stopped briefly in Central Park so that Bob could be photographed at the wheel, standing on the running board, gazing toward the western horizon, etc., and shortly after one o'clock we barged away."

Whizzing along at thirty-five miles per hour, they reached Ephrata in western Pennsylvania that night.

"But for Ephrata there would be no United States of America," Faust wrote Dorothy in California. "This is the reason. After the Declaration of Independence was written, our fathers remembered that a great slice of the citizens did not read English, so they looked about them for a man who could translate it into the seven necessary languages. They found him in Ephrata. You can imagine that this is all clover for Bob. He is out now interviewing a self-taught painter in oils, and a cripple who can't leave his room and about whom all Ephrata whispers great things."

Faust had brought his typewriter as usual and was pounding out stories each night while Davis wrote his columns.

After spending two memorable hours on the Gettysburg battlefield and crossing the Potomac at Harper's Ferry, they found spring just coming to the Shenandoah Valley. "The willows actually have trailers already, the elm trees are getting fuzzy in the branches, and some of the bushes have touches of red."

Faust thought the Virginians a shade on the sour side, compared with the good-natured western Pennsylvanians of the night before, and there was enough of the southern aristocratic element "still tainting the air to make them resent Bob's bluntness. There wasn't much sleep last night because we had a double room and I had to listen to Bob snoring in sharps and flats all night long. By the time I reach the coast, I'll be either dead, or in excellent working habits."

Poetry was never far from his mind, and he worked at his style by studying the "wealth of feminine endings" in Shakespeare's *Henry VIII*.

They left Virginia, dropping out of beautiful mountains into "districts that remind me of central California as it was twenty-five years ago. I don't mean the appearance of the country so much as the people, their tone and their ways. Everyone is boosting. 'We like you, come again!' read the signs on the far side of the towns. I suppose boosting is a virtue, but my God, what an unattractive one."

He teased Dorothy with descriptions of the charms of southern girls, while making firm resolves to be a better husband in the future. He was truly afraid of losing her. It seemed to him, he said, that his shortcomings, potential and actual, might someday cause her to see what he called "the appalling truth" about him, and to turn a cold cheek when next they met and say she had found the real love of her life. He even promised to take her out to tea when they got back to Florence.

At Winston-Salem, the tourists visited the Reynolds Tobacco Company and were astonished to find that the firm paid the government $500,000 a day, five days a week, for tax stamps to put on cigarette packages. They met Reynolds himself, "as fine, and kind, and simple an old boy as you'd meet in a year's traveling. It was amusing to see Bob warm him up. Bob has the brass of a piratical broadside in the good old days."

Faust found it exhilarating to meet top executives and their assistants. "I don't want to compare small things with great, but I suddenly was able to understand how such men as Washington, Jackson, Lee, J. E. Johnston, and all the rest came out of the South. They were without bunk, perfectly simple, and knew their stuff."

Davis gave an interview to a local paper, saying that he was traveling with "the celebrated novelist, Max Brand." Faust exploded, and Davis promised not to reveal his identity again.

In the racing horse country near Lexington, Kentucky, they stopped to see Man o' War. Faust found him "a royal beauty."

"It was sacred soil that he walked on. Think of seeing the greatest horse that ever lived and actually rubbing his nose!"

Faust also saw Morvich, Dress Parade, and other four-footed celebrities. "There was a foal out of a mare with the funny name of Ringlets by Sweep, that looked like a lightning flash. I've never seen such wonderful long legs, and shoulders and quarters, as square as a Percheron's."

Sensing he loved horses, the Negro groom led him from stall to stall and finally to an old mare named Masquerade and asked him to guess her age. "I saw the point that was coming. Her temples were sunken two inches deep and her lower lip hung loose and her backbone was raised and her belly sagged, but I politely guessed that she was about ten. They whooped with joy and told me she was twenty-four. 'But sir, you're not the first real horseman that's missed her age!' "

Elizabeth Dangerfield, who supervised the care and training of Man o' War and other horses owned by the Riddle Stables, entertained them at tea.

137

"She's very nice, with the horseman's straight-looking eye. She lives, breathes and dreams horses. She speaks of 'scholarly horsemen' and 'lucky ones,' and 'cheap' ones. Some have only a smattering. Some have nothing but good fortune. I learned from her that Man o' War is too high behind, to suit some, and that his action was too high off the ground, to suit others. But to her he's the perfect machine. Lexington is the flaw in his ancestry which keeps him out of the English studbook."

They went on toward the West by way of the Deep South. At Lake Bruin, Louisiana, they stayed at an exclusive hunting and fishing club where well-to-do residents of Monroe retired for weekends and vacations. It was surrounded by lovely woods, "all drenched with grey Spanish moss, and the lake itself is quite charming. Wherever we go, I'm staggered by the wealth of every community. We are now in the Black South with a vengeance, with superstition, and the crass ignorance which pervades every part of the 'cultured South' specially on deck here. Once more, the Negroes are far more interesting than the whites. They rise a bit to meet the whites, who can only sink to meet the blacks."

Faust found the hospitality astonishing. "It would be quite perfect except that they are pretty self-conscious about it all. Let these people occupy themselves with dogs and horses and bear hunts and turkey calls, and they are all right, but all subjects where information must be recruited out of books are to be strictly avoided."

On the shores of Lake Bruin they camped near the place where Theodore Roosevelt had hunted in 1907. The caretaker of the camp was a Negro who had hunted with Roosevelt. He told with enthusiasm about Teddy's nine cups of strong black coffee a day, his dislike of meat, his love of fish, his swimming every morning in the icy winter water of the lake, his sportsmanship, his good riding.

"They loved him here. He must have been a man, in addition to being so much of a faker. It was Governor Parker of Louisiana who ran with him on the Bull Moose ticket."

Faust had picked up quantities of information that might turn readily into stories. At the same time he was becoming homesick for chianti, for nightingales and the peace of his *podere*, and for his children. Davis was getting increasingly on his nerves and he on Davis'. From Monroe, Louisiana, to Dallas, Texas, the road was rough in more ways than one. Faust's dynamic driving did not help matters.

"Bob wriggled in the seat, clasped his hands, rearranged his hat, and every time the rear spring let us whang down on the axle he'd groan, 'Jesus!' Finally I invited trouble by asking him if he was nervous. He was so delighted to have the door opened in this way that he hardly could speak for a moment. Then he began something as follows:

" 'It's a pretty plain thing to me that the only reason you want to drive a car is to torture the people that are with you on a trip. Every time I nearly put my foot through the floorboards to ease around a corner, I can see you laugh and step on the accelerator. A motor trip with you is worse than a Belgian atrocity. If you haven't cut off my hands at the wrists you've cut off my heart at the roots. For Christ's sake have a little compassion on an old man. If you have anything against me, use a gun and not an automobile.' "

Faust was monitoring his daily production of prose by the day and by the hour. At the end of a forty-five page day he crowed to Dorothy, "If I keep on at this rate, by the time I meet you in Los Angeles I shall have written between eleven and twelve thousand dollars' worth of stuff. That's a rate of a hundred and forty-four thousand a year. And nothing this side of hell is going to interfere with my schedule."

He had planned a raid on the gold of Hollywood and asked her to stand by to pick up the loot.

By the time he and Davis reached the Baker Hotel in Dallas, Faust's daily output had leveled off at twenty-five pages. He was touching no liquor and feeling fine. "Suppose that alcohol should become actually repugnant to me?" he speculated to Dorothy, and told her to prepare to have another baby. But his enthusiasm for Davis and the U.S. was nearly at an end.

Near El Paso they picked up an oilfield worker who "gave us a grand story about capping gushers, and how the great eight-inch bit is blown over the top of the derrick by the force of the gas spouting, and how he saw a gusher catch fire, and how he saw thirteen men burn horribly to death. But the best thing was how Texas Thornton puts out the fires, which is by backing up a truck to within twenty feet of the flames and then catapulting great tubes of nitroglycerin into them. The explosion blasts out the fire. Tex gets a thousand dollars for one of his performances. Why he is still alive, no one knows, including himself. But better than the oil fields was the old fellow's talk about horses. He assured me that if you take time and pains, a horse can understand more of one's speech than most men, and he told me of a beautiful blood-bay he once owned, which used to come and waken him at night if anything strange was happening on the prairie."

Faust used the horse as prototype for a fictional horse called Parade in a number of subsequent western novels. Parade and others were lineal descendants of the imaginary stallion his father had once stolen from the imaginary southern mansion.

And then in El Paso one evening as he and Davis saw the blazing marquee of a threater proclaiming, SEE CLARA BOW, THE "IT" GIRL, MAKE WHOOPEE! Faust decided he had had enough. Not even the gold of Hollywood was going to keep him from getting back to Italy as fast as possible.

They managed to jolt on rapidly to Los Angeles, where Dorothy met them. Davis returned East by train. The Willys-Knight was disposed of, Yuba City quickly visited, and the Fausts fled back to Florence, where he wrote, "The sense in Europe of the many crowding generations is beautiful to me and I am carried along on a river of existence; whereas in our own country that river seems to me always pouring over a great brink of darkness. Such matters as war and famines, in Europe, are merely temporary, like gestures illustrating a moment of speech. There have been worse things before; there will be worse things to follow; and man still exists. Peace such as I've never known in America comes to me in Europe. Returning to Italy, I noticed that the peasants working in the twilight fields were the color of the earth; and an ocean of peace rose up around me."

15.

DESTRY RIDES AGAIN

ONCE again Faust had failed to penetrate the "real West," but one result of his trip was an unexpectedly successful piece of work.

Written during and after his travels with Davis, *Destry Rides Again* turned out to be one of the most popular western novels of all time. Its setting is somewhere in a West that Faust had failed to reach in actuality but which he continued to know imaginatively. Harry Destry is the "rootin'est, tootin'est, scrappin'est youngster" yet known in the town of Wham, situated near the Crystal Mountains. Wham is something of Modesto, the Crystal Mountains are something of the Sierra Nevada, and Destry perceiving Wham is a bit of Faust perceiving Modesto. "It was mapped in his mind; he knew every street sign, and the men behind the signs, from the blacksmiths to the lawyers, for Destry had grown up in the place. He had squirmed his bare toes in the hot dust of the main street; he had fought in the vacant lots; and many a house or store was built over some scene of his grandeur. For the one star in the crown of Harry Destry, the one jewel in his purse, the one song in his story, was that he fought; and when he battled, he was never conquered."

Destry is framed by a local Machiavelli named Bent who as a boy had been defeated by Destry in a Tom Sawyer-like scuffle such as Faust had engaged in in valley towns. Destry is so naive he thinks Bent is his best friend, but Bent is also Destry's rival for the affections of pretty Charlotte Dangerfield. So closely does the tale reflect the 1929 trip with Davis that Faust not only used the Dangerfield name but transformed one of the Riddle thor-

oughbreds—perhaps the foal that looked like a lightning flash—
into Destry's superlative mare, Fiddle.

As consequence of Bent's treachery, Destry is sentenced to
prison on false evidence and the perjured judgment of twelve
peers, who happen to be, like Bent, men he has cheerfully bested
in various contests when they were boys, and who secretly hold
grudges against him.

"Twelve peers? Twelve half-bred pups," Destry tells them to
their faces, leaning into the jury box when their decision has
been made known. "When my ten years has come up, I'm gunna
call on all of these here, and if they ain't in, I'm gunna leave my
card anyway!"

Come back he does, leave his card he does, win Charlie Dangerfield he does, and thereby hangs the tale.

It introduced the concept of the reluctant western hero, a hero
as reluctant to engage in violence as Faust was to experience the
realities of the West. The reluctance of the literary Destry turns
out to be a mask, but the concept of reluctance and naiveté in a
western hero was new, appealing, and it caught on.

The novel appeared serially in *Western Story*, beginning February 1, 1930, under the title of *Twelve Peers*, and in book form
as *Destry Rides Again* on August 22. It is characterized by the
bounce and good humor that Faust felt during much of his
transcontinental motor tour with Davis. It is almost farce. The
bloodshed cannot be taken seriously. Men die, but they die as if
shot down in a musical comedy. This is in fact comedy. It bur-
lesques the western syndrome. The author is poking fun at himself, Davis, and their entire trip. At the end of the book Harry
Destry symbolically puts away his Colt and devotes himself to
other subjects, as the United States and Faust were about to do.

Among western novels, only Zane Grey's *Nevada* and Jack
Schaefer's *Shane* reportedly have sold more copies than *Destry
Rides Again*.

After negotiating for nearly a year, Universal bought film
rights. The delay was partly due to efforts to sign Walter Huston

to play the leading role, but Huston had wanted $40,000 and Universal had balked. The rights were finally purchased from a financially hardpressed Faust for $1,500.

The three motion-picture versions of *Destry* have featured in turn Tom Mix (1932), Marlene Dietrich and James Stewart (1939), and Audie Murphy (1954). Except for the Mix version, Faust's essential message of reluctance, fun, and farce remained unchanged. The Dietrich-Stewart version is generally considered to have established a trend toward western-film satire and toward the "new" or "adult" western which now includes the anti-hero.

In the 1950's, *Destry* proved an attractive subject for a David Merrick musical comedy starring Andy Griffith and Dolores Gray. By then, the novel was enjoying its fourteenth printing.

Faust spent the summer following his western trip with Davis at the village of Forte dei Marmi on the Tuscan seacoast near Viareggio. It was a lovely bit of unspoiled shoreline, close to the spot where the poet Shelley's drowned body was recovered and burned. Behind it rose the Carrara Mountains where Michelangelo quarried the stone for his statues. Faust took a house in a pine grove and brought Dorothy, the children, Monty, the cook, a maid, and the chauffeur from the villa. Leonard Bacon and Aldous Huxley and their families occupied houses nearby. There were walks and talks—memorable conversations by beach bonfires "when the words soared upward with the sparks," and the dim outlines of the Carrara Mountains were lit by the moon.

As Bacon's daughter Martha described it later in the *Atlantic Monthly*:

During a Mediterranean summer everything that is serious happens at night. In the early morning before the heat begins we are in pursuit of music and art. At eleven we swim, at noon we eat figs and *prosciutto* and drink wine. The rest of the day we sleep under white nets to keep off the mosquitoes. At twilight we rise, as the evening primroses, taller on their long stalks than we are, open their yellow eyes to

Arcturus in the west and to Capella coming over Carrara, escaping the sharkstooth range by inches. The sand is cool now and we have lit a bonfire on the beach. We are grouped around Faust, who with his worker's hands and scholar's lips translates into his own terms the universe.

"Do you see that necklace of stars almost directly above you? That is called Corona. Those are not stars of the first magnitude. They are thousands of light-years away. There is Polaris, there is the Great Bear, the Little Bear, Io and her son. Later on in the year you will see Orion and the weeping Pleiades. There will be Sirius and there, invisible, will be the dark companion whose atomic substance outweighs our solar system." And the voice continues, impressing upon us the precise number of light-years at which we are standing off from Vega, whom we are approaching, as it happens, at a really nerve-racking pace.

. . . Faust makes the stars real. Faust makes it possible to believe that time is what it is, a great ring of pure and endless light that comprehends the dinosaur, the drowned body of the author of *Prometheus Unbound*, the undrowned bodies of the authors of *Point Counter Point* and *The Furioso*, who at this moment sit clasping their thin knees on the other side of the fire, their glasses gleaming like four stars, admonishing us drily not to fall into the flames.

Faust could now believe in the stars. Eight years after he had been given up for dead by many doctors, his heart was causing him less and less trouble. Behind him lay a record prose production and an astonishing popularity with film makers. His faith that he could finally produce something worthwhile in poetry was growing as he entered his fourth year of work on his epic of Dionysus in the underworld. His love for Dorothy and the children was at its height, and in his circle of friends he was finding the kind of people he had searched for.

Near-zenith was followed by near-nadir. After a solid year of happiness and intensive work at the villa, Faust, with Dorothy, the children, and Monty spent the summer of 1930 on a farm at Wiesenfelden, in Bavaria near Munich. It rained nearly every day. He had loaned $5,000 to a friend and was obliged to work doubly hard to make up the loss of available funds. Something cracked in him. Perhaps it was the result of overwork, or perhaps it was a recurring mood of depression about his poetry. Perhaps it was the sense of limitation some men feel on nearing the age of forty.

He spoke later of "a rising despair over Dorothy's preoccupation with childrearing" and of her "unwillingness to use the hands of her mind, unwillingness to make any effort, physical or mental." He also spoke of a "sudden conviction" that he had been wrong in his method of rearing his children, that the burdens he had imposed on them had been too heavy and had impeded rather than advanced their development.

His comments have the tone of physical and mental exhaustion. Toward the end of an August hot spell, he returned to Florence alone ahead of the others. The garden, a precious thing to him, was dry and burned. "Even Italy which always had been a blessing seemed a curse."

Meeting an experienced young American woman, he went off with her to Rome. There was no evidence of affection, he said, but simply a feeling which he likened to a loosening of fetters. "To my amazement, I felt no shame. I looked back with surprise and saw that it was the first time I had stepped off the straight road in thirteen years."

Faust was quite capable of hurting other people, even those he loved. He was able to convince himself of the validity of almost any action he wanted to take, just as he was able to convince readers of the validity of actions his characters wanted to take. His failure to understand the consequences of his actions, both in life and in writing, constituted one of his major shortcomings.

When his defection was discovered, Dorothy flew into a jealous frenzy. There were bitter scenes. Faust said that men since

Homer's time had had more than one woman. She replied that he did not love her. He retorted that he did and would never divorce her, that he was simply practicing the "European standard" of sexual morality he had long regarded as most suitable. Dorothy suffered another of the nervous breakdowns that constantly threatened her.

He tried to lose himself in poetry and the children; and as the subject for his next affair he chose a visiting society matron from San Francisco, known for her good works and Christian endeavor.

Monty had sided with Dorothy. One evening as Faust was leaving for an assignation, Monty resolutely barred the front door with outstretched arms, declaring, "Mr. Faust, you shall not leave this house tonight!"

What seemed high seriousness became low melodrama. The idyllic villa became a hell. Like Dionysus in the underworld of his poem, Faust plunged on through it.

Dorothy left him in January of 1931 and went to live in London alone. Nevertheless, her devotion to him remained absolute. Though many men admired her, she wanted only Faust, and he could not bring himself to let her go. He wooed her back with eloquent letters.

"Spend all the money you can," he wrote to Brown's Hotel and later to the Hotel Rembrandt. "Stop in Paris and buy some dresses." And he added with more relevance, "I think this separation may form a little precedent that may be of use to us both. We simply live too close together."

A trip to Greece in April and May was partly an attempt to reunite their marriage; but essentially it was the realization of another dream, as their first visits to England, Florence, and Ireland had been.

"Odysseus landed in a cave of Corcyra," Faust confided to his notebook, "wild old olive and a green meadow with thick patches of brush. The monastery above. The cliffs: streaks of light up the rocks. Remember the atmosphere (brown) of sun and sky. Thick-packed mimosa yellow-green and green-yellow."

147

They were cruising the Ionian and Aegean seas on a small yacht, "The Afros," in company with Berkeley friends, the Walter Morris Harts, and a Florentine couple, the John Sprangers. Hart was a scholar of considerable reputation, a professor of English and medieval literature—and a former vice-president—at the University of California. Spranger was a cultured businessman of English and Italian ancestry, and was an official of Magona Steel, one of Italy's largest firms.

Hart had been helping Faust with his epic poem and Faust was helping him with a scholarly paper on Dante.

"Wherever there is Greece there is magic," Faust wrote. "And when mountains or islands appear blue, there is usually a silver or golden slope shining through the mist. One rarely finds a landscape that is all dark."

As pastime, he and Hart were developing a popular-writing partnership which soon resulted in the sale of a story to *McCall's.*

Spranger attended to practical matters of the voyage, and contributed from a wide knowledge of history, languages—including Modern Greek—archaeology, and navigation.

The stock market crash of 1929 had not been seriously felt in the farther reaches of the Mediterranean, nor in the inner citadels of publishing, and Blackwell had paid Faust a record $5,000 for a single story. It exactly made up for the unpaid $5,000 he had loaned his friend. Appropriately, the story was titled *A Friend in Need.* Faust's immediate surroundings put all such problems from his mind.

"Cephallonia. The anchor chain of five-inch links under the water swings lightly as a string . . . . The houses are surprisingly big, dark cream in color, roofs of red tile. Small wind . . . a little tremble and run in the water. Images of the town sink part way into the bay.

"Aegina. A three-foot boy goes by with a five-foot tray of buns on his head. He yells at every third step. I hear him for four blocks and he never sells a bun.

"Cos. I sat in the shade of the fig tree which grows where the temple of Aesculapius stood and I listened to the voice of his fountain, still sounding after thirty centuries." At Cos, where Dionysus too had sat, Faust believed he penetrated the mystery of the beauty of Greece. "It is nothing but light, collected by the naked mountains and the sea. Perhaps, also, the water is continually lighting the sky, and the sky the mountains."

At Crete, Sir Arthur Evans conducted them on a tour of his most recent excavations at the Palace of Minos, explaining how the discovery of a gold ring in the neighborhood had led him to the finding of the Temple Tomb, which his workmen were engaged in excavating.

Faust wandered through the Vale of Tempe, visited the Acropolis in Athens by moonlight, floated on among the islands upon the wine-dark sea famed in poetry and song. It was almost more than he had dreamed of, and he worked it into his epic.

His poetic theme had been familiar to men since Homer's time, and most citizens of Athens of the Age of Pericles would have understood it clearly. Its climax was depicted in sculpture on the wall of a famous temple at Cyzicus, on the shore of what is now called the Sea of Marmora. Semele, a mortal, was shown ascending bodily to join the gods on Mt. Olympus, as the result of her release from the dead through the efforts of her immortal son, Dionysus.

The myth suggested by the sculpture on the temple wall was of major importance to the ancient mind. Semele's ascension to the company of the gods had a significance comparable to that of the Virgin Mary's ascension to heaven in many modern minds.

The mythical story was briefly this: Semele's death had been caused by the jealousy of Hera, wife of almighty Zeus. Disguised as a mortal, Zeus had become Semele's lover. Hera tricked the pregnant Semele into asking Zeus a favor. In response to his promise that she could have anything she wished, Semele asked for an undisguised look at her mysterious lover. Though he knew that no mortal could behold him in his true radiance and live, Zeus could not break his promise. Semele was consumed to ashes, but Zeus snatched her unborn son to safety. Dionysus became the most popular, most human, and most nearly Christ-like of all ancient Mediterranean gods, in addition to becoming the god of poetry and of wine.

In Faust's poem, Dionysus begins his search for his mother by entering the waters of the bay of Troezen near Athens, in order to descend to the world of the dead. With him goes a band of gay and laughing devotees. Dionysus is prepared to demand the release of his mother from the underworld on grounds that not sin but the malice of Hera caused her to die—and on further grounds that as mother of a god she is entitled to live with the immortals on Olympus.

When the group reaches the River Styx at the boundary of Hades proper, they are met by Hermes, conductor of souls, who guides them onward. Dionysus asks Hermes if he may see the shades of the famous dead described in the poetry of Homer and Virgil. The shades appear; but only that of Odysseus, gifted with superior perception, realizes the presence of the visitors. Given even greater perception by a taste of Dionysus' wine, Odysseus understands "the thin reality of the death in which his great spirit is enclosed." He expresses a Faust-like wish to live again and achieve an even larger experience.

The underworld explorers next meet beautiful Eurydice, beloved of Orpheus. She tells them she hopes someone will eventually release the spirits of the glorious dead. Next Hades, ruler of the underworld, is encountered. Beside him sits his wife Persephone, the spirit of spring.

When Hades is deaf to Dionysus' plea for the release of his mother, Persephone intercedes. Hades relents and admits that not he but only the Titan, Prometheus, who is suffering torture in the farthermost reaches of the underworld, can provide the information Dionysus needs in order that Semele may be reembodied and released. Dionysus presses on through many adventures, including a meeting with Prometheus, the creator and friend of man; and Semele is eventually released and ascends bodily to

Olympus, where she is thereafter known as Thyone, goddess of joy.

In a final scene in which Dionysus confronts his father, Zeus appears more like a sympathetic parent than a harsh tyrant. Zeus reveals his own pain and uncertainty because of the doubt (introduced by Prometheus) that is turning the realm of the Olympians into the substance of bodiless thought. Zeus fears a greater power, namely truth. In the end, Dionysus is satisfied about himself and his origins and has had a sobering glimpse of the future.

Faust's personal identification with his poem comes through clearly. With Dionysus, he represents poetry and wine. He searches for his own dead mother, finds his father as well, and glorifies them both. At the same time he discovers that happiness is fleeting, that pain and doubt prevail, and that in action there can be an end to both pain and doubt. But again Faust makes the mistake of imitating literary masters too closely. He leans far too heavily on Dante, Virgil, and Homer. Tone as well as subject matter seem ostentatiously poetic.

Dionysus in Hades was a majestic failure. Its 2,155 lines suffered not only from perfervor and ornateness but from a kind of murkiness that characterized much of Faust's poetry. On the whole, he was not coming through clearly. He had not found himself in verse, just as he had not found himself in life.

Walter Hart, to whom Faust dedicated the poem, told him frankly, "Your difficulty in finding a publisher is going to be that these are dark times for classical studies. Interest in antique poetic themes is at a low ebb, and the fact that no one has tackled yours for at least twenty-four hundred years is not going to help."

Events bore out Hart's prediction. No U.S. publisher expressed interest in *Dionysus in Hades*. Faust finally published it at his own expense through his favorite bookseller, Basil Blackwell, at Oxford, who was a publisher of distinction. Blackwell's imprint did the work no harm.

Faust consoled himself with the thought that many writers had paid to have their work published—Tolstoy, Stephen Crane,

Vachel Lindsay, and Edwin Arlington Robinson, among others.

The first of five hundred copies of *Dionysus* was in Dorothy's hands on December 19, 1931, inscribed "My dear Dorothy, you saw it through." Though Leon Richardson, professor of classics, reviewed *Dionysus* favorably in the *University of California Chronicle*, praising its "beauty of line" and "fine imaginative quality," and saying "it will take its place on the uncrowded shelves of good books," the work went almost unnoticed and unread in a world gripped by economic depression, Marxist dialectics, strikes, lockouts, riots, and threat of revolution.

It was one of the cruelest blows Faust ever suffered. Six years of what he considered his best effort seemed wasted. The trip to Greece, which realized a precious dream, became a mockery. The defeat shook his confidence, but did not change his dedication to verse or his conviction that really important poetry should be "elevated" above ordinary life and talk, as were the epics of ancient times.

Faust divided his forces and fought on under his various pen names (they now numbered ten) but not yet as the legitimate Frederick Faust.

16.

EDITORS AND AN AGENT

ECONOMIC depression had by this time caught up with the U.S. publishing and film industries. There had been little alarm at first. During the period immediately following the 1929 crash, some publishers believed that unemployment would mean more leisure for more people and thus more time to read. Similarly, some film makers had thought that people might go to see reasonably priced movies, to occupy their time or forget their troubles. But by 1932 it had become apparent that rising unemployment, rising readerships, and rising film audiences did not go hand in hand. At the offices of Street and Smith, where Frank Blackwell had become editorial director, and where *Western Story* had been a mainstay of Faust's bank account, payments declined sharply toward a record low of $112.80 for a single Faust offering.

Simultaneously his sales of motion picture rights to Hollywood stopped completely. As far back as 1928, *Variety*, a leading film-industry publication, had adversely criticized Tiffany-Stahl for presenting Richard Talmadge in Faust's *The Cavalier* at a special run Broadway theatre, on grounds that it was merely "a western dressed up in Spanish costume." The popularity of the simplistic or straight western was declining. Nevertheless, Fox had released George O'Brien, Louise Huntington and George Brent in *Fair Warning* (based on *The Untamed*) in 1930; and in 1931, O'Brien, Sally Eilers, Rita LeRoy, and Humphrey Bogart appeared in *A Holy Terror*, based on *Trailin'*. Bogart drew favorable comment for his portrayal of a sinister but interesting ranch foreman.

A significant change came on April 4, 1932, with the release of

Destry Rides Again. Tom Mix played it straight, with the help of Claudia Dell, Zasu Pitts, and Andy Devine; and it was a failure. It was among Mix's first talking pictures, and it was a major step downward in a career which ended soon after. Mix had risen and fallen with Faust's stories. The carefree days of Tom and Tony at the White House, of jubilant juvenile America, and of shoot-'em-up westerns opening at first-run Broadway houses were over. So were Faust's bonanza sales to Hollywood.

Along with most of the rest of the world, he was obliged to face new facts. Although reluctant to leave Europe again, he was forced to consider revisiting the U.S., meeting the issues, and effecting remedies with the help of his literary agent, Carl Brandt.

Faust had become a client of Brandt's in 1925 on the suggestion of Stephen Vincent Benét, who had found in Brandt a personal friend as well as an excellent critic and businessman. Like Faust, Benét was supporting himself financially by writing popular prose fiction while at the same time writing serious poetry, and Brandt had proved extremely helpful. Though Brandt had represented Faust for seven years, there had been little personal contact. Faust had lived aloof in Italy, dealt directly with editors such as Blackwell; and Brandt had handled such details as renewal and assignment of copyright, sales of motion picture rights, routine contracts with book publishers, now and then "clicking off a new note" as Brandt expressed it, such as a sale to *Ladies Home Journal*, but leaving control and direction very much in Faust's hands. Now this was to change.

"Just a note to catch the "Majestic,' " Brandt wrote on January 29, 1932. "I have spoken to Blackwell over the telephone and as soon as he has your letter we are going to get together." Blackwell had rejected 400,000 of Faust's words, roughly the equivalent of six books, in the past twelve months. Something had to be done.

Brandt had been urging Faust to make a serious effort to enter the more prestigious and better paying hard-paper magazine market, in which he had casually appeared from time to time. Max Brand stories were now being seen by *The Saturday Evening*

Post, Collier's, Liberty, Country Gentleman, and *The Delineator,* as well as *McCall's,* and *The Ladies Home Journal.* Yet despite rejections, Blackwell and *Western Story* were still publishing hundreds of thousands of Faust's words annually, paying him scores of thousands of dollars, and must remain a mainstay for the moment.

Don Moore at *Argosy* had offered five cents a word for 200,000 words of Faust fiction in 1932, an offer representing $10,000, providing *Argosy* had first look at material submitted. Moore's five-cent rate was better than Blackwell's depression rate of four, yet *Western Story* would take six or eight times more words than *Argosy.* Out in Hollywood, H. N. Swanson, editorial director of *College Humor,* was in close touch with RKO Studios, who were calling for a football story; and it seemed Faust might have just the thing. Fawcett Publications, publishers of *Triple-X Western,* as well as *True Confessions* and a host of other magazines, wanted to see Faust's fiction. So did George Delacorte, Jr., at Dell.

In mid-January, 1932, Faust had written Brandt that he was going to Egypt and needed cash for the trip. Could *Western Story* make an advance? Blackwell was in the habit of making Faust advances up to four and five thousand dollars for material received or in the mail, but not yet read or accepted. If it was rejected, Blackwell sent it over to Brandt for sale elsewhere and deducted the amount of the advance from the next Faust payment. He now advanced $2,000 and Faust and Dorothy went to Egypt. But the serial Faust sent to New York, *The Red Pacer,* didn't please Blackwell. Over to Brandt's office by special messenger went the serial. Faust mailed a new book-length serial by fast boat, as he neared Cairo, and Brandt sold *The Red Pacer* to *Argosy* for $2,800.

Brandt was totaling up prospects for the coming year and wrote Faust, "It strikes me that we have 1,140,000 words at five cents, which would equal $57,000 gross, or if you paid 5% commission would be roughly $54,000. 300,000 words at four cents would be $12,000, less 10% would be $10,000, and the scattering sales of stories that would have to go in the magazines which pay less would probably mean another $5,000 all told, which would give you a net income from magazines of practically $70,000." Brandt's final figure could be doubled or tripled to represent purchasing power in a later day. Book and film sales could be added, proportionately, in order to get a true perspective on Faust's annual earnings.

Brandt was working overtime with editors and publishers in a manner approaching a fine art. They were buying him almost as much as they were buying Faust, but Brandt felt that he needed support, and he kept urging Faust to come to the U.S. and see the situation first hand.

Faust, however, was looking at the pyramids and writing in his notebook, "Belief is the thing, whether of the subject in the king or of the king in himself. When Zoser was carved in limestone as Osiris, is it not clear that the sculptor and the pharaoh both believed that he was the king of death?" And Brandt was writing that he had reached an understanding with Blackwell whereby *Western Story* agreed to take eight serials of 70,000 words or more, plus twenty novelettes of 25,000 words or more, or a total of approximately 1,140,000 words in 1932, "as opposed to between 1,300,000 and 1,400,000 words that you have been giving him, but Frank says that these stories must be your best work. The other 200,000 or more leeway I can take care of through the Munsey group (*Argosy*, etc.) under the name of John Frederick."

Blackwell had also agreed to restore the five-cent rate. So Faust was again geared to write and publish between a million and a half and two million words a year, written, as he liked to think, with his left hand. The painful irony to him was the continued, almost overwhelming, acceptance of his prose and the non-acceptance of his poetry; but he had long aspired to seeing Egypt, and there he was at last, aged forty, with a heart still beating.

"Today we at least have escaped," he wrote in his notebook where he was keeping a running dialogue with himself, "There is no pulse in your body that is not mine. Yet perfect love is not perfect understanding of one another but of other things. The moment that can contain us both is love." He and Dorothy had refound their devotion for each other.

Page 201 of *The Red Pacer* was missing; and Brandt cabled half-way across the world to tell him to rush the missing page to *Argosy*, adding that he was depositing $5,920 to Faust's account.

Still Blackwell was unhappy. Readers were complaining. "Dear Boss of the Round-up," one wrote, "I have been a reader of Street and Smith Western Story Magazine for a number of years, so I think I am entitled to register a complaint. I am getting tired of seeing Max Brand and George Owen Baxter take up so much room. Why don't you give them two a vacation for about ten years? If you want them two to write a story, why don't you change the name of your magazine to Street and Smith fairy tales?"

Blackwell joined Brandt in urging Faust to abandon the pyramids and come to the U.S.

The April 2, 1932, issue of *Western Story* featured a novel, *Speedy's Crystal Game,* by Max Brand, *Lucky Larribee,* a six-part serial by George Owen Baxter, and *The Golden Spurs,* a six-part serial by David Manning; and on April 3, Faust, back in Florence, was writing Brandt that it would probably be good to give Blackwell a rest.

"He ceases to be a market for me when he refuses 400,000 words in a year as he has just done. I can't continue writing seventeen hundred thousand words a year, as I did in 1931." But on April 6 he told Brandt to nail down Blackwell to 1,240,000 words for the next year, and added, "As far as I'm concerned, I'm ready to go." Spurring him on as usual were the financial and emotional demands of his establishment, his dependents, his dreams—and in addition, a new drug. "For the first time in eleven years I have found a dope that keeps my rotten heart from going crazy—digitaline and quinine—and I now can work at least twice as hard as I ever did before, and three or four times as hard in a pinch."

The seventeen hundred thousand words of 1931 had been a

partial effort (*Dionysus in Hades* had been finished and published that year), yet it was the equivalent of more than twenty-five books.

Faust now hungrily asked Brandt about the marketability of gangster material and underworld stories. "I know a good lot about gangsters, and I have plenty of background, personally experienced."

Brandt replied that he thought he could reopen the gangster-detective-murder mystery market which Faust had entered years before but had not appeared in since 1925. Faust informed Brandt that he was going to write 4,400 words or two eight-page chapters a day, "That will give you 132,000 words a month to dispose of. Also, instead of writing 2,000 words an hour, I'll spend twice that much time, which will make five hours' work in place of two and a half. The stuff ought to be proportionately better in quality." He then inquired with sudden humility, "Can you really criticize stuff as badly written as my pulp paper fiction? If you can, of course it will be a vast advantage to me."

Faust still balked at the thought of traveling to New York. The trip was always a physical as well as a mental and emotional ordeal. "Personal conferences with editors have never gained me a thing and have lost me much. I did millions of words for the Munsey Company, in the old days, at a third of the price I should have received, merely because I knew the editor so well."

Nevertheless, on April 13, 1932, Blackwell received a cable saying Faust was arriving in New York on the twenty-sixth and to please tell Brandt. Blackwell met him at the dock. Brandt, who had been obliged to play host at a squash-club dinner—"squash is the chief thing that keeps me sane"—was unable to be on hand; but the next night he entertained Faust and Blackwell at his apartment at 310 Lexington Avenue. They made plans to roll back the depression.

Faust settled at the Hotel Gladstone, at 114 East 52nd, and got to work furiously on a serial, "something newer, faster, tighter, that will embody these new times and tensions."

On May 8, *College Humor* rejected an adventure story, *Michael Carmichael*, but the associate editor, Patricia Reilly, asked that Max Brand stories keep coming her way. Not taking no for an answer, Brandt asked her to specify criticism and rush it to him, because "Max Brand is in town for only a few days before he disappears into Italy again." She wrote back, "My only criticism of Max Brand's material is that it is almost too well written." She wanted to know who the mysterious stranger was, how old he was, and what he had done; but Brandt forewarned by Faust, would tell her nothing.

On May 9, Faust lunched with Dixie Fish and Gene Tunney, recently retired from the world's heavyweight championship. Tunney made a strong impression. "He's gentle, straight, and decent and working frightfully hard to make of himself a cultured man of the world and succeeding amazingly well. He has brains and he ought to come through unless the society bastards break his heart." Faust also lunched with Jim Corbett, conqueror of John L. Sullivan, and with Sam Levin, once manager of the fighter Sam Langford; and Bob Davis arranged a dinner with Geraldine Farrar, the opera star, and a lunch with Roy Chapman Andrews. Andrews, lately returned from collecting fossilized dinosaur eggs in Mongolia, delighted Faust with his account of chasing Mongolian antelope across country in a Dodge touring car at sixty miles an hour.

Meeting people who had performed well or interestingly always excited Faust. Thinking in terms of achievement, he wrote Dorothy that Dixie Fish was "probably among the handful of top surgeons in the U.S." Fish had established a practice in New York City and was consulting urologist to several hospitals.

Dorothy now joined Faust in New York, then went by train to California, while he continued working at high speed in Manhattan. Their love was, if anything, deeper than before; and he wrote her at Yuba City, "This is too damned ridiculous. I mean to say, after a man has been married fifteen years, he ought to be able to navigate quite well with his woman out of sight. Don't stretch the visit to the coast a minute longer than you have to. I want you to wire, the instant you receive this, the exact day and hour of your return. I have just heard that you can make the entire trip, now, by aeroplane, and in about thirty hours. So why not return that way?"

He was seeing Brandt regularly and reported much benefit from their conferences. Brandt had agreed with many of the editors that Faust was writing "too well," that story disappeared behind characterization. To correct the deficiency, Faust was—and he knew it—to lose a little more of his artistic integrity.

On May 24, 1932, *Argosy* sent a check for $2,800 for the North American magazine rights to *The Dead Man Steer*, which Blackwell had rejected. On the same date a letter from Harry Maule at Doubleday, Doran—Maule was the editorial director of *Short Stories* and *West*—said that he was loaded with good western stuff but looked forward to seeing Max Brand material. *College Humor* was offering $300 for the football story *Tippity Witchett*, which Ron Oliphant at Street and Smith's *Top Notch* was reading too. While Oliphant was reading, *College Humor* bought another football story and withdrew its offer, so Brandt put the heat on Blackwell to take the story for $300 and "use it somewhere," and Blackwell did.

On May 27, Faust and Dorothy boarded the "Europa" at Pier 4, Brooklyn, Faust taking with him a serial he had been working on under Blackwell's supervision. By June 10 they were back in Florence, Faust writing Brandt that on shipboard he had had good talks with Cass Canfield of Harper. Canfield said that Zane Grey's sales had fallen off to 30,000 copies annually and he thought Faust might be able to "take up the slack." He wanted to know if any publisher ever had put any "real money" behind a book of Faust's. "He seemed so interested that I told him in view of the new way I'm trying to work, that I might eventually be able to write a really good romance, and that when Carl Brandt and I both felt I had done something that was amusing, we would give him a look at it. His idea is to start a new name because he thinks that Max Brand has severe limitations in the minds of booksellers."

The new name developed into Evan Evans. Under it Harper was to publish a number of Faust's westerns.

But in mid-July Blackwell rejected a novelette. Brandt learned that Blackwell was nursing a grudge against Faust for beginning the serial *All For One* under his direction in May when in New York, then suddenly departing for Europe without finishing it. Blackwell had taken the departure as a personal affront. He felt that Faust, to whom he had paid hundreds of thousands of dollars, had slighted a benefactor in favor of unrealistic retreat to a dream life in Europe. Faust was furious. Summering in a vine-covered country house at Giverny near Paris, he wrote Brandt that he would work for a cent a word for any competitor of Blackwell; but almost in the same breath he completed the long serial *All For One*, and Blackwell immediately bought it, cabling his wish that Faust continue to write for *Western Story*.

Brandt quoted Blackwell as saying that *Western Story* was so dependent on Faust that if it was to continue to publish, Faust must continue to write for it. "But you have got to provide the cure for its ailments, or we will all go down the drain together. We are fighting with our backs to the wall," Brandt added, "and we need all the ammunition we can get. You are too far away to serve up the type of shot and shell we need at any particular moment. Why not enlist for the duration?"

Brandt was borrowing money to pay his office help and was covering Faust's overdrafts at the bank. *Western Story* had again cut Faust's rate to four cents.

In the hot days of August, when sales declined and collections grew harder, the chorus demanding the expatriate's presence once more became loud.

Faust sailed from Le Havre on the "Columbus" on September 5, 1932. On the boat with him was Howard Vincent O'Brien, author, columnist, and until recently literary editor of the *Chicago Daily News*. O'Brien offered to put him in touch with magazine editors, in particular Kenneth Littauer of *Collier's*, and said that what was in fashion at hard-paper magazines was "editorialized short stories—that is to say, stories to cheer up the depression, stories to denounce divorce, etc. etc."

Despite painful insomnia, homesickness, and difficulty in breathing—some nights he did not sleep at all—Faust completed, while on shipboard, a serial about a buccaneer on the Spanish Main and worked out two plots, one for a crime story and one for a western. O'Brien had convinced him he must leave the pulps and try the hards, but he understood that breaking into the latter was going to be difficult. They had their regular writers and their established policies.

Bad news met him when he landed in New York. Blackwell had refused a serial. "I'm seeing Gibney, the manager of the Munsey forces, tomorrow," Faust wrote Dorothy. "My idea is to sell the pulp paper rights to my soul to him. He is interested in large ideas, and my 'pulp paper soul' is a large idea as ideas go in this business."

With Brandt's help he played off the Munsey people against Blackwell, while laying the basis for his shift to hard-paper production. His second sally into the U.S. within four months must pay off. "I am going out of town to work, probably to a quiet little hotel in Rye, where living will be cheap and the telephone will not exist for me."

Dorothy had returned to Florence after placing John in boarding school in Switzerland. There she found problems arising between Monty and the four-year-old Judy.

On September 12, Faust took up residence at The Holmewood Inn, in New Canaan, Connecticut, and prepared to convert himself into a new kind of writer. He liked Holmewood. "Think of finding a place where sleep comes at night out of the air, and where there is quiet all day for a man to work!" Forty-two pages were behind him. Next night he wrote, "Supper over, but only twenty pages done; and thirty more to do before the infernal novelette is finished. But it is running like a song, and why should

I care about working until twelve? I really think that it is a good thing for a man to have a strenuous challenge. Hard times ought to come, or else all but the vital organs of life will go to seed and be covered by fat."

He spoke of walking down a New York street and seeing a hundred laborers standing and watching twenty who were actually at work, "watching like poor dogs staring at fresh meat, eating their hearts up with desire to work and gloomily criticizing the skill of the lucky devils who have jobs." He said it was the sort of thing that made for revolution, and it convinced him that the state had an obligation to all of its members. "And therefore, I, we, owe an obligation back to the state." His ideas on economics had been in theory conservative, individualistic, and anti-big-government but they were changing.

His personal economic needs were enlarging too. A maiden aunt of Dorothy's had lost her teaching job in California, and he put her on his payroll as a researcher. His sister was clamoring for an advance of $100 on her allowance. Dorothy was at the bedside of John, who was in a hospital in Lausanne with a severe case of scarlet fever.

Brandt had made an appointment for Faust and himself to lunch with Kenneth Littauer, fiction editor of *Collier's*. On September 18, Blackwell bought a serial at four cents a word; and Abe Merritt at *The American Weekly* asked permission to dramatize *Luck and a Horse* over the new medium, radio—a medium that the Democratic party's nominee for President, Franklin D. Roosevelt, was using with surprising effect.

Faust got on well at lunch with Littauer, and with Howard Bloomfield, editor of Munsey's *Detective Story Magazine*. Bloomfield was ready to buy the crime fiction Faust was prepared to write. Like *Western Story*, many detective story magazines were published weekly to help provide the mass entertainment of the type later provided by radio and television.

Meanwhile, Brandt's book department, under direction of Bernice Baumgarten, wife of the novelist James Gould Cozzens, kept pushing out galley proofs of new books to the Hollywood studios. This time it was *The Jackson Trail*, which Dodd, Mead would soon publish.

Argosy bought serial rights to *The Naked Blade* by George Challis, a pen name Faust had first used for a costume piece in *Western Story* in 1926. *The Naked Blade* was the buccaneering adventure story he had completed on the boat. Its hero's name was Kildare, the name of a county in Ireland and of the favorite horse of the late Edward VII of England.

On October 3, Brandt touched *Argosy* for a $1,000 advance on *The Naked Blade*. On the fourth, Blackwell bought *Coming Clean*, for *Western Story*. On the sixth, at 4 P.M., Faust met Cass Canfield at his office in the Harper building at 49 East 33rd to discuss production of westerns. On the fourteenth, Littauer wrote Brandt, encouraging Faust to write for *Collier's*. Brandt rushed a copy of *The Jackson Trail* to Warner Brother's New York office and added he was sending the manuscript of the new Max Brand book, *The Masterman*, in a few days. He sent a Faust poem to *Harper's Magazine*.

"Remember that I am anchored to you by invisible cables," Faust told Dorothy, "and if my anchorage goes adrift, where will this foolish airship blow?"

His establishment, stretching from New York to Lausanne, from Florence to California, was spread rather thin; and he was fighting to keep it from collapsing. He had had to borrow $2,500 from his father-in-law. At the same time, Arthur Acton made a generous offer to defer rent due on the villa, saying he would rather have Faust's company than immediate cash. They had formed a substantial friendship over books, flowers, and the amateur painting Acton did and asked Faust to criticize.

After giving him trouble on the boat, Faust's heart was behaving. He had seen Dr. Halsey and was taking Luminol at times for sleeping, while resisting dependence on the drug. He now occupied an entire cottage at Holmewood and was producing forty or fifty pages on good days, valiantly declining invitations to social occasions and temptations to hard liquor, falling off the temperance wagon only once, for a period of two days.

Dorothy cabled desperately from Switzerland for funds and for his presence. He wrote her rather touchingly that he was going to have to lean on her more heavily than ever when he got back, for advice of all sorts. "The last flicker of independence has gone out of me during this stay in New York." Conforming to editors' demands was taking its toll.

On October 31, 1932, Faust moved to the Hotel Croydon at 12 East 86th, in New York, preparatory to sailing for Italy within a few days. He found that if he completed four 50,000-word novelettes, really four books, in sixteen days, he could sail on November 15. He decided to aim for this goal and to repay half the loan from Dorothy's father before leaving American soil.

A group of short poems was submitted to *Forum*; Howard Bloomfield bought a crime serial, finished at 11:15 P.M. a few nights before, for *Detective Fiction*; Irita Van Doren at the *New York Herald Tribune* got a Faust poem from Brandt; Franklin D. Roosevelt was elected President of the United States; and Faust sailed home on the "Leviathan" on November 15, missing an appointment with Roy de S. Horn of RKO Radio Pictures but mailing a check to Dorothy's father.

He left turmoil in his wake. "The Blackwell novelette will go down to him just as fast as the three typists can copy the parts that have to be copied," Brandt wrote by earliest transatlantic mail, "and *The Naked Blade* will go to Moore shortly thereafter. My brother is taking down the insert for Bloomfield himself today at luncheon."

Faust had kept three to twelve editors and three to twelve typists busy, not to mention Carl and Erdman Brandt. He had swept in and out of the U.S. twice at a high cost of money, time, and self. While apparently winning the constant battle, he knew that he had only begun the change from pulps to hards.

On November 18, a Faust poem went to Henry Seidel Canby at the *Saturday Review of Literature*, and arrangements were completed whereby Harper would publish the first of a series of western novels, *Montana Rides*. On the twenty-second, Brandt sold the novelette, rejected by Blackwell, to Rogers Terrill of Popular Publications for $250; and Blackwell scheduled *Montana Rides* for *Western Story* prior to its publication by Harper. The author's name, for magazine publication only, was to be Evin Evan.

On November 24 Faust cabled Brandt from Lausanne, where John was still critically ill in the hospital, "Did Blackwell buy?" —referring to a novelette left with Blackwell. Brandt cabled back, "Blackwell not buying until further revise. Returning manuscript joint letter Florence earliest boat."

For the first time in his life Faust was revising and rewriting. On November 28, Blackwell received the first of the Silvertip series of westerns. The series contained realistic material, including the stallion Parade, collected by Faust on his western trip with Davis. Blackwell rejected it. Brandt made suggestions. Faust rewrote. Blackwell bought. A new character was launched. Money poured in. It was not enough. Keeping Faust going financially was like keeping a small nation afloat.

"What advance can I get from Blackwell, book publishers, or you? Sorry to ask," he cabled from Florence on November 30.

On December 3, *Harper's Magazine* bought a poem for ten dollars. Brandt cabled the news with congratulations. The poem, titled *Only the Young Fear Death*, expressed a middle-aged cardiac's acceptance of the fact of death—at the moment when his activities were reaching whirlwind tempo. Again Faust had the momentary satisfaction of knowing, with the sale of the poem, that he was at least partly refuting the warnings of friends and critics, such as Bill Benét and Canby, who had questioned the wisdom of writing serious poetry and pot-boiling prose simultaneously. But he "ground his teeth a little" at the thought that he must work for *Western Story*, *Argosy*, and *Detective Fiction* in order to exist. At times he wanted recognition and prestige, even for his prose.

Among editors and publishers, word was spreading that Faust was looking for markets and had golden potential. Immediately following the sale of the poem to *Harper's* came the sale of a pure pulp yarn, *The Devil Walks*, to *Top Notch*, for two cents a word.

By December 15, 1932, Blackwell was friendly, Harper was publishing a book and a poem, Brandt was happy if exhausted, Faust was impoverished as usual, and the U.S. was heading toward the March 1933 bank holiday and the depths of the depression.

Brandt had been taking only a five per cent commission on everything Faust sold Blackwell, rather than the usual ten, because of Faust's long-standing arrangements with *Western Story*. Now, at Faust's insistence, the percentage was increased to ten. "I'm glad to have you as buffer state between me and Blackwell," he wrote Brandt.

Brandt deposited $500 in response to yet another desperate cable and on December 19 he queried Harry Maule at *West* about the Max Brand serial Maule was reading. Faust wrote from the villa that he was working on short stories for *Collier's*. The trips to the U.S. had inspired and sharpened him, he declared. "Thanks for getting the additional six hundred and fifty to the bank. It was a drop of water to a man speechless with financial heat."

Maule could not use *The Blackness of McTee* in either *West* or *Short Stories* because he was stocked up. "If the Foolkiller finds me, my life will be short," Faust complained; and in response to a request from Harper for a biography of their new author Evan Evans, he told Brandt, "I simply can't write a biography of Mr. Evan Evans. I've really tried. Can you do it for me? Have him born in Wales and bred in Mexico, if you want to, and raised on frog's milk."

On December 22 Brandt cabled, "Blackwell buying *Great Enemy* novelette. Depositing $1750. Merry Christmas." On the same date, Fox Studios asked for a chance to see "Max Brand's new one"—*Slow Joe*, which was on the Dodd, Mead list for early

January. On the thirtieth Harry Maule bought *The Quest* for $275, and on the thirty-first a cable informed Faust that Don Moore had said go ahead for *Argosy* on the writing of the story of a white boy reared by Indians.

The revised Silvertip serial was being polished by Brandt's typist for cramming down Blackwell's throat on the day after New Year's. During 1932, Faust had appeared in every weekly issue of *Western Story*, and had published all together 1,660,000 words—a record.

"Do try and get a moment for your slick-paper stuff," Brandt pleaded, "And remember story, story, story. It's not enough to have action and color; there must be character, progress, and a solution; and above all, sympathy for your people; the reader must *care* what happens to 'em. Here endeth the lesson. I've gotta nerve, eh, kid? Happiest of New Years."

Faust was finding in Brandt a friend who not only spoke his language, but whose life had had many parallels with his own. Both had lost fathers early. Both had struggled up the hard way, earning their own living and education, stoking coal, working on farms. Neither had managed to graduate from college. Both enjoyed making money, establishing their influence, and surviving challenging crises. Both drank heavily at times.

17.

ORDEAL BY WRITING

NINETEEN hundred and thirty-three seemed to dawn brightly as the Silvertip series of westerns got off to a good start with Blackwell, but on January 10, *Argosy* wrote mentioning a two-cent-a-word rate, a new low. On the thirteenth, Thomas B. Costain, a *Saturday Evening Post* editor, later known as a novelist, rejected a story, though he asked to see others. On the sixteenth, Brandt cabled, "Kid mailed week ago. Blackwell reading Hunting Silver now. Personally afraid will want changes but Marriage Dark swell. Will cable earliest."

Brandt's cable bills were running into three figures, he asked Faust to register a short cable address, such as "Maxbrand." Faust, working too fast to keep carbons properly, cabled that he had none of *Hunting Silver* and asked Brandt to send the original manuscript back over the ocean for changes.

Blackwell bought a story called *Marriage in the Dark*, and Faust poems went to Alfred Dashiell at *Scribner's Magazine*. "What about Prison Shakes?" Faust queried by cable, and Brandt replied, "Blackwell booking Prison Shakes today," meaning that Blackwell had bought it. Faust cabled every few days asking what had been sold. Brandt said the latest manuscript, entitled *The Green Beetle,* could have gone to the hards if Faust had been there to make one or two minor changes. Don Moore called Brandt from *Argosy* to say it was the best thing of Faust's he had read. The name was changed to *The White Indian,* and Moore paid $2,800 for it. Some of Faust's best work of this period dealt with Indians, he relying for much of his background on the experiences of James Willard Schultz and George Bird Grinnell.

Signs of Faust's new writing personality were appearing, and Brandt was so disconsolate at the thought of what might have been done with *The White Indian* that he wrote a three-page letter asking that Faust give Costain at the *Post* and Littauer at *Collier's* a chance at the next story like it. Yet, ominously, on this same date, March 3, Brandt cabled Faust, "Bank moratorium holding up Munsey collections. Argosy hopes to pay Monday or Tuesday. Will cable immediately collected."

The banks had closed. Faust was marooned in Italy with no money and expenses mounting. On March 10, Brandt wrote grimly, "The situation over here is such that everyone has had to take even further cuts. Blackwell has kept your rate at four cents longer by months than that of any of his other writers and is only now asking that you should cooperate with him for a time on what would approximate a three-cent rate. The situation is an extremely serious one for you as it means the cutting of the major part of your income by 25%."

Brandt added that it would be difficult for Blackwell to continue *Western Story* without Faust, but he might be forced to, should Faust refuse the cut. Faust took the cut.

Like the rest of the country, Brandt was looking for the upturn that did not come. Faust was working at hard-paper fiction in the morning and pulp fiction in the afternoon. There was almost no time for poetry. "In sixteen years I've never written so badly over such a long period, and it has never been so hard for me to turn out copy of any sort whatever," he wrote to Brandt in a rare moment of complaint.

On April 5 there was a favorable turn. Littauer at *Collier's* wrote an encouragingly detailed criticism of a story. Each story was a precious bit of ammunition in what Brandt described as "a special kind of battle in which you cannot afford to waste a shot." But Faust gambled on a six-thousand word scenario of a crime-mystery novel, *The Night Flower*, and sent it across the Atlantic, along with a four-hundred-line poem about the mythical, hundred-handed giant, Briareus.

No money came in. Finances were so desperate that Faust tried to break the trust he had established for Dorothy and the children years before, but he had foreseen just such an eventuality and had made the trust unbreakable.

Brandt, nearly as hard-pressed as Faust, wrote to Blackwell a few blocks away, regarding *Silver's Search*, "Frank, your reader quit at page 115 with the comment 'pretty tiresome.' I've now read the manuscript for the third time and it still holds my interest and whips up my mental excitement. If your reader had pursued his reading until page 126, Silver would have come back into the game with six-guns and quick flashing action. From here on I'll try to finish out the synopsis for your reader." And Brandt did. And Blackwell bought. It was a turning point.

By August, 1933, Lee Hartman, editor of *Harper's Magazine*, was very keen about a new story; and *Montana Rides*, the first Harper western novel, was selling well. Abe Merritt at *American Weekly* liked one of Faust's science-fiction serials but wanted to talk to Faust about it; since Merritt was leaving for Europe, he took the manuscript with him to the villa. Brandt and Howard Bloomfield of *Detective Story Magazine* put their heads together over *Night Flower*, a lurid story of the New York underworld. Brandt wrote Faust that "Beer is Best," which he had just received, "is one of the finest Max Brand efforts so far. You really seem to have experienced this one."

Faust replied with a single-spaced letter of approximately three thousand words outlining a plot for a book. Brandt replied with a letter nearly as long urging Faust to come to the U.S. again. "You are almost on the spot of doing these hard-paper stories. What you need is to have Ken Littauer or me or both sitting next to your elbow just for a time. We're going to yank the doors wide open once we get going."

Suddenly there was a real opening. Hartman at *Harper's* bought a story for $250. It meant little in cash, but much in prestige. It would make other editors take heed. The story, titled *A Special Occasion*, concerns a middle-aged New Yorker named

Campbell. Campbell, once a promising young architect, is now an alcoholic with a disillusioned wife, a disloyal mistress, and tarnished dreams. He is a rich failure overwhelmed by his inadequacies. Faust reveals himself in Campbell. "Merely to be known, merely to be understood is what most of us desire, as though a divine ray will surely dazzle every true observer," Campbell says bitterly, knowing that no such ray will strike him.

As he sits in despair in a luxurious easy chair in his library, Campbell's eye wanders to his books. "The Rabelais was distinguishable because it was done in unstained levant morocco, and the polished vellum of a photographic reprint of Caxton's Chaucer shone like a lighted candle; but he could not find Thucydides, the clear thinker. The dark red of that leather was lost among sober shadows. But even Thucydides, calm and great, would be little help to him. He had forgotten almost everything except the seventh book, and that was an empire's ruin. He had forgotten too much. In his youth he had done his reading; afterward he had bound the volumes and put them away on shelves."

Yet Campbell has a young daughter who loves horses. Her homecoming is the special occasion on which the story centers. And beyond the last sad drink, the last unsuccessful attempt at deception, the last crystal of morphine, there may perhaps be a place for aging sinners who accept each other, because there is really nothing else to do.

In addition to being revealing, *A Special Occasion* is one of Faust's best pieces of work. It strangely prefigured experiences he was going to have, as well as some he had had.

As a means of extracting the story, Brandt had bet Faust five dollars he couldn't write something that *Harper's* would buy. To go him one better, Faust wrote another story of the same type, *The Wedding Guest*, and Brandt sold it to *Harper's* too.

Faust could probably have continued to publish in *Harper's* and other quality magazines, but it was not the kind of writing that interested him and he could not live on the money it paid.

Faust and Dorothy arrived in New York in the fall of 1933, he convinced he was working harder than ever, his inner life still tormented by a single hope. "If I could write one powerful poem, no matter how short, it seems to me that dying would be an easy matter." The more immediate reason for the New York visit was the rapid weakening of the pulp market and the necessity for an immediate transition to the hards.

Brandt had made ready a room a short distance down the hall from his office at 101 Park Avenue, a tall building situated two blocks below Grand Central Station. The room was furnished with a typewriter, a chair, and a cot for resting between long sessions of work. For Faust, it was now or never. With Dorothy at hand to guard him from excesses—his own and those imposed upon him by others—he hoped to whip the depression as well as find his new writing personality. He was learning, he said, that writing for the hard-paper magazines was not simply a matter of writing better, that excellence had little to do with it. It was a matter of attitudes and ideas.

He found time to write to his son John at school in England, "This will reach you on your fourteenth birthday. Out in the West, when I was a youngster, boys were men when they reached fourteen. At that age they were entrusted with plough teams and sometimes they would even take the road with eight-horse teams and haul loads of hay or grain to town. They began to swear like men, and swagger like men, and drink their beer like men. They learned to smoke cigarettes, and even chew tobacco. They were a bit funny and a bit pathetic. I don't want you to become a man all at once. It is better to grow up by degrees and keep young as long as possible."

Thomas Costain said on behalf of the *Saturday Evening Post* that there was a lot of fine writing in Max Brand's latest, but the *Post* did not buy. *Detective Fiction* did buy the *Night Flower*. The Fausts took a house at Katonah near where they had lived in the twenties; and Monty and the three children joined them for Christmas—an expensive trip, financed by an advance from Brandt, but considered necessary because the parents were not expecting to return to Europe for five or six months. The *Post* rejected still another manuscript. But *Collier's* started out 1934 by buying a story; and Richard Halliday at Paramount Pictures' New York office discussed with Brandt the possibility of Faust's adapting the novel *Shanghai Express* for the screen. "We desperately need a picture for Marlene Dietrich."

In that first week of 1934, Brandt and Faust planned the production and marketing of their output for the coming year. (Faust had published more than 1,830,000 words in 1933—a new high.) They were like two generals planning a campaign. So many units here. So many units there. The first of three 20,000-word novelettes for Rogers Terrill. Whole armies to go marching off toward *Western Story* and *Argosy*, with special forces aimed at *Collier's* and the *Post*. Brandt was making editors feel they were missing something by not buying Faust.

On January 18 Brandt sent a memo to Katonah. "Oppenheimer is in town looking for something for Anna Sten" and added that Jock Whitney, who had ventured into films, wanted to do a big picture on Wagner's *Tristan*. Faust was excited at the prospect of helping his favorite Arthurian material into films and hastened to interpose his own version of the Tristan legend. Nothing came of it; but a hard-paper monthly, *The American*, bought a horse story.

Yet by April, after a nine-months stay in the U.S., it seemed to Faust that no ground had been gained. As a last-ditch stand he and Dorothy took refuge at the Farmington Country Club near the University of Virginia.

Throughout the spring of 1934 it was touch and go, Brandt hitting the road to drum up business and stopping at Falmouth, Massachusetts, to see Fulton Oursler, editor of *Liberty*, and in Virginia to see Faust. Brandt had numerous clients as important or more so than Faust—Benét, Conrad Aiken, Edna St. Vincent Millay—but it sometimes seemed that he was working for Faust alone. Faust's latest request for an advance of funds had been received rather breathlessly by Brandt because Brandt had just saved a client from going to jail by advancing a considerable amount of money—"more than I had any real business to do." Nevertheless, Brandt found the necessary funds for Faust.

"My idea is to have you as free from financial worry as possible," he said with rather wonderful generosity. "I know it can't be done in entirety as yet, but I'm sure it will be."

In late April he wired from New York that he had sold a story called *Mr. Christmas* to the slick-papered *Liberty*. It was an appreciable dent in enemy defenses. Faust was wrestling with a serial aimed at *Collier's*.

By great effort the *Collier's* serial was finished. A 20,000-word novelette for Rogers Terrill at Popular Publications was to be begun next day. The crime story aimed at the *Post* was started, and Faust was about to leave for Europe. His nearly year-long effort in the U.S. had been predicated on the assumption that to survive emotionally and to write well he must live in Italy. Dredging deep into his energy he produced in three days a 20,000-word crime novelette for Terrill. Brandt sold it. But the *Collier's* serial did not succeed. Faust revised, cut 15,000 words, and sailed on the "Saturnia" on May 25. On May 29, his birthday, Brandt cabled that *Pictorial Review*, a highly successful slick magazine, was buying a story.

18.

FICTIONAL SUMMITS

To be back in the villa was a joy to Faust. He had bought a little time. Summer in Italy would be no rest, but at least he would be working and overworking in surroundings he loved, among the books that were a special source of inspiration.

One of his favorite volumes concerned an eighteenth-century fox-hunting squire of the Tom Jones era, named John Mytton, who inherited 500,000 pounds sterling and ran through it in fifteen years. Mytton operated on gigantic scale, keeping two packs of hounds and two stables of horses, one for hunting, one for racing. The Christmas parties at his Shropshire estate lasted till Easter. At his table, eating, drinking, and enjoyment assumed Rabelaisian proportions. Mytton was a heroic horseman, a generous landlord, a loyal friend, loved at first sight, and died as he had lived, "in dread of nothing human or divine." Three thousand persons attended his funeral and he was mourned throughout the countryside.

According to his old friend John Schoolcraft, who visited the villa in the summer of 1934, Faust dreamed his way into this book as thoroughly as he had into the Arthurian legends; and the role of John Mytton became one of many that he played to some degree in life as in fiction.

The library that supplied such dreams now numbered approximately 5,000 volumes and was comprehensive enough to be the nucleus for the library of a small liberal arts college, although it was weighted rather heavily toward sports and prizefighting.

Brandt, who understood Faust's historical bent, was now discussing a project with Al Gibney, of the Munsey interests, and

Fred Clayton, editor of *Argosy*. "Clayton and Gibney think you should use the Italian Renaissance notion you outlined to them for a series of novelettes laid in Italy," Brandt wrote to Faust. "Our hunch was that you might work out a character something like Cellini who would run through all the stories and he would be something of a big shot in the gang world that you said you felt had many things in common with the gangs of the present day."

Faust created the character, The Firebrand, who ran through a series of serials and books that made the era of Benvenuto Cellini credible to the 1930's man in the street. Faust enjoyed himself while reliving a period he knew well. But *Detective Fiction* suggested that he needed to keep in closer touch with the terminology of the contemporary police and crime world, and he determined to do so through Edward Mulrooney when next in New York.

Brandt was meeting continued deficits at the bank. Faust suddenly found himself in debt to Brandt for $4,000. He wrote a story about a hay-baling crew and a young boy, himself, who makes good at a man's job; and Brandt sold it to *The American*. Not since Modesto days had Faust felt so desperate, he said. The title of the story, *The Sun Stood Still*, expressed the memory of endless weariness of time in the San Joaquin Valley. It also reminded him he had escaped seemingly insurmountable difficulties and might escape again.

Like the U.S., he was haltingly pulling out of the depression while threatened with backward slippage at any moment. With what he described as nausea, he was revising the sophisticated serial that *Collier's* might buy. At least with the pulps he could write myths and enjoy himself, at times. Not so with the slicks. They were buying his mind, not just his story-telling skill.

In September the financial pressure eased when *McCall's* bought a story involving an aircraft carrier and a sailing ship; and *Liberty* became keenly interested in the society serial, *House on the Hill*, which *Collier's*, *Post*, and a number of others had refused. Cass Canfield of Harper wrote that he would reach France in October and come to Italy in November, adding that the pre-publication sale of a second Evan Evans western had been good.

Argosy was aglow about the Cellini-Renaissance series. One of the editorial staff commented, "What a pity Faust feels constrained to make $25,000 a year instead of $15,000, because he undeniably has the touch of genius."

To serve as patterns of what was being published in slick magazines, Brandt sent Faust copies of published stories by Mildred Cram and I.A.R. Wylie, Brandt clients. Faust wrote a synopsis for a novel for Harper. Frank Blackwell of Street and Smith bought a western by "Hugh Owen," and commented to Brandt, "As I understand it, Hugh Owen is 'mine own' author, yes?" and Brandt replied, "Yes, Frank, you are quite right about Hugh. He is your ewe lamb." Owen, one more Faust pseudonym, was thus officially born.

On October 8, *Cosmopolitan* nearly bought *The Christopher of Luigi Pastorelli*. It was indicative. On the ninth, *Liberty* bought the much-refused, much-revised *House on the Hill* for $5,000. It was the first big money Faust and Brandt had made with the slick-paper magazines. Brandt saw it as a breakthrough. While agreeing, Faust felt keenly how much work it had cost to transform his writing personality. Nearly every day he felt a sense of shame that he was not writing something that could be bound and placed among the volumes on the shelves around him.

Blackwell was paying only two cents a word for a "Hugh Owen" story. The financial corner was far from turned. Brandt, however, had talked again with Fulton Oursler. *Liberty* would raise Faust's rates and give him editorial guidance on his next stories.

Then came another break. Erdman Brandt, till now an active partner in the agency with his brother, went to *The Saturday Evening Post,* still the top-paying, top-rated, slick-paper fiction outlet, as associate editor.

Into the Brandt office to replace him came a young Dartmouth graduate, Collier Young, later known as a Hollywood motion-picture and television producer.

During the fall and early winter of 1934, Brandt shepherded Faust toward newer, higher-paying markets while keeping the old ones going; and Faust worked at a new long poem about the poet, Sappho. *Cosmopolitan* offered $800 for short stories and asked to see Faust's, while Duncan Norton-Taylor at *Detective Fiction* bought *The Electric Touch* for $680. Faust was preparing a second serial for *Liberty,* a series of South Sea Island stories for *Adventure,* and short stories for *Collier's.* He was also working on a historical novel about Richard the Lion Hearted, which he called *The Golden Knight,* and which he hoped would make the top slicks, "but Jesus, Carl, how can I do anything good when I'm starving for money?"

"Two Spies arriving Europa with Playboy strongly protest alteration central theme Invisible Man," read a cable to Brandt in early January, 1935. Cable office employees sometimes knew plots and characters before stories were written, and Brandt's cables going to the villa contained some of the most magnificently garbled Italian-English recorded.

In late February, Brandt and Faust made an all-out attack on the Curtis publications, which included *The Saturday Evening Post* and *Ladies Home Journal,* Brandt choosing as their most likely point of penetration a magazine where Faust had been published previously. "In thinking over our talk," he wrote Harry Paxton at *Country Gentleman,* "it seems to me that there is one thing which is obvious that could be done and should be done—that is the proper development of Max Brand for your book. Let's look at the matter seriously." Brandt followed with a two-page persuasive view of his client. "He is, without doubt, the most circulation-compelling writer in the pulp field. I see it happen week in and week out. I have also seen him progress from western and costume stories, to modern day stories, stories of crime, and just recently to stories of the South Seas. By this I mean that he has trained and fitted himself to write these different forms of stuff for his regular markets."

Brandt continued. "Besides this he has gone into the slick paper field; into McCall's, with two stories of human emotions under distress of shipwreck; into Liberty, with a serial laid in the hunting country of Virginia; into The American with stories of horses and one of a boy on a hay-baling press, which latter one would have been swell for you; into Pictorial Review and Collier's, and into Harper's with a couple of highbrow stories . . . .

"It won't be long before you will see long stories of his in Cosmopolitan and The American. I think it is a very real chance for the Gentleman to have the first crack at Heinie of the Curtis magazines," Brandt concluded his sales pitch.

"Will you tell Heinie how much I like the last two stories in his great spy series?" Duncan Norton-Taylor, editor of *Detective Fiction*, informed Brandt; and Faust's international agent Anthony Hamilton was launched. Having mastered the crime genre, he now mastered the spy story. His man Hamilton moved freely on several continents as Faust himself had been doing. But Dorothy's maiden aunt in San Francisco had been producing some compelling research in response to Faust's weekly checks, and Faust proposed to Brandt a "limitless" series of adventure stories about an American in the Napoleonic upheavals in Europe. It seemed a good chance to use the two-million words of research notes on the French revolutionary period he had amassed in Paris fifteen years before and never fully exploited.

By February 29, he was sweating out the last of some South Sea tales for Bloomfield at *Adventure*, and outlining a long tennis serial for Gibney at *Argosy*, while complaining, "my elastic brain that used to pound out the six-thousand-word days is no more. I feel a mass-production day now. I feel it like hell."

Brandt laughed at him. "We're just getting started."

Faust was planning another trip to Greece, partly to show it to his children, partly to do research for a long poem on Sappho.

Sale of another serial to *Liberty* for $5,000 helped begin 1935 on a positive note and helped finance the new Greek expedition.

By April a story had sold to *Esquire* for a mere $150—Brandt getting the last $25 out of Arnold Gingrich, the editor, with a personal pry—but there was a certain prestige attached; and a cable arrived in New York, "White Indian sailing today. Regret delay." The white Indian was not Faust, who was sailing for Greece, but the long and successfully revised serial for *Argosy*.

Readers of *Detective Fiction Weekly* had voted Faust's spy stories their favorites for 1934. Harper was bringing out another Evan Evans western novel, and *Argosy* was to run it as a serial first. Brandt was offering bottom-of-the-barrel western material, that would not sell elsewhere, to Blackwell or to anyone else who would take it, under the name of Hugh Owen. The western pulp market was nearly finished and so was Faust's writing of westerns.

He and Dorothy were planning to come to the U.S. in the fall, put the two older children in boarding school, and take a house at Katonah. The time had come, they felt, to Americanize the family.

Esquire published *Hummingbirds and Honeysuckle*, by Max Brand, in July, 1935. The magazine used his true name without his knowledge, as well as some partially true, partially erroneous biographical material, in a biographical sketch. Faust protested angrily to Brandt, who said it was a misunderstanding; but it was also indicative of the rising attack upon Faust's anonymity. The story involved was a good one, if highly fanciful. The central character is a sailor-castaway in a strange land where the only inhabitants are women, a region perhaps calculated to appeal to *Esquire* readers.

As the date of the Fausts' arrival in the U.S. drew near, Dorothy was in her usual nervous state about her husband. She connived with Brandt to arrange the room down the hall from his office again, as a kind of cage for Faust to work in. Brandt had several clients with similar needs who used the room at various times. It had no telephone, no address, no identity, and virtually no means of entrance or exit except under Brandt's watchful eye.

Argosy for August 23, 1935, carried installments of book-length serials by Max Brand and Dennis Lawton, and a long story by George Challis; but no ordinary reader would have guessed that they were written by the same author. The promotional blurbs accompanying the contributions were safely diverse in the subject matter each described. "A White Indian Among the Cheyennes!" "When the South Seas Were Young!" "Tizzo Matches Swords With Caesare Borgia!"

Arriving on the "Rex" on August 29, the Fausts went first to the Hotel Fairfax on East 56th. As if in honor of their arrival, *Collier's* bought a story. Then *Cosmopolitan* bought two. All that remained was to exploit the breakthrough.

They took an apartment at 25 East End Avenue, placed Jane in Miss Spence's expensive finishing school in New York City and John at the Hotchkiss School in Connecticut.

Argosy bought *The Golden Knight* for four cents a word, bitterly disappointing Faust, who had hoped to make his version of the story of Richard the Lion Hearted acceptable for publication in a better-paying magazine. Ninety thousand words at four cents brought $3,600. It was well that they did. He was $5,000 in debt to Brandt. He was thoroughly trapped, and still liked to think that it was against his real will.

"Are you driven to the wall?" he asked Brandt. Brandt patiently assured him that all they needed to do was work hard and reap the golden harvest they had sown.

By Christmas the Fausts were settled in a colonial cottage called Bedford Farmhouse, owned by Mrs. Arthur Iselin, the cottage being an adjunct of the historic John Jay residence near Katonah. The new and highly prosperous Sunday magazine supplement, *This Week*, edited by Mrs. William Brown Meloney, was buying what was to become Faust's best-known short western story, *Wine on the Desert*. It is about a Nordic killer, Durante, who is outwitted by a Mediterranean man of peace, Tony, whom he has abused while fleeing from the scene of a murder. Proceeding into the desert, Durante opens his canteen expecting to quench his thirst with the cool water placed there by Tony, only to find he is drinking wine from Tony's vineyard. He dies in mid-desert in a drunken delirium.

The story shows Faust's narrative power and lyric yet popular style to good advantage.

Next, *Cosmopolitan* bought a story about a young doctor. The idea for the character had been in and out of Faust's mind several times. One evening he was talking with Brandt at Brandt's apartment at 270 Park Avenue, recalling experiences Dixie Fish had had while an interne at Roosevelt Hospital, some of which Faust had shared. Some of them dealt with the underworld. When Faust used the phrase "internes can't take money," Brandt jumped to his feet and exclaimed, "There's your title and there's your story." So Doctor Kildare was born.

Internes Can't Take Money concerns a country-bred doctor escaping a background very much like Faust's. As the story opens, Kildare, a young interne, is having a drink in a bar near his hospital when a young man with a badly slashed arm enters and faints from shock and loss of blood. Acting on the spur of emergency, Kildare stops the flow of blood, hurries to the hospital, obtains necessary instruments and materials, sews up the young man, and saves his life. Kildare is then confronted with the consequences of his charitable act. The young man is a criminal. With his associates, he offers Kildare a large sum of underworld money in payment. Kildare's reply is the title of the story.

Cosmopolitan bought it for $800. Brandt sold motion picture rights to Paramount for $5,000, a relatively substantial sum for the times. Perhaps reflecting the heightened tensions of success, Faust sustained a severe attack of paroxysmal tachycardia, the result of his local physician switching him from digitalis to a new heart-control drug. He switched back, duly reporting full details to Dr. Halsey, saying he was playing tennis again.

Collier's bought a short story for $800, and Richard Halliday at Paramount's New York office asked to see the material on Sappho that Faust had prepared in connection with his poem. Faust's eloquence at luncheon at Pierre's had convinced Halliday that the seventh century B.C. Greek genius could live and breathe in a style that might appeal to Hollywood.

On May 5, 1936, after four years of intensive siege, *The Saturday Evening Post* capitulated. The price they paid for Faust's story, $750, was not high; but the prestige was worth vastly more. En route to the recognized top of the popular fiction market, the Faust-Brandt team had cracked the highbrow prose and poetry markets, as well as films, radio, and Sunday supplements, while continuing supreme in the pulps; and Faust was the possessor of a new writing personality that he did not particularly like but was obliged to live with.

On June 20, he and Dorothy and the children were aboard the "Champlain" bound for Italy as *The Kinsale*, by Frederick Faust, led off the fiction in the *Post*. The story takes place in a contemporary, yet mythical, valley close to New York City, a valley inhabited by fabulous Irishmen, fabulous horses, pretty girls. It was a fairy tale laid not somewhere in the West but somewhere in the East, and was so convincing that a number of readers wrote the *Post* inquiring where the valley was located.

Faust had thought the tale good enough to sign his true name to it. At forty-four, he was becoming hungry for an identity he did not have and a recognition which, if deferred longer, might never come.

19.

A FAUSTIAN OLYMPIAD

CONCURRENTLY with his ascent to the summit of the popular fiction market, Faust had continually attempted to realize his favorite values of the ancient Greek and Roman worlds in life as well as in literature. One of these attempts was indeed strange. It involved such diverse elements as his trip to Greece in 1935; the Italian 1936 Olympic team; Sappho; and Professor Walter Hart, Faust's companion on the first Greek expedition.

"Six years ago, summering at an Italian beach," he wrote Brandt in the winter of 1934, "I was staggered by the physical splendor of the Italian men and wondered why they never won the Olympic Games." On inquiry Faust learned that the Italian Olympic teams had never been competently coached. He took it upon himself to remedy this historic lack. "It happens that I know well the best coach in the world," he informed Brandt, "Boyd Comstock, coach of Southern California, Yale, and writer of Spalding's ten volumes on track athletics." Faust had met Comstock while an undergraduate at Berkeley and had known him later in New York. Comstock, in fact, had an excellent reputation. He had once come to the Penn Relays, then the East's biggest intercollegiate meet, with a four-man team, and won the meet. He had coached Charles Paddock and Frank Wykoff, known as "the world's fastest humans." If anyone could help Faust correct the deficiencies in Italy's international track and field effort, Comstock was perhaps the man.

"I got his abstract of a course for coaches that he gave at the University of Chicago, had it translated into Italian, presented it to the most influential Italians I knew," Faust continued to Brandt, "waited five years, nothing happened because the selfish bastards saw no political advancement for themselves. Then I ran across the Marchese Ridolfi, high in Fascist circles, and talked to him. Ridolfi is boiled up with excitement. I want to bring Comstock over at my own expense and see what he can do with Italian athletics."

Faust hated Fascism and he had not become involved in anything approaching Italian politics. The controlling factor in his involvement now was his admiration and affection for the Italian people and the belief that, given a chance, they would perform creditably in international athletic competition. Another factor was certainly his enthusiasm for the Greek Olympic tradition and for the vision of its renewal in modern Italy.

He asked Brandt to hold back a thousand dollars of his money to pay Comstock's expenses. "When I cable you, 'Comstock one thousand,' or 'Comstock five hundred,' you can send it off at once to him by wire. Don't tell me I'm a damned fool. I knew that twenty years ago. The point is," Faust continued, "I don't want Dorothy to know. She'll go crazy if she hears I'm spending more money on other people, considering my present list of the lame, halt and blind."

If the scheme did not succeed, Faust was to pay for Comstock's return to the U.S. Until the Italian government took over, Faust was to pay Comstock's salary. Until Comstock and his family found other housing, they would live at Faust's villa.

Brandt accepted the inevitable but spoke his mind. "I've got nothing against the Italians or the Italian race. But I've got a decided interest in your being in a position to do the fine work of which you are capable and which you have to slur because of the pressure brought on you by your doing Quixotic things of this sort. You can't, Heinie, uphold the world like an Atlas but I do agree that you make a damn good try at it."

Faust replied, "I've been talking again to the Marchese Ridolfi, the Italian athletic head, and have cleared the way on this side of the water. Can you wire $350 to Comstock, Palos Verdes Estates, California?"

At the same time, his friend and confidant, Walter Hart, was suggesting in fatherly fashion that Faust stop writing poems about mythical gods and giants. Faust replied, "It isn't really a preference for those themes, but a lack of all other themes that determines my choice. Since modernity is impossible, what remains?"

Hart served as a connective between Faust's dreams and his practices in classical literature and life. He was a father figure in whom Faust could confide. They had known each other slightly during Faust's Berkeley days. A chance meeting in Florence had ripened into warm friendship, developed by regular correspondence and trips to various parts of Europe. Faust saw in Hart the scholarly knowledge and objectivity he needed. Hart admired Faust's imaginative power and success in the popular writing world, a world which Hart, like many academics, secretly longed to enter. Both had suffered at the hands of the University of California. As vice president, Hart had been prominently mentioned as Berkeley's next president in a long tradition of scholarly leaders from liberal arts fields. He was bypassed in favor of Robert Gordon Sproul, first of a line of business-executive presidents. In Florence and Faust, Hart found compensations. In Hart, Faust found partial recompense for his lack of a college degree and for his lack of self-realization in verse. They had shared an actual experience in Greece and continued to share its traditions, including its athletics.

Now off for Greece again, Faust instructed Brandt in a series of code signals to be used in cabling information regarding a spy series, a western series, or King Richard the Lion Hearted, and concluded, "What about a small illustrated booklet based on Comstock's theory of walking to be called 'The Graceful Woman,' or some such title?"

Brandt, a non-walker, was unimpressed by the graceful woman proposal. "Taylor withdraws objections. Go ahead on Japan against America," he cabled Faust, with reference to an international spy story.

While sitting at an open-air cafe in Constitution Square, Athens, Faust and Dorothy learned of the new pen name, Dennis Lawton, which Brandt and Fred Clayton of *Argosy* had devised for a South Sea serial to be called *The Blackbirds Sing*. Faust and Dorothy had a drink of *retsina* on the strength of the sale of *The Blackbirds Sing*. With the two older children, they were cruising the northern Aegean on a converted trawler, "The Kyma," and Faust was hard at work on his poem about Sappho as well as his daily quota of popular prose.

From Constitution Square they walked around to the east side of the Acropolis to the theater of Dionysus. There the *Oresteia* of Aeschylus was first presented one spring day in 458 B.C. They were seeing it on a brilliant April afternoon. Faust sat on a 2,400-year-old stone bench and thought about Aeschylus—who had fought at Marathon and at Salamis, had dominated the Attic theater for forty years, yet who wanted inscribed on his tombstone only the statement that he had fought for liberty against tyranny.

Faust felt that by encouraging Comstock and the Italian Olympic effort, he was doing a little bit toward bringing what he considered the greatest of all periods back to earth.

On May 12, 1935, Dorothy wrote Brandt from Delos, the sacred island of the Cyclades, that Faust was studying the recently planted palm tree commemorating the one mentioned by Odysseus in Homer, but had refused to become interested in his income tax returns. Could Brandt help?

During three weeks in May, Faust lost himself in the Aegean world. He preoccupied part of his mind with the theme of Prometheus, the life giver, a theme dealt with in his *Dionysus in Hades*, but actually worked at his poem on Sappho, visiting her city of Mytilene on the island of Lesbos.

His long Sappho poem was unsuccessful and was never published. His notes for it communicate more than the finished work.

188

With every height of Mitylene I wonder how high your heart leaped. Then I remember that you were like other women, with a green girlhood behind you, and as you grew up, too few men, too many women.

Driving through the sweeping, naked valleys of Lesbos, it was hard to think of Sappho there until I saw the sea.

We haunt the places where divine men have been before us. Why is there only one woman?

I notice that Mytilenean flies are small and bite hard. The rocks of Eresos are neither very bare nor very noble.

The trip to Eresos does little but make one feel the great difference that has come, and the significance that has gone away.

Sappho: In my lengthening years, with the gentle hands of a daughter to attend me, love ran over my body like spring over cold earth; love in my heart betrayed me. Love who cannot be closed out by shutting the eyes, but lies within beating against the lids, love which lifts up the heart with wings through the daylight but sinks into loneliness at night, weltering down through the unending hours like a stone through the darkness of the sea.

There is much material like this which evidences the tragic division in Faust. He was a man almost bursting with poetic feeling and not finding adequate means of expression. In such fantastically complicated and burdensome schemes as his support of the Italian Olympic team, he found one more outlet for his frustrated energy.

Brandt had set up what they called "the squirrel fund," into which odds and ends of royalties went. He cabled a $2,000 surprise dividend to Faust in Greece. Faust had taken Brandt fully into his confidence about his short life expectancy, and Brandt made extra effort to utilize assets as soon as they became available and to protect his client.

"I'm not shooting $250 of your dough off in thin air to Tracy Richardson without finding out where that old lad is," Brandt said, in response to a cable from Faust ordering help for his old friend from Canadian Army days. "I usually find that these starving lads—and I have at least fifteen on the list—can be kept fed for less than your lavish means."

Brandt finally located Richardson in Albuquerque, New Mexico, and satisfied his needs at reduced rate.

Faust wrote affectionately, "You make it easier to sit in a rolling cabin every day and bat out my fifteen pages."

He visited Ephesus in Asia Minor and looked mournfully at the bog where the Temple of Diana, a wonder of the world, had once stood.

He could look forward to a year of hard work in the United States which would repay the advances that had made possible the Greek trip and would underwrite Comstock.

The 1936 Olympic Games were scheduled to begin in Berlin on August 1. Faust, back in Florence in late June, was eager to see what Comstock had been doing with the Italian team. In the previous year, Faust had acted as co-coach during the awkward, early days of training. The beginning had indeed been awkward. Comstock, who spoke no Italian at all, and Faust who spoke comparatively little, had begun their coaching operations at the Giglio Rosso field in Florence chiefly by smiles and sign language. Soon they noticed a growing discrepancy between what they were saying and what the athletes were doing. Their chief interpreter was interpreting their instructions to suit himself. After they fired him, performances improved.

Comstock believed rhythm essential to good track and field performance and appealed to the Italians' sense of rhythm by having his trainees sing or hum tunes as they ran, hurled, or jumped. There were humorous comments from observers about grand opera on the athletic field. Confidence was another problem. Faust and Comstock made a special effort to overcome what they believed to be a sense of inferiority that had plagued Italians as result of defeats in battle, like that at Caporetto in 1917, and in international games throughout the years.

Training took place at a number of fields, but Florence was a center. Faust's custom-made Isotta-Fraschini was frequently seen parked at the Giglio Rosso on the Viale dei Colli, and his large figure moved here and there among the thinly clad athletes. With Comstock, he patiently invoked, cajoled, lectured, demonstrated, praised.

The press on both sides of the Atlantic got wind of what was happening. It was publicized widely if inaccurately in the U.S. in articles in *Collier's, The Reader's Digest,* and elsewhere. Comstock and the United States were given credit for "helping Italy over the hurdles," as one writer put it. Faust, as usual, remained incognito. Brandt complained bitterly that the least Faust should receive in return for his immense expenditure of time, energy, and money was due credit.

Instead Faust received a cable in late July announcing the rejection of a book-length serial, *Six Golden Angels,* by *Collier's.* Again an editorial and financial crisis threatened. He was in New York making money to help pay for Comstock and the Italian Olympic effort when word came that the Italians had achieved a close second to the United States (sparked by the Games' quadruple gold-medal winner Jesse Owens) in the 400-meter relay, and had placed well up in the 1,500-meter race, the discus, and other events. Generally speaking, Italy gave its best Olympic performance, scoring $32\frac{1}{2}$ points as compared to 13 in the 1932 Olympics. Comstock received a six-year contract from the Mussolini government and instructions to build a winning team for 1940.

Faust accepted a decoration from a government he held in contempt politically but from a people for whom he had the deepest affection. He became "Cavaliere Faust," Faust the Honorary

191

Gentleman, adding one more alias to his growing list. But Hitler's refusal to greet American Negro athletes had helped convince him that Fascism and racism were probably making war inevitable. Jews were being persecuted even in Italy. Dark clouds were lowering over his Mediterranean dreams.

20.

TWO WOMEN

WHEN Faust sailed toward the United States in August of 1936 on the "Rex" ("too broke to bring even one member of the family with me"), he rose at five the first morning, "with the Balearics about four hours astern," and took stock of his affairs. "One solid month of work in New York really may put us on Easy Street for the time being," he wrote Dorothy. It will entail the revision and sale of *Golden Angels*, *The American* (the French Revolution story, the revision of which I'm sure that I can make a saleable yarn), the Florentine murder story which I'm bringing along, and the spy story the writing of which I'm starting today." He told Dorothy he would bring her and the children over by installments as he could afford it. In the course of the past twenty hours he had outlined all the characters, the main actors, and many of the scenes and dialogue cues for the spy story.

Faust shared a cabin with the art critic Richard Offner, whom he had met in Florence. Offner restimulated his imagination by talking about the light that Masaccio had let into painting. "When shadows begin to fall inside the picture, something happens to the spirit of the spectator," Faust reported to Dorothy. "It's a sort of fourth dimensional idea. Giotto is Offner's great among Italians. Rembrandt is his greatest of all time; Velasquez his most *perfect* painter; da Vinci a marvelously facile *mind*, but a weak artist. Imagine my delight," he crowed, "to hear so many considered judgments that agree with my own taste!!!"

Over the years Faust had bought and mounted many dozens of expensive prints in a personal art collection that included volumes on Rembrandt, Michelangelo, and Leonardo, as well as earlier painters and the early Greek sculptors. The giant albums containing the Alinari prints reflected his appetite for size as well as subject matter. Each was 20 by 14 inches, contained 50 pages, and weighed about 25 pounds. He and Dorothy had followed the program he envisioned during his exploratory trip to Paris in 1921. They had visited museums, galleries, churches, and private collections. A substantial section of his library was devoted to books on art.

He reached New York in time to revise *Six Golden Angels* successfully and sell it to *Collier's* for $12,000, and he learned that Columbia Pictures wanted copies of the Kinsale stories that were appearing in *The Saturday Evening Post*. Seeking other stimulus, Faust bet Cass Canfield five dollars he could write a story with a strong female interest for a slick-paper magazine and sell it under a feminine pen name. The story, set in Africa, had as its heroine a Negro girl named Mwemba; but Faust wasn't sure whether under the terms of the bet the story could be sold to any slick or just a woman's slick, and asked Brandt to "check with Cass. The story must be sold in September or I lose my bet and a lot of glory." Faust lost. "Mwemba" was never published.

Brandt was asking Universal $15,000 for film rights to *Six Golden Angels*. The pre-Olympic Games setback in Faust's affairs had proved fleeting. Hollywood suddenly sprouted with offers for his work and services. Fifteen hundred a week was the salary mentioned. But he refused to consider a job that would take full time. He had had lunch to good purpose with Canfield and Gene Saxton, a Harper editor, and they had developed plans for a book about an American in a small Italian hill town. Meanwhile Brandt was opposing his going to Hollywood under any circumstances, on grounds that it would likely destroy him as an imaginative writer; but Faust was flattered by the interest and expounded glowingly to Dorothy on the usefulness of a steady income of even a thousand a week. "Fifty-two thousand a year— with time free to work at verse and stories." He added that the approved procedure in negotiations was to disregard first and second offers and become serious only after the third.

Brandt next arranged a meeting between himself, Faust, and Edwin Knopf, director of writers and chief talent scout for writing at Metro-Goldwyn-Mayer's Hollywood studios, whom Faust described as "a good guy whose left hand had been blown off when he saved a child from an explosion of firecrackers" and who was "smoother than silk."

Though Dorothy and Judy had to wait, John and Jane were brought to the United States one at a time, as finances permitted, to enter Hotchkiss and Spence; while Faust worked steadily in a room high up in the Hotel Vanderbilt. His career was approaching a climax in several ways. Friendship with the Lovetts, Benéts, Barrys, Charles Fullers, Myerses, and others had ripened; also with the Gerald Murphys—the prototypes for the Dick Divers of Fitzgerald's novel *Tender Is the Night*. Faust did not particularly care for the kind of international social life represented by the Murphys but said he found Murphy's keen interest in the poet Gerard Manley Hopkins stimulating.

At a party given by the Henry Siedel Canbys, he locked horns with avant-gardists over his dogmatic assertion that serious poetry could be written only on ancient themes. One modern asked him, "When did you die?" Stephen Benét and Archibald MacLeish had won Pulitzer prizes for poetry and Leonard Bacon would soon do so. Faust's own poetic achievement by contrast seemed miniscule, and his self-esteem suffered.

At a party at the Cass Canfields' he met a small, brown-haired, large-eyed, intelligent, sensitive woman thirteen years younger, recently divorced, and fell passionately in love with her. Her response was immediate and in kind. As usual with Faust, the case had unusual dimensions. She was the daughter of a man who, had such a poll been conducted, would probably have ranked among the dozen or so most respected in the United States. Such distinction plus other factors had removed him from close contact with his daughter. In addition to this remoteness, she believed an older sister to be his favorite. She saw in Faust a combination of father, lover, and husband she had never had. He saw in her the passionately unquestioning admiration he craved, an admiration which included absolute belief in his powers as a poet. The prolonged enforced absence from Dorothy, whose devotion was absolute but who believed his poetry to be too intellectual and too contrived, plus the strain of constant work, and the loneliness of a solitary New York room, were contributing factors. Under his guidance, his mistress began to write. They read poetry aloud together. As he watched her groping attempts at self-expression, she seemed to him like a person struggling to emerge from under water. She was in her way an image of himself.

Dorothy saw the matter differently when she arrived in November, in company with Judy and the Russian governess who had succeeded Monty, and joined Faust in the apartment at 25 East End Avenue. Dorothy had a keen intuition. She sensed how matters stood even before she was told by friends. Again there were painful scenes. Faust patiently explained that he loved only one woman as his wife, assured Dorothy the affair had no bearing on his basic feeling for her, and refused to consider the divorce she again offered him.

She could not accept what seemed to her his basic dishonesty and said she would not be able to feel the same about him again. This in turn angered him. He appears to have allowed his mistress to think in terms of their eventual marriage.

His personal problems were reaching maximum complexity as his professional career approached a climax. The *Post* had bought another story. The editors at *Cosmopolitan* wanted him to meet Bert Acosta, the transatlantic flyer, and do a series of aviation stories; and associate editor Don Moore added, "Don't forget we'll need a spy story soon!" and sent Brandt a thousand dollars for the one they were taking.

Faust was becoming a chief supplier to the slicks as he had been to the pulps. He was not concentrating on one outlet as with

Western Story but was spread across the board. Such quality magazines as *The Forum* were asking to see his verse and prose, and *This Week* bought a story for $500 and a serial for $5,000.

As sales to top markets were reaching new highs, Edwin Knopf wrote in early March, 1937, that he wanted to make a deal with Faust for MGM. While the Hollywood deal was pending, *The Saturday Evening Post* for March 6 carried a Faust novelette, *Johnny Comes Lately*, as well as a story by Scott Fitzgerald.

Hoping to mollify her wrath, Faust called Dorothy's attention to the fact that for the first time since the spring of 1932 they were nearly out of debt.

On Wednesday, April 14, he lunched with Thomas B. Costain, who had left the *Post* to become editor of *American Cavalcade*, a magazine newly established by Pocket Books Corporation. Costain, too, wanted aviation stories; and they discussed a series based on the Quiet Birdmen Club, a little-known New York group to which most prominent pilots in the United States, including Charles Lindbergh, belonged. Faust got busy at once and produced four stories which Costain bought, and he and Costain established a personal friendship.

In response to an inquiry from *Black Mask*, Brandt replied that Faust was no longer doing pulp fiction. Yet *Argosy* on May 29 began publishing a book-length science-fiction serial, *The Smoking Land*.

"You are quite right about Frederick Faust's Sappho poetry. It has an exquisite quality, but it is not for us," said *This Week*, but wanted to see his sonnets.

On Tuesday, April 20, Knopf, on his way to Europe, lunched with Brandt and Faust. Afterwards Brandt made clear his continued opposition to the Hollywood venture, on the grounds that it would jeopardize Faust's now very good magazine market as well as his talent. He was convinced that Faust could make more than $1,000 a week by sticking to magazines.

Knopf, however, wrote Brandt from Metro-Goldwyn-Mayer's London studios that he was looking forward to continuing the negotiations with Max Brand; and Brandt wrote Faust, who was en route to Europe, that he had seen the film Paramount had made of the first Kildare story, Joel McCrea playing Dr. Kildare; and Brandt reported that "a lot of tears were shed by Barbara Stanwyck, but that can't be helped. She weeps easily."

Cue reported: "*Internes Can't Take Money* is a fast-moving, tense, thrilling melodrama in the best Alfred Hitchcock tradition (although directed by Alfred Santell). It is packed with action and overflows with cinematic chills—a good 85 minutes' worth of gripping film entertainment."

Brandt radioed the "Rex" to say Costain needed an aviation story by June 4, adding that he, Brandt, had been to the Mascot Restaurant and found the maitre-d'-hotel and Gene Tunney swapping stories about Faust. Faust reported his typewriter broken, rendering his days on shipboard somewhat of a loss. Brandt suggested he carry a spare typewriter and proposed that they pick up $5,000 from a mystery novel titled *The Seventh Day*, "an old discard from Cosmo," if Faust could bring himself to revise it. But Faust couldn't. He was sick of slick fiction and looked forward to Hollywood as an escape to a new medium.

Twentieth Century-Fox thought the Halcyon Club series appearing in *American Cavalcade* would make splendid film material; and Henry LaCossitt, a producer, wanted to go into the matter on behalf of the film magnate, Joseph M. Schenck. *Seventh Day* sold unrevised to *MacLean's Magazine* in Toronto for $1,380.

A mystery story, featuring a sophisticated detective playboy called Bombi, sold to *Liberty* for $5,000. "I can raise them to $7,500 next time and probably to $10,000 on the one to follow," Brandt reported. Thus a new "series" character was born.

Elks Magazine bought *Virginia Creeper* for $225; and Frieda Lubelle, Brandt's financial manager, sent Dixie Fish at 755 Park Avenue $130 Faust had borrowed to keep his financial nose above water.

Faust reached his villa paradise nearly exhausted from overwork, domestic conflict, a particularly personal problem he had brought with him, and the dilemma represented by the Hollywood offer and Brandt's opposition.

"I'm dissatisfied with everything I'm doing," he wrote Brandt. "Listen, Carl, the only guy that ever had a right to write *Of Mice and Men* without a let-down ending, is Heinie Faust. Why the hell can't I do something? Why can't I see you and talk about something except cheese to fit the *Collier's* market? I'm sick. I don't like life. All I want to do is to write verse which makes everybody else sicker than I am. Just now, I think I'm writing better than Milton. Which means that I need a brain doctor." More and more he was falling into the bitter but ambiguous tone of self-accusation, the complaint of a writer self-caught in his own lures.

Brandt replied forcefully, "It seems to me that your growing pains are becoming acute and that even you will have to recognize that you are an artist and a craftsman. You, you big bastard, are the only one who doesn't truly believe it. And your living in Italy is only the remaining thread tying you to what will soon be apparent to you as your outworn romanticist phase. The kind of poetry that you burn to write is born of a passionate desire you have had to identify yourself with a color and an age in which you know people to have loved, sung and held high wassail. But you can no more wake that spirit in this age than you can reverse your incarnation and go back to be at Lorenzo's Court." Brandt then gave some hardheaded advice. "When Milton and Pope wrote their heroics, all educated people knew their mythology, were adept in symbolism—do they now? No, and goddammit, they don't read Milton any more either—not after they've been physicked with him in colleges and schools.

"Put that music into songs of our mythology—Billy-the-Kid, Fremont, Washington, Robert E. Lee, Paul Bunyan, Buffalo Bill—make us hear our common language sung. If anyone is the mouthpiece for the emotion of his contemporary race, you are he. When you try to sink yourself into an old-world background you

199

are as apparent a fake as a Jewish peddler dressed in kilts at a Vatican reception."

Purposefully or inadvertently, Brandt did not respond to a request Faust had added to his letter. "When I say the word," Faust had requested, "write me that I've got to come to the U.S. immediately on important business."

The reason for the subterfuge was that Faust had not gone alone to the villa ahead of Dorothy and the children to closet himself with heavy work, as he had said he was going to do. He was traveling with his mistress. They had sojourned in Venice, even visited Florence and the villa. She had gone home alone, and Faust wanted Brandt to give him an excuse to return to the U.S. and rejoin her.

Meanwhile with what seems almost incredible misjudgment, he was telling Dorothy that his two women should meet and accept each other in what he considered the highest traditions of civilization.

Other aspects of civilization were at the same time impinging their realities on Faust. Plumed-helmeted, black-shirted, *fascisti* were marching the streets of Florence. Everywhere on walls were the militant slogans signed "M" for Mussolini, in the manner of Napoleon's "N." Hitler had marched into the Rhineland. The Rome-Berlin axis was being solidified and was looking toward Japan as a third member. The summer of 1937 was an eleventh hour in world history.

A deeply unhappy Heinie and Dorothy returned to the U.S. in September to establish a household at Bedford Farmhouse at Katonah, while the two older children went to live for a year in Vienna. Judy remained with her parents and the Russian governess.

21.

DIONYSUS IN HOLLYWOOD

THE fall of '37 brought an accentuation of Faust's problems. Leading a double life between his wife and his mistress, and another kind of double, or triple, life between his slick-magazine writing, his pulp fiction, and his writing of verse, he converted his days into labyrinths of complexity. A professional success that would have delighted most men became increasingly repulsive to him, as he worked hard at a major poem on the subject of Christ at Gethsemane, while sketching out a shorter one about St. Francis' divinely inspired sermon to the birds.

His heart, which gave him yet another kind of strange and special identity, somehow managed to stand the strain of all this, though there were constant small attacks. He had been hospitalized for a week in the spring of 1936 when under lesser duress. His resistance was proving equal to the punishment to which he subjected himself.

However, by the end of 1937 he had reached the depths of self-disgust. After promising Dorothy that his love affair was over, he continued it. At the same time he was reaching out artistically for the symbols of greatest virtue, Jesus and St. Francis. He found that the conflict involving his two women was one that his nature could not easily shrug off. He had become convinced that he was, in his own words, a great sinner.

By early January, 1938, he was on sale to Hollywood for $1,500 a week, a going rate for big names. Brandt had waited until after the third offer from Knopf and then moved into serious negotiations under instructions from Faust. Brandt's heart was not in the matter; but Faust was financially hard-pressed, "bedeviled by revising stories for editors," and thought he saw in Hollywood solutions to both problems.

In 1937 he had earned $42,712.44. It was a giant step up from depression lows but still insufficient for him, and far below his hundred-thousand-dollar marks of the 1920's.

According to the plan evolved by Brandt and Knopf, Collier Young, Brandt's associate, was to precede Faust to Hollywood as advance man, a sort of courier announcing the arrival of the illustrious and mysterious Max Brand. Young was charged by Brandt with the responsibility of keeping Faust reasonably sober, behaving at least somewhat realistically, and in funds. Young would work through the Myron Selznick Agency, and Brandt would continue to direct over-all operations from New York, and to sell stories to magazines and superintend the production of books. Faust's books, all hardbacks, had been appearing at the rate of six or seven a year in the United States alone. A particularly interesting serial with the working title of "Marijuana" had been sold to *This Week*. It was published as *Flower of Hell*. Several studios rejected it for film use because of its "dope angle," which they believed would be distasteful to audiences.

Following lunch in Philadelphia with Erdman Brandt and Wesley Winans Stout, editor of *The Saturday Evening Post*, Faust caught "The Broadway Limited" bound for Chicago and California. He knew he was turning away from summits only recently achieved after bitter effort, but they had provided him with nothing he felt was essential except money, and he felt he could make more money in Hollywood.

He had esteemed his prose production so little during these hectic years that he had signed his true name to only some half a dozen pieces, including the stories in the *Post* and in *Harper's*. In Hollywood he intended to implement a tentative arrangement agreed on with Knopf, whereby his mornings would be free for verse and he would devote afternoons to film writing.

Yet he had high hopes for his Hollywood career. He had seen

two pictures he believed to be great, *Mayerling* and *Grand Illusion*. They had shown him, he thought, the possibilities that lay in the art of film making and had inspired him to dream of bringing Sappho and Homer to the screen. The many successful films based on his work would help, though there had been a hiatus of several years for which he blamed Brandt. The fact remained that he was by no means unknown in the film capital, and the recent success of *Internes Can't Take Money* should do him no harm. At the back of his mind was the idea of a motion-picture series based on Dr. Kildare.

As he rode westward, serious Hollywood interest was developing in his historical romance of Richard the Lion Hearted, just published in book form. Throughout the fall and winter of 1937–38, studios had been asking to see galley proofs of his books as well as manuscripts of his stories in advance of publication. Most active in this respect had been MGM, Columbia, and RKO.

To refute Brandt's argument that film writing would destroy his talent, he could cite the example of Steve Benét, Sidney Howard, and others who had moved in and out of Hollywood, on an experimental basis, to make money. He was planning to try the experiment for six months.

Giving him additional confidence was the publicity he had just received in *Publisher's Weekly*, the leading magazine devoted to the book publishing and book selling industries, in the form of an article written by Edward H. Dodd, Jr., of the Dodd, Mead firm. The article, appearing on March 26, 1938, titled "Twenty-Five Million Words," publicly revealed in detail who Max Brand really was. It told how he had become "King of the Pulps," claimed that he wrote a book every three weeks, used at least a dozen pen names, published 1.7 million words a year, and since 1917 had published altogether about 25,000,000 words. "It would take an Einstein to calculate the number of times all these words are read," Edward Dodd affirmed and proposed a figure of 22,959,000,000,000, "which shows what happens when Einstein isn't on the job, and is probably more people than ever lived or will live, indicating that a few generations of mid-Western grasshoppers must needs be devoted Western fans." Not only was Max Brand popular in the U.S., according to Dodd, but he was the best-selling American author in most countries of central and northern Europe.

The article reflected the fact that during his five-year struggle with the depression and the editors, Faust had divided himself into additional pen names: Frank Austin, so that Dodd, Mead could publish westerns under that name as well as under Max Brand; Frederick Frost, for mysteries going into book form under the Macrae-Smith imprint; Walter C. Butler, for novels of crime and the underworld published by Macaulay; while Harper continued its westerns under the Evan Evans pseudonym.

Dodd's revelations seriously endangered an incognito that was being penetrated from other quarters. The incognito and its penetration had become a kind of detective story that enhanced the mystery surrounding the name "Max Brand." A New Yorker named Philip Richman seems to have been the first reader to guess the truth. After reading the work of Brand, George Owen Baxter, Peter Henry Morland, and David Manning for many years, Richman became impressed by similarities of tone and style and began to suspect that the authors were one and the same person. When *Western Story* refused to enlighten him, he did research at the New York Public Library, and, by means of Library of Congress catalog cards, discovered the truth. As others followed Richman in solving the mystery, they constituted a hard core of fans, collectors, and readers who received a special kind of double pleasure from everything Faust wrote. Many engaged in a sleuthing game of seeking out pen names and tracking down published work of Faust's previously unknown to them.

Most agreed with Dodd and other authorities that Faust had published more prose fiction than any other person on record.

Collier Young met the train at Pasadena and drove Faust straight to the MGM lot in Culver City. Immediately beyond a guarded gate was a drive-in compound surrounded by a number of buildings, one of them the recently completed, two-story, New Writers' Building. In the background were the sets, the make-believe jungles, cabarets, frontier towns, and grand hotels, forming a maze resembling the stories in Faust's brain.

It was one of Hollywood's most fabulous eras, often called the golden age of films. On and off the MGM lot at this period were Aldous Huxley, to do the screen play for Jane Austen's *Pride and Prejudice*, and Vicki Baum, author of *Grand Hotel*. Nelson Eddy and Jeannette MacDonald were making musicals. James Hilton, a mild little man with hair parted in the middle, had come from England to assist in the screen version of *Good-bye, Mr. Chips*. Katherine Hepburn was to play "Jo" in *Little Women*, and Spencer Tracy would make *Dr. Jekyll and Mr. Hyde*. Sinclair Lewis was working with Dore Schary and Sol Fielding on *Storm in the West*, a western burlesquing Hitler, Stalin, and Mussolini, never released. William Saroyan would write the story for *The Human Comedy* in which Mickey Rooney would star; and Ingrid Bergman was to make *Gaslight* with Charles Boyer. Marlene Dietrich and Ronald Colman would appear in *Kismet*, and Greta Garbo was about to make *Two-Faced Woman*, with Melvyn Douglas.

Ocean Wave Lucas, Mary Pickford's goddaughter, who had played opposite Will Rogers in the stage production of *Ah, Wilderness*, handled publicity for MGM; and Greer Garson had come from England to play in Hilton's *Mr. Chips*, with Robert Donat. Frank Sinatra was getting a start, as were Judy Garland, Ava Gardner, and Lana Turner. Cary Grant and Wallace Beery were stars, Beery and Garland being regarded as the biggest money-makers on the lot. But James Stewart was rising fast, thanks in no small degree to Faust's *Destry*, soon to be released by Universal. Tyrone Power was playing opposite Norma Shearer in *Marie Antoinette*; while Vivian Leigh, Leslie Howard, Clark Gable, and Olivia de Haviland were being signed for Selznick's *Gone With the Wind*, for which Sidney Howard was writing the film story. Last but not least, Johnny Weismuller was playing

Tarzan to Maureen O'Sullivan's Jane, supported by Cheetah, the big chimpanzee, and two dozen human dwarfs acting as monkeys.

One writer, accomplishing apparently nothing in what seemed a multimillion-dollar madhouse, took a plane to New York and stayed there. Six weeks later a letter from the MGM finance department was forwarded to him. It asked him to please stop by and collect his paychecks, which were piling up at the rate of $1,500 a week.

Presiding over all these activities was Louis B. Mayer, the former junk dealer born near Minsk in Russia and reared in Canada, and his general manager, once his bodyguard, a big, tough, shrewd, red-necked Irishman named Eddie Mannix. Mannix was reputed to have a telephone in his apartment studded with $30,000 worth of jewels. Every time he picked up the phone, he picked up $30,000.

Young took Faust to the office of Edwin Knopf, who gave him a cordial welcome; and he was soon settled in living quarters at the Beverly Hills Hotel and in writing quarters in a second-floor office with two desks and a thick beige rug at MGM's Writers Building. The building housed more than a hundred writers, including Aldous Huxley and Scott Fitzgerald.

He immediately began work on a story in which the central character was a dog. He had agreed to a starting salary of $1,000 a week, in return for the freedom to work at home as he chose and to retain publication rights for work done for the studio. "It is obvious what they expect of me is quantity and not quality," he wrote Brandt in some disgust. They in fact intended to use Faust's mass-production abilities to produce the masses of so-called "B" or inexpensive pictures that were major money-makers.

He was working with Harvey Gates and Chester Franklin, who had helped produce successful *Rin-tin-tin* dog films and more recently a sentimental woodland idyl, *Sequoia*, featuring Jean Parker and many wild animals. The new picture was to be the first of a series, but Faust found it "the lousiest sort of melodrama," and when Gates and Franklin stuck to their plot despite his objections, he told them he could be of no further help and rang Knopf and told him what had happened. Instead of showing him the door, as he had half expected, Knopf expressed appreciation for his opinion, and suggested he work with two other producers, J. J. Cohn and Carey Wilson, and try an entirely new plot, keeping an atmosphere of crime detection—and the dog.

Faust kept the dog, changed the main human character, produced a plot which Cohn and Wilson liked, and agreed to write it into a full story in fourteen days. "I was brought here as a prestidigitator and I have to give them a sample of white magic. They ask me if it's true that I have other people working for me and if I'm not, in fact, the head and title for a corporation. That I don't dictate but beat out the copy with my own fair hands, is the crowning touch for the miracle. I love you dear," he concluded this letter to Dorothy, "and love you and love you. Are you missing me as I'm missing you?"

Dorothy had put Judy and the governess on a boat to Italy where they would join Jane and John, who had left Vienna following unpleasant experiences during the Nazi take-over. The two older children had been staying in the house of an impoverished Jewish baronness who had come first under suspicion, then under discrimination as the anti-democratic, pro-totalitarian elements in Austria gained the upper hand. With her youngest on the boat and her other children safely back in Florence, Dorothy flew to the bedside of her mother who was dying of cancer in a San Francisco hospital.

Faust's continued need for wife as well as mistress was profound and genuine. It seems to have been an aspect of his craving for company and dread of loneliness that probably dated back to childhood bereavement. It also reflected a basic insecurity.

Knopf took him to dinner with Thomas Mann, who had recently left Nazi Germany; and the meeting led to closer acquaintance with both Knopf and Mann. Knopf soon suggested that Faust do a story about the life of the composer Offenbach, in which William Powell would play the leading role. Faust was elated. Offenbach seemed not far from *Mayerling* and *Grand Illusion*.

Meanwhile he produced the new dog story, 75,000 words, in a record thirteen days, which set the lot talking. He found the copy flowing more readily than it had for years and informed Brandt, "You sold me to them as a fast worker. I'll prove the point and then take things easily."

Brandt asked him to send the 75,000 words to New York so he could sell them.

Faust described Hollywood as "our onion" and set about eating the onion all in one bite. "Yesterday the underground wire buzzed in my ear that a survey of the scenario department had revealed that between five and six million dollars worth of material lay discarded on their shelves and that hell was to pay, with the gun at the head of Knopf and, above all, at the head of Kate Corbelay. (She has been here longer.) So I rang Knopf and reminded him that in New York he had talked about giving me some of their dead to bring to life, and that I would like to have a few manuscripts to browse over, some of their more spectacular failures, where several hundred thousand dollars were tied up in a worthless script. Knopf was very much excited by the idea, admitted that he had Lazarus in large numbers, and said he thought I might be exactly the guy needed to raise the dead. I said I wanted the comments and history on each piece I took and he said that the producers were now being asked their special reasons for refusing each of the important scripts in the past. . . . It looks as though it might work out for me far better than our most enthusiastic dreams."

The scripts were soon placed in his hands. Two mornings later he sent Knopf a new plot for *Tell It to the Marines*, a "big service picture"; and in the afternoon he dropped in to tell Knopf a new plot for *Dolly*, a picture MGM had been seeking a story for for six years. At the same time he reported that his Offenbach story was going well.

Suddenly, according to Faust, Knopf threw up his hands. "My God, man, you're an oil well that never stops gushing. Where do you get these stories? We frankly don't know what to do with you. We've never had anybody like you, and no other lot ever has had anybody like you. You're giving me more trouble than any other ten writers put together. Usually I assign a man to a story and forget about him for three or four months while he hatches a few ideas and assembles them into a yarn which may or may not be used. But I assign you to a story and it's finished in two weeks. I ask for a complete story idea and you have it in twenty-four hours. If I had three or four writers like you, I'd have to spend all my time keeping them busy with new work!"

Knopf asked if he would like to have a number of writers working under him executing plots, and Faust said it might be a good idea, though he declined a scenario writer, not wishing to share credits. He had by now acquired a personal secretary of his own, Francis Gallagher, a small, dark, intense man several years younger than himself, who had formerly been Philip Barry's secretary and whose own plays had been produced. With Knopf's help Faust and Gallagher had found a cottage on Second Street in Santa Monica and were doing their own housekeeping, while working late into the night nearly seven days a week. Faust used Gallagher as a kind of sparring partner for ideas and plot contributions, and Gallagher worked on his own things on the side.

Faust was pleased by Knopf's attention and what seemed to be studio admiration, but Collier Young was worried and informed Brandt that Faust was moving in all directions at once instead of concentrating on the one successful picture, whether "A" or "B," that would establish his reputation. But Faust had already offered to tailor a picture to suit Joan Crawford who was looking for one. Scott Fitzgerald had been working on this project but nobody, including Fitzgerald, liked the result. Meanwhile Joan was idle on studio time and costing "hell's own fortune," as Faust expressed it. Knopf received his last suggestion with frigid silence. Faust had stuck his neck out so far that it was in danger of being lopped off.

At the same time he was writing deeply affectionate letters to Dorothy, which revealed the ambivalent depth of his dependence on her. "I don't blame you for being angry with me," he admitted, after flying to San Francisco to be with her and her mother and father over the weekend (as Belle Schillig's death approached, there was a fresh gardenia on her pillow every morning, from Faust). "I don't mind looking myself in the face, these days. And I see lots of bad things. But I'm not despairing. On the other hand, I'm in no frantic hurry to change. The fact is that I'm too busy working at things that seem to me much more important. Can you possibly see that?" It was hard for Dorothy to see. "Physically, as you know, something definitely has gone out of me. In one sense that is an unhappiness for you; in another sense it ought to be reassuring in that it means the old string-halted, blinded horse will not be jumping into strange fields and pastures new." He said that basic to the physical change was the growing concern for his work and for the "ideas that are valuable to me for their own sake and a ceaseless source of happiness."

Faust may have burned himself out physically in the terrible excesses of work, or the satisfactory relation with a younger woman who adored him without qualification may have made a similar relation with Dorothy impossible for the time. Whatever the cause, Dorothy believed that it reflected inadequacy on her part and continued to suffer, while her mother died slowly day by day.

Back in Hollywood, learning that a friend from college days was in immediate need of $10,000 to keep his business from failing, Faust marched into Knopf's office and offered to sell motion picture rights in ten, twenty, or if need be thirty of his books for an immediate ten-thousand in cash. Knopf was flabbergasted, concealed his feelings, put Faust off momentarily, and telephoned Collier Young. As Young told it to Brandt, "Eddie called me and asked what manner of man Mr. Faust was and told me about this insane proposition. I went to see Eddie and we agreed I had better beard Mr. Faust in his den. This I did and minced no words in calling Heinie a lot of names with real emphasis. I told him he was offering to sell virtually his entire estate for ten thousand dollars, which was not only crazy but far from fair to his wife and children. I told him that Knopf had refused to make such a deal. He then begged me to go to several other studios which I would not do."

The producer Sam Zimbalist was looking for someone to make instant alterations in a script starring Robert Taylor, for an international friendship picture about the U.S. and Canada, *Hands Across the Border*. Faust came to Knopf's mind. But Faust, after seven grueling weeks of work without a single drop of alcohol, had gone to Ensenada in Mexico, "and pretty well drunk the place dry," as Young put it, only to return and be greeted by the challenge from Knopf and Zimbalist. He guessed, correctly, that his future at MGM might be in jeopardy. His work had amazed more than it had pleased. He had bothered people. Seven weeks at a thousand a week had yielded few tangible results.

Lying in a semi-trance, full of hypodermics as the result of a heart attack brought on by his Ensenada excesses, Faust dictated alterations in the Zimbalist script, alterations which Young described to Brandt with awe as, "the fastest thing ever birthed on the lot."

Zimbalist was delighted. The picture went into production. Faust got out of bed despite the doctor's orders and played tennis.

"I have worked out the theme for the sermon of St. Francis to the birds," he wrote Dorothy excitedly. "Briefly it is: When God made creation, the last act was the making of the birds who are the direct musical voice of ecstasy, and the silent song in the sky through their lovely grace. Because they were perfect, as an unconscious expression of the highest will of God, he was inspired to create man after them, and enclose in flesh some of the divine spirit. Birds are, therefore, our nearest glimpse of God, more than mountains or the sea. . . . Love me, darling, but don't miss me as much as I miss you. I'm growing terribly jealous of San Francisco."

"That man was born to excess," Young said. "Nine of ten ideas he throws out at a story conference may be sheer nonsense. The tenth is apt to be a stroke of pure genius."

The tenth idea this time was for a series of films about Doctor Kildare. "They intend to run it for years and spend many millions on the pictures," Faust wrote Brandt happily. "Their first concern was to get a gripping new character in the hero, surrounded by intriguing and novel circumstances. Finally, this morning, I gave Cohn and Wilson just what they wanted, and they literally pranced around the room, Cohn clasping his hands over his head and exclaiming, 'We've got it! We've got it!' And Wilson was inspired to say, 'Shut up, Joe. Wait till you realize just what it means!' More amazement because I got an entirely new idea between Saturday and Monday for the beginning of the series."

Faust had won through, once again by a cliffhanger, and his future at MGM and in Hollywood was assured.

In midsummer of 1938 he returned to Italy to close the villa. Dorothy was establishing their new household in a modest two-story house they had bought at 317 Burlingame Avenue, in the hushed and leafy residential section between Sunset and San Vicente boulevards in the Brentwood district west of Beverly Hills. She was glad about giving up the villa. She had long urged her husband to live more simply and write more honestly, saying she would gladly undergo whatever privation was necessary so that he could do work that satisfied him. Though the 317 Burlingame residence was not privation, it seemed to her a step in the right direction. She hoped it would bring improvement in their personal relationship, too.

Faust sailed on the "Statendam" on August 5, as Radio Station WOR, New York, was broadcasting one of his stories and Don Kennecott at *Blue Book* was buying one. Abe Merritt at *Ameri-*

can Weekly was putting an option worth $10,000 on one of two plots Faust had worked out during a hectic week in New York, and *The Saturday Evening Post* was expressing interest in the other. Lennon Mitchell, a radio producer, wanted to discuss the possibility of a radio series based on the Kildare stories. Also during that hectic week—Faust termed it the hardest of his life—he rewrote the Kildare film story for magazine and book publication. Just before leaving Hollywood he had, in a further burst of virtuosity, written a complete screen play to accompany his original film story.

Faust's screen play did not suit MGM's taste, and the film eventually followed a play written by Harry Ruskin and Willis Goldbeck which, however, adhered closely to the spirit and much of the detail of Faust's version.

The picture, titled *Young Dr. Kildare*, was going into production so rapidly that there was no time for the editors at *Cosmopolitan*, who wanted to buy the story, to publish it before release of the film, so Brandt sold it to the weekly *Argosy*, who could start running it simultaneously with film release. This in turn permitted earlier book publication.

While Faust was on his way to Europe, MGM became worried lest the name "Kildare" sound too much like somebody who "would dare to kill." Faust cabled a willingness to change; but the studio decided to keep the name, because it had become well established.

Faust lay in a stupor of exhaustion during much of the crossing, passed through Paris, and went straight to Florence. To abandon the villa and leave Italy was a painful end to his most precious dream. In the August sunlight he said good-bye to the cypress trees he had planted, the Ampelopsis vine now covering half the villa, the hydrangeas in their giant terra cotta pots, the espaliered lemons, and the rose garden he had planted for Dorothy. He wrote to her in loving if sad detail, though first giving a cheerful report on the children. They were thriving; but talking with Jane and John he had learned firsthand of

Germany's brutal conquest of Austria, of the flights of bombers droning over defenseless Vienna for days preceding the invasion, of the secret imprisonment or death of young men who opposed union with Germany, of the fear and the terror. Judy, touched by tuberculosis, as Faust had been at her age, had recovered nicely after spending the summer at Vallambrosa in the Apennines.

He supervised the packing of twelve tons of belongings. Most of the weight was represented by his books; but it also included the telescope Leonard Bacon had given him, which had been mounted on the roof of his tower-study and through which he had studied the stars.

All the additions and improvements to the villa and grounds remained, and he arranged with Arthur Acton to begin paying by installments the $2,600 of deferred rent. His feelings were touched by what seemed Acton's sincere regret on his leaving. There were additional good-byes to last remaining friends. Old Jo Dietrichstein, a figure from another world, came to dinner; and Dick Blow and his wife Marya Mannes came for both tennis and dinner, she seeming to Faust "a woman in pain but during dinner I managed to rouse her . . . though I never got her to the old roaring point." He was still able to call up reserves to give others pleasure. Blow was in good spirits, having just sold one of his paintings to the Metropolitan Museum of Art.

As Faust left the villa, the household staff stood in a line on the sunlit terrace to shake hands, tears streaming down their faces, as down his. He promised he would be back.

On the way home he heard of the Munich agreement whereby Hitler in effect gained a free hand to destroy nearly all that was left of the Europe he had known and loved.

Back in New York, he took the 12:25 A.M. plane on Thursday, September 29, arriving in Los Angeles at 5:15 P.M. He stepped back into mounting success. By October 14 the reviews of the preview of *Young Dr. Kildare* were out in *Variety*, *The Reporter*, and elsewhere. Comments were highly favorable. The habitually restrained *Variety* said, "Metro has the makings of another fine series in 'Young Dr. Kildare' . . . . This story of the medical profession is surefire for adults . . . . 'Dr. Kildare' . . . is rather frank and almost entirely devoid of the hokum with which the healers are usually fed the public in book, or other entertainment form." Lionel Barrymore as Dr. Gillespie and Lew Ayres as Dr. Kildare were praised, as was Lynn Carver, who played Kildare's sweetheart. The screenplay, "from an original story by Max Brand," was termed an A-1 job.

Motion Picture Herald was even more enthusiastic. "Putting it bluntly, 'Young Dr. Kildare' is a surprise picture . . . . Intelligently written, acted and directed, the picture was produced with a constantly evident aim to establish a new standard. For spot showmanship angles it might be noted that the show is based on a story by Max Brand, popular among fiction readers and possessor of several film credits . . . . Previewed at the Uptown Theatre in Los Angeles," the review concluded, "the crowd caught the spirit of the story almost immediately . . . . The applause was whole-hearted. Then a short trailer announced that this was the beginning of a series in which Ayres and Barrymore would be featured. It was the first time this writer ever heard a trailer applauded."

Metro-Goldwyn-Mayer decided to release the film as an "A" rather than a "B" picture. Carl Brandt, on his way to Radio City Music Hall in Rockefeller Center to see the grand premiere opening, wrote Faust for heaven's sakes not to have his head turned by Hollywood grandiosity and to remember that he was a writer, not a celebrity. Magazine and book markets were crying for his output. Dodd, Mead had just published a western, *Dead or Alive,* and *Young Dr. Kildare* was a smash hit at the Music Hall.

Brandt also cautioned about the "casual" writing of checks by both Faust and Dorothy, checks that had a way of turning up in

New York when there was nothing in the bank. "I've had to send down $3,400 to the bank this week." But Joe Cohn and Carey Wilson went to bat for Faust at MGM and were instrumental in getting him a new contract at $1,250 per week, and he could put in his time very much as he pleased.

22.

DEEPENING CONFLICTS

UNDERLYING the brightness was an increasing despair. From time to time Faust would drop in at Bob Campbell's bookstore in Westwood Village, ten minutes' drive from his home, and say, "Bob, I need the entire Everyman's Library." Or he would buy the latest scholarly editions of Shakespeare, Goethe, or James Joyce. If he needed background for a story about Shanghai or Van Dieman's Land, he would ask Campbell to get him what he needed. Occasionally they had deeper discussions. "Cervantes didn't do anything worthwhile till he was over fifty, Bob, maybe there's hope for me," Campbell recalled his saying once.

At forty-seven, Faust increasingly mentioned writers such as Cervantes and Malory who had not produced their best work until aged fifty or older. Meanwhile he received a bonus of $3,500 from MGM for the next Kildare film, and Brandt sold the story to *Cosmopolitan* for $3,500.

Faust discussed with Alfred Hitchcock the possibility of working on a film based on Daphne du Maurier's *Rebecca*, but nothing came of it. However by May of 1939 his story about a girl of overwhelmingly pristine innocence moving in the midst of evil—he called it *The Nightflower*, apparently forgetting he had published a crime novel by the same title—was in the hands of Universal, and Danielle Darrieux was under consideration for the starring role. The idea for the story had come straight to Faust's head from the character of Miranda in Shakespeare's *The Tempest*.

"I have a feeling the Kildare doctor stories can be made to last

217

indefinitely," he told Brandt. "As Don Moore points out, there is the detective element of interest which is rather new, though it is distinctly medical; and there are as many Kildare stories as there are detective stories that can be given a medical twist. After all, a diagnostician *is* a detective."

Faust was getting technical medical advice for Kildare stories from Kenneth Eikenberry, a Los Angeles doctor who had become his personal physician. In return for a modest fee, Eikenberry provided facts covering such esoteric subjects as the insulin shock treatment for schizophrenia. Eikenberry also helped Faust through difficult times with Dorothy. When she discovered that Faust was not only writing regularly to his mistress but had seen her during a quick trip to New York, supposedly on business, Dorothy tried to commit suicide by taking an overdose of sleeping pills. Eikenberry once asked them point-blank why they didn't divorce rather than cause each other continued anguish, but neither would divorce the other. Faust was struggling with what he felt to be his responsibility toward two women, both of whom he knew he had treated unjustly. Recurrent drinking brought on attacks of fibrillation. At one point in 1939 his entire family and himself were hospitalized by influenza complicated by pneumonia or heart trouble, and Collier Young wrote Brandt, "I think it would be much wiser if Heinie sold his house and bought the Santa Monica Hospital because the family are in it almost constantly."

By July, Faust had concluded a deal worth $5,000 by which he undertook to write a film story based on James Fenimore Cooper's novel *The Deerslayer* for Gene Towne, a producer at RKO, in thirty days. His path had by now crossed Cooper's at several points. Both wrote extensively of the West while in Europe. Both lived and worked on the John Jay estate at Katonah, Cooper completing *The Spy* on the front porch of the house there. Both saw the American West in terms of myth—Cooper's the myth of the perfectible man at last finding self-realization in a virgin land, Faust's the myth of the timeless man, reliving the age-old, cyclical stories of the son in search of an illustrious father or the warrior who had an Achilles heel.

Carl Brandt and Collier Young were urging Faust not to pose as a lightning worker but to spread himself in small measure, to act importantly. He would not listen. His ego demanded playing the incredible role; and a colloquial intimacy, and speed, were essential to his performance.

He had taken leave of MGM for the summer but returned in the fall, visiting the studio as a rule only in the afternoons, working at home on his poetry and fiction in the morning. He had completed the work at RKO in the allotted time.

Asked the source of his apparently instantaneous supply of plots, Faust replied that plots were everywhere if you knew how to look for them. "Perhaps the best way to go about it is to ask one's self what there is about a theme that invites the writer. How much is background and how much is character, how much is action? Then you should ask yourself what kind of action develops the character most perfectly. There is a certain logic in the working out of stories, a sort of mathematical necessity in the operation of order to get the right answers, and I think you can surrender to the nature and the kind of emotion with which you are dealing. It will lead you to the right denouements."

He recalled that when he started doing stories each seemed the last he could find. But then by degrees his story-finding faculty had increased. "You spot stories in the air, flying out of conversations, out of books." Stories also arise, he said, out of the inversions of things as you find them. "You sit at the rich man's table; well, what if he were broke and this were the last time he could entertain? Or suppose the beggar suddenly inherits wealth? Or what is it that might tempt the just man to acts of injustice? What is it that the Texan finds most non-Texan?" He recalled that Stevenson used to get characters from among his friends. He would add or substract one characteristic and then was furnished with a living creature whose mind he knew. "When you read a story, pause when you are halfway through; finish the story in detail out of your imagination; write it down in brief notes. Then read the story through to the end. Often you will find that you have a totally new final half of a story. Fit in a new beginning and there you are."

Esquire bought *The Taming of Red Thunder*, *Photoplay* took a Kildare novel. *This Week* bought a short story.

In addition to lightning-fast studio stories, much time was going into personal correspondence. There were the long business letters to Brandt and to editors, sometimes running to five- and ten-thousand-word outlines of plots; and there were personal letters to friends, relatives, dependents—single-spaced typewritten bits of his life totaling hundreds of thousands of words annually. Among his many correspondents were children, such as the son and daughter of Carnes Weeks, a New York doctor, to whom he wrote regularly as though they were adults. They collected albums of his letters, as did others. He wrote also to members of the academic community, such as Professor Frederick C. Mills at Columbia, and Roswell Ham at Yale and Mt. Holyoke; and at Berkeley there were Walter Hart, Ivan Linforth, whose field was classical Greece, and others. Among professional writers, besides Bacon, Howard, and Schoolcraft, Phil Barry and the Benéts, he developed a particular relationship with Grace Flandrau, whose stories were appearing regularly in *Harper's* and *The New Yorker*. Eventually much of his adult life was recorded in letters.

His philanthropies continued to grow. He was paying for singing lessons for the daughter of his cleaning woman. He took her to John Charles Thomas, the noted baritone, for an audition, and when Thomas' report was negative continued the lessons anyway.

"Send Collie and Valery Young $500 as a Christmas present," he wrote Brandt. "Don't say it is too much. I promised it to Collie for the help he gave me on stories in New York." Young had among other things loaned Dorothy money to pay household bills. "And tell Miss Lubelle," Faust concluded to Brandt, "to send $55 to those two young men—I forget their names—on 57th or 37th Street."

He continued to practice a gregarious relationship with people of all kinds. An itinerant pianist from a local night club, a merchant mariner home on leave met in a bar, might practically live at his house. He developed a special feeling for Texas Negroes and retained several as butlers, chauffeurs, and cooks, often departing from a rigorous work schedule to talk and drink with them most of the night, to Dorothy's mortification and despair. It was idle to point out that such conduct broke down lines of relationship, ruptured household routines, impaired his health and working schedule, not to mention those of others in the house. Whatever seemed the most interesting living thing or situation at hand was still apt to dominate his attention or engross him completely at the expense of all else.

From these contacts, he was fed in basic ways, absorbing character, speech, attitude, ideas that could be developed into magazine or book fiction, poetry, or film stories.

World War II had broken out. Germany again threatening the peace and freedom of the world made Faust feel that the wheel had come full circle. He was violently for the Allies and for immediate U.S. involvement, while wondering how he might become involved himself.

The year 1939 ended with the big success of the second film version of *Destry Rides Again*. Marlene Dietrich was acclaimed, as was James Stewart. *Motion Picture World* announced, "Destry Rides Again and So Does Marlene Dietrich!" In the screen story written by Felix Jackson and based on Faust's novel, Marlene played the part of a barroom entertainer, gyp artist, and girl friend of the town bad man. "The knockout battle between Miss Dietrich and Una Merkel, so widely publicized in the cinema columns is wilder, hotter and longer than they said it was," *Motion Picture World* continued. "Nothing since Pola Negri's 'Passion' has approached it. The lady also wins Mischa Auer's pants from him in a poker game . . . ." Dietrich's throaty singing was a memorable feature of the performance.

The unusual review-in-advance-of-release was advertised on *Motion Picture World's* front cover, and was accompanied inside by a spread of color advertising predicting that "The Whole Country Will Go . . . To See Dietrich Let Herself Go." Very nearly the whole country did, and musical comedy westerns, satirical westerns, and adult westerns were thoroughly launched. Faust gained no money, having sold motion picture rights to Universal previously, but there was considerable prestige attached, especially when the success of *Destry* was added to the mounting success of the Kildare series.

To his son John at Harvard he wrote philosophically, "Mr. Spinoza still takes my mind with his profound common sense. You remember how the gods, from time to time, purged the eyes of heroes of their mortality and enabled them to see the divinities? Diomedes, for instance, when Athena was encouraging him to be a bad boy? Well, I wish I could wipe the mists from my eyes as Spinoza has from his. He's a delightful companion."

To Grace Flandrau in New York he wrote, "To revert to the Cosmopolitan story, the source of this and of all my fiction which has sold (or nearly all) has been an escape from reality. There was perhaps too much reading and too much actual pain in my childhood. It made me build daydreams, bubbles into which I could escape and find a bright and blue and golden world all for me. I denied pain. So in my stories men may start bad but they must wind up good. Women are angels and men are heroes. And a certain number of child-minded people, even millions of them, read this brainless drip and like it. Their minds don't have to budge . . . . Now and then in short stories I've barely rubbed elbows with painful truth, but I've never liked that truth; it's always seemed horrible to me."

He had terminated his love affair. As part of an effort to live and write more honestly, he began planning his first serious novel. It was to take place at the time of the Civil War and to have a

Northern hero and a Southern heroine. He assigned Dorothy's maiden aunt, Miss Florence Greely, who had been on his payroll so many years, to help him and his assistant, Francis Gallagher, with the research. "I'll need books like *Hardtack and Coffee*, as well as the memoirs of Grant, Lee, Hood, Longstreet, Sheridan, and others, and even unpublished manuscripts of soldiers who fought on both sides. And of course I shall read all of Douglas Southall Freeman." Faust's Civil War library grew until it covered one wall of his study. Saxton and Canfield at Harper were encouraging. There was a series of letters and conversations, and work on the project went forward.

He and Dorothy entertained frequently, despite his statements that he wanted only privacy and work. The extraordinary hospitality which had characterized their life at Katonah and Florence was transferred to 317 Burlingame Avenue. Troops of guests invaded the book-lined living room and lawned back-garden, which was surrounded on three sides by a tall cypress hedge and which became a sort of outdoor stage for Faust's gargantuan performances of talk, outdoor cooking, croquet, putting, or symposiums on gardening, viniculture, insect control, the life of the ant, or California architecture. Indoors the guests settled into comfortable easy chairs that seemed especially made for them, and sometimes they did not leave until morning.

Few motion picture personalities appeared at these gatherings and the Fausts were seldom seen in the homes of the stars, although they enjoyed a tea with Myrna Loy, whose performance with William Powell in Dashiell Hammett's *The Thin Man* Faust much admired. There was, however, a cordial relationship with an English theatrical pair, Philip Merivale and Gladys Cooper, she a famous pin-up girl from World War I days and a *grande dame* of stage and screen. Gilbert Emery, another actor of excellence, was a more than occasional dinner guest, and perhaps served as prototype for the hero in *The King*, Faust's best short-short story, written at about this time but not published until after his death. *The King* appeared in the November 21,

1948, issue of *This Week* and in the 1967 edition of Faust's best stories. Perhaps Faust himself was at the heart of this incredible but convincing vignette, in which an aging Hollywood actor who has played only aristocratic roles refuses a large sum to play a lesser part, though he is starving. Elements of prophecy and fulfillment from Faust's inner life show themselves in the story.

He and Dorothy were seeing a good deal of Aldous and Maria Huxley, who had a cabin in the high desert, overlooking the Victorville-Lancaster area and the Joshua trees. Retreating with the Huxleys to this hideout for a weekend, they found much in common, especially the old days in Florence when Maria had been typing Lawrence's *Lady Chatterly's Lover* and there had been the walks and talks on the beach at Forte dei Marmi, and the bonfires with Bacon and the children, including the Huxleys' son Matthew. Dorothy and Faust became enamored of the desert retreat and planned to acquire one like it. Their project got lost in good intentions and pressing necessities; and they continued trapped, as Faust often saw it, in the suburban prison at 317 Burlingame. His attitude toward this house, as toward much else, was ambivalent. Though it had eleven rooms and Dorothy had added a study over the garage with an outside staircase, and even though the big telescope Bacon had given him was installed on the third-story sundeck, Faust did not fit in. Often those seeing him observed his restlessness. He missed his villa. He needed other-world surroundings, and his search for them was essential to his life's effort.

He sometimes found escape in music from what seemed increasing limitations. Acquiring one of the Lansing sound systems used at the studios, he played Mozart, Bach, or Gregorian chants by the hour, occasionally all night, taking notes, tears sometimes streaming down his face at the beauty of what he heard. The dream of the beautiful people and the beautiful land that he had envisioned as a child was still with him.

His daughter Jane had married and gone to live, ironically, in the valley from which he had tried most of his life to escape. Revisiting the valley and Modesto, he overdrank, overconversed, visited his parents' graves—and though the return had been in many ways triumphal and he had been hailed as a celebrity—he ended it depressed, with chiefly the thought of the fruit trees in blossom to sustain him. He pondered over the trees, and confided to his notebook that they thought they were going to die, because they had been pruned back, and in response had put forth their blossoms in a supreme effort to survive.

Increasingly he turned to two older friends for intimate counsel and support. They were Walter Hart, in Berkeley, and Professor Charles Rieber, now of the philosophy department at the University of California at Los Angeles. With them he could talk calmly about what seemed the eternal verities. He flew to Berkeley on several occasions for conversations with Hart, and he talked nearly every week with Rieber, who lived not far away— filling the perennial pocket notebook with ideas, many of which were poured out into verses and stories. Conversations and friendship on a dinner basis with the Robert Millikans—the head of the California Institute of Technology and a Nobel Prize winner for his work in cosmic rays—helped stimulate Faust's scientific and academic interests.

The University of California offered him an honorary degree but he refused it, for the same reason he had refused the invitations to join the Berkeley fraternities that had once rebuffed him.

He was at the height of his career in many respects. In the eighteen months between the release of *Calling Dr. Kildare* on April 28, 1939, and the appearance of *Dr. Kildare's Crisis* on November 29, 1940, six major films based directly on his work had been released, or an average of one picture every three months. The Kildare stories and others were making popular reading in a variety of magazines, and in 1940 he published seven books in the U.S. alone, two of them anthologies. One anthology was a collection of his more serious stories, *Wine on the Desert*; one a collection of western material, *Fiction Rodeo*.

Faust had left MGM and was now at Columbia, first concluding an arrangement whereby MGM would continue making Dr. Kildare films, and he would receive a fee each time the characters he had created were used. In all, fourteen Kildare pictures were produced. Featured players in addition to Barrymore and Ayres included Lana Turner, Laraine Day, Robert Young, Van Johnson, Susan Peters, Gloria de Haven, and Ava Gardner.

At Columbia he wrote the story for the studio's first big technicolor success, *The Desperadoes*, filmed in Utah and starring Randolph Scott, Glenn Ford, Claire Trevor, and Evelyn Keyes. He sold Columbia the title to one of his books, *The Valley of Vanishing Men*, under which the studio made a fifteen-part serial—fifteen separate pictures—starring Bill Elliott, Slim Summerville, and Carmen Morales. While at Columbia Faust became involved in a typical professional crisis. He offered to do a screenplay in six days for a picture which was to star Humphrey Bogart and Rita Hayworth. Since his offer meant doing eight-weeks work in one, it antagonized most of the studio's writing staff and raised serious doubts in management circles; but his producer backed him and on a Monday morning they set to work. Faust had already submitted six successive revisions for the script, a crime story titled "You Only Die Once." This was to be the final version.

The producer, a stumpy little man who had once played professional football, began rushing around the room exclaiming, according to Faust's record of the event, "Where's our dark hour? For God's sake Frederick, nothing's any good unless it has a dark hour." (The critical darkness before dawn at the end of a melodrama.) Or again: "It's a man and woman story, see. We gotta have a woman in there. We gotta have her hot." Faust assured him that he did not write "bitchy" scenes, even if there was a Hayes office to censor them. "Yeah, but thicken the soup, will you, Frederick? Thicken the soup, for God's sake. This Rita is a gal that the boys of the U.S. would like to roll in the hay. So she's got to seem like she could roll, don't she?" And finally: "Now we haven't got any menace in here. There's a whole reel and a half without any menace in here, and that's no good. We can't sell *that* to Harry Cohn, can we? Let's *do* something about it."

The result hung in the balance and then succeeded; and Faust was assigned to work on another starring vehicle for Rita Hayworth, this one titled "Cover Girl."

Dorothy's once blonde hair had turned dark brown and was shot through with gray, and her once renowned beauty had been lined, but she retained a remarkable charm and grace and a figure that made men turn their heads. Faust's black hair was graying and thinning and his rough-hewn face had grown more lined and jagged. They presented a brave front to the world and few guessed their hidden problems.

Though he had terminated the destructive love affair, the children had learned of it and had sided with their mother; and Faust stood discredited in their eyes as well as in his own.

Amid highly personal ruins, he started rebuilding. "Nothing I have done has been any more shameful than this Hollywood work," he wrote Dorothy while in New York for a conference with Canfield and Brandt, "and on it as a basis your life cannot be happy. It is true that our friends would be more numerous and more interesting if I had not been intoxicated or at least loose-tongued too many times. But at the best they would include chiefly actors, etc. And the amusement world is a dreadful thing. We could see the Huxleys more, and the Thomas Manns more, and we could see a few others and build up a more real circle of acquaintances. I think we must try to do this, with a quite self-conscious effort, and you will see that everything goes much better when I'm not woozy with liquor, noisy, argumentative, full of insistence and many words."

The uphill pull was not easy, but their mutual determination to preserve the marriage elevated, and alleviated, to a degree, the suffering and discouragement. He pushed ahead steadily on the Civil War novel. U.S. entry into the current war set him working at ways to get in himself.

A poem, "Distance," in the January, 1942, issue of *Harper's* expressed his loneliness. The long poem about Christ remained unfinished, though it had put Christianity in new perspective for him.

"As I looked into the beatitudes which always had seemed to me a foul mass of weakness and shameful and slavish surrender to superior force, I began to see that they expressed the only axiomatic truths which could enable human beings to live happily together. 'Blessed are the merciful . . . the pure in heart . . . the peacemakers,' expresses an ecstacy of truth. The hell of fire is reserved for one sinner only, he who says to his brother Thou Fool."

He played tennis with the veteran amateur champion May Sutton Bundy and developed an on-court and off-court friendship with the former Helen Wills and her polo-playing husband Aidan Roark. For wholly masculine recreation he went to Jim Jeffries' Barn in the San Fernando Valley, where the onetime world heavyweight title holder operated a ring for young fighters. Faust antagonized Jeffries by recalling more about his fights— especially the famous struggles with Tom Sharkey and the disastrous encounter with Jack Johnson—than Jeffries cared to. One evening they squared off against each other semi-amicably, with the help of a few glasses of beer. Faust won the bout on words but lost on tact. The affair was, in its way, typical.

Drinking continued to be a major problem. Sometimes he disappeared from home for a day or two, to be brought back by Collier Young or some other friend. He went into conferences with producers and directors when he had been drinking, and this exasperated some people and antagonized others, often threatening the stability of his tenure at the studios, but the phenomenal success of his films argued in his favor.

He had moved on to Warner Brothers and was writing to Grace Flandrau, "Dostoevsky convinces me—he convinces me that man exists, he convinces me that there is a god in man, however perverted that god may be by environment."

He saw in Dostoevsky a fellow sufferer in the depths of sin, and like Dostoevsky squandered his money. To make ends meet on an income of $75,000 a year, he hired a business manager. The business manager put him on an allowance of $35 weekly—and embezzled his funds. He hired another—with the same result.

While at Warner's Faust worked on *In Our Time*, which starred Ida Lupino and Paul Henreid; *Uncertain Glory*, featuring Errol Flynn, Paul Lukas, Jean Sullivan, and Faye Emerson; *The Conspirators*, starring Hedy Lamarr, Paul Henreid, and Peter Lorre; and other successful films including *The Adventures of Don Juan*.

At Warner's he met a number of writers: Ayn Rand, Frank Gruber, Steve Fisher, W. R. Burnet, the two Englishmen James Hilton and Richard Aldington, and William Faulkner, the latter recently removed from the studio's blacklist for drinking and intransigence and now working for a meager $250 a week.

Faulkner was at a low ebb in personal fortune and not widely known to the general public. His work was yet to enjoy its post-World War II popularity. Emerging from his first-floor office below Faust's, Faulkner would sometimes join the group in the studio restaurant at noon, when, according to Frank Gruber, Ayn Rand argued politics vociferously with Dalton Trumbo, John Howard Lawson, and others. Faulkner was markedly silent. Faust joined the group occasionally but as a rule drove "over the hill" (Warner studios were then as later located in San Fernando Valley) to Hollywood for lunch in lavish style at Musso Frank's, sometimes not returning till three or four o'clock and then often far from sober. Faust was making $2,000 a week at this time and was regarded with admiration and envy by many of the other writers.

The Warner Brothers management took a rather dim view of its rather brilliant writing staff, perhaps for good reason. Writers were expected to work from 8:00 A.M. to 5:00 P.M. like other employees. Appearing at the studio about nine o'clock, Faust would complete his work—usually fourteen pages—by about eleven and spend the rest of the day in having lunch or in agreeable conversation with Aldington or some other friend, or in pitching coins at a crack in the floor, a recognized pastime in the Writers' Building. Frank Gruber recalled the grand manner in which Faust regularly lost ten to twenty dollars a day pitching coins, apparently to help writers operating on a less grand salary than himself.

As at MGM, legends grew up around him. Hearing that a fellow writer thought him snobbish, he walked into the man's office unannounced and, finding him at his desk, took his head gently between both hands and said pleasantly, "Listen, you son-of-a-bitch, I hear you hate me." Five minutes later they were enjoying a drink in the bar across the street. Other legends told how he spent hours helping other writers with their work. According to some who knew him at Warner's, Faust kept a Thermos bottle of whiskey in his desk and used it throughout the day. One friend recalled a lunch when Faust consumed fourteen drinks. At home he never drank while writing.

Faust was too much of an original to fit long into any studio's operations; and the managements at MGM, Columbia, Warner's, and elsewhere seem to have regarded him more as a phenomenon than a durable asset. His growing disgust with himself and the type of work he was doing at the studios was a factor in their attitude as well as in his own. *Mayerling* and *Grand Illusion* remained as far out of reach as ever, and his production of magazine and book fiction was dwindling toward a record low.

Working through Brandt and Cass Canfield, he stepped up his efforts to get into World War II. He had missed combat in 1918 and the failure still rankled. A series of letters exchanged with Canfield in mid-1942 aimed at securing Harper influence in getting him to the front "so he could write stories of individuals in action" got him nowhere, though Canfield, who was serving in Washington as Chief of the Blockade and Supply Branch of the Board of Economic Warfare, of the Economic Defense Board, interceded valiantly with other government agencies.

Spurring Faust on was a contact arranged locally for him by his friend Pinckney McLean, formerly of the *Baltimore Sun* staff and now attached to the Marine Corps air base at El Toro, near Los Angeles. McLean arranged for Faust to meet pilots of the 212th Marine Fighter Squadron returning from Guadalcanal, where they had been the first Americans to engage the Japanese in aerial combat. Though heavily outnumbered, the Marine pilots had defeated the enemy, devising tactics whereby their slower and heavier Grumman Wildcats could be used effectively against the more maneuverable and faster Japanese Zero fighters. They had made Japanese air attacks on the Guadalcanal beachhead too costly to sustain.

Their leader, Joe Bauer, received the Congressional Medal of Honor posthumously after being shot down while attacking five enemy aircraft alone; but surviving members of the squadron, including the much-decorated "Cowboy" Stout and "Tex" Hamilton, came to 317 Burlingame to tell the moving and decisive saga of the 212th.

The book that resulted, *The Squadron*, did not immediately find a publisher as Faust had hoped. It suffered from what he was suffering from: secondhand experience. To make the book appealing to a general audience, Faust realized, he should have been flying a Grumman himself, or at least been present on Guadalcanal while the fighting took place.

Brandt now arranged for him to be dropped from an airplane over Yugoslavia and join the resistance forces of Draža Mihailovich, at that time a leading anti-Hitler element in the country. The Yugoslav government in exile in London was backing the project; but it fell through—much as the fifty-year-old grandfather might have fallen through had his 220-pound body with its bad heart been lowered by parachute to the Serbo-Croatian back country.

Dorothy, the children, and friends protested these seemingly ill-considered efforts at involvement but to no avail. Faust followed the course of the war in intense detail, his spirits rising or falling with Allied fortunes, his whole being sickened by Nazi atrocities. It was through Warner Brothers that his opportunity finally came. A Colonel W. F. Nee was representing the Army as film advisor to the studio. Through him, Faust arranged to be sent to the Italian front as correspondent for *The Infantry Journal*, a service magazine devoted to the interests of the foot soldier, and for *Harper's Magazine*. Canfield and Brandt worked out the details. He was to live with a platoon of combat infantry, in action and out.

Adverse reports were being published concerning the performance of U.S. infantrymen and of Allied forces as a whole in Italy. The Italian campaign, following initial landings at Salerno and later at Anzio, had bogged down. Morale was low. Hard fighting in the fall and winter of 1943–44 resulted in little progress. The Army was willing to have someone of Faust's talents give true and hopefully good publicity to the infantry. Faust was more than willing to return to the country he loved, and thus complete one more of the circles that seemed to be gradually determining his life.

Perhaps he would make his way to the villa and Florence. It would indeed be a triumphal thing if he could help liberate the place and even the building that he loved best in all the world. In so doing he might liberate himself from the limitations that seemed to hem him in. As once before, he would try to find his true self in Europe.

Nobody had done exactly what he was going to do—live side by side with infantrymen for a protracted period as an actual member of a combat unit. Even such correspondents as the distinguished Ernie Pyle had not done that. As usual, what particularly appealed to Faust was the chance of doing something hazardous and out of the ordinary.

There is no doubt that he evaluated the risk and was prepared to die if necessary. The infantry, especially the rifle platoons such as he would be joining, sustained most of the war's casualties. He had no illusion, either, about his physical handicaps. But he believed, with characteristic optimism, that he could condition himself sufficiently so that he could keep up with younger men.

The processes of war and change had affected his circle of friends, as they were affecting him. Stephen Benét was dead from overwork in the war effort. Sidney Howard was dead, crushed against the wall of his farm shed as he cranked his tractor while it was in gear. Friends such as McLean and Blow were in uniform; and others, like Bacon, were engaged in civilian service. It was with a sense of fatalism as well as commitment that Faust boarded the train for New York, Italy, and the battle-front in mid-February of 1944. At long last he was going to war, but it was not the war of his youth.

He carried letters of introduction to a variety of Allied military personnel, including General Richard McCreery, commander of the British Eighth Army in Italy. There was a letter from Bob Lovett, now U.S. Assistant Secretary of War for Air, to General Ira Eaker, commander of Allied air forces in the Mediterranean. Another letter was from Richard Aldington, a veteran of nearly three years in the trenches with the British Army during World War I, to Brigadier General Theodore Roosevelt, Jr., now with U.S. troops in England preparing for the Normandy landings in June. There was also a letter from Aldington to C. P. Snow, the novelist, wartime head of England's scientific manpower procurement.

"Dear Snow," Aldington wrote. "This will introduce my friend Frederick Faust, who is crossing to Europe as a War Correspondent. Fortune or the haggish Norns of the War Department may send him to England and thence to Cambridge. Little or nothing has been published in America about England's scientific contributions to this struggle, and I think it might be rather a good thing if you would point out a little of what has been done. Nobody is better qualified. Apart from this you will find Faust a valuable and pleasant companion, though full of crochets and eccentricities which you will discover and pass over. You have not written to me for some time, you scoundrel, and I hope you have a good excuse."

Aldington had become Faust's closest friend in Hollywood. Both thought of themselves as exiles from places they liked better, such as Florence, and from work they liked better, such as writing poetry. Faust had been sharing painful labor on his Civil War novel with the former soldier, Aldington, reiterating that what he called "real composition" was as difficult for him as for anyone. Aldington, although past his prime as poet and novelist, had recently achieved renewed distinction as critic and editor with the publication of *The Viking Book of Poetry of the English Speaking World*, and he had also recently published an autobiography, *Life For Life's Sake* (dedicated to Leonard Bacon and Howard Lowry), and was working on an intimate biography of his friend D. H. Lawrence.

Aldington also wrote a warm introduction for Faust to D. L. Murray of the *London Times* staff.

There were additional advance arrangements. The children's former governess, Monty Lamont, was now hostess and manager at "Chequers," the country residence of English prime ministers, not far from London. If Faust went to England, Monty planned to arrange a meeting with Winston Churchill.

When Faust left Los Angeles, he carried with him an uncompleted epic poem about the Titan, Prometheus, as well as other verse on which he was at work; and he had sent ahead to New York what he believed to be the final draft of the first two hundred pages of his Civil War novel. He had worked closely with Cass Canfield for more than two years on outlines and revisions and hoped for a good verdict on his first sustained attempt to write serious prose.

As he boarded the train he could look back on closed circles in his life, on the escape from the valley and his return to it, on the twenty-five to thirty million published words which had brought him to summits from which he had almost completely retired (only two magazine stories had been published in the previous year), on the more than sixty films with which his name had been associated (the number would grow); but instead of achieving satisfaction or fulfillment, he had simply, it seemed, exerted himself furiously.

He left Dorothy in the usual financial difficulties. The household had been geared to an income of $2,000 a week. There were pressing debts. It would be some time before money arrived from the dispatches or articles, or the book about his war experiences that he intended to write, or from the Civil War novel. But more pressing to her was the unspoken conviction that they were saying good-bye for the last time.

As she waved from the platform in Union Station, heavily crowded with wartime traffic, she sensed that it was her last sight of him alive. She said afterward she believed him to be escaping a life that had grown intolerable. But he left in apparently high spirits, vociferously attacking her gloom as usual and assuring her, as he had for twenty-seven years, that everything would be all right, that just around the corner was promised land.

He had the flu as he left, plus inoculation reactions of various kinds, was exhausted from last-minute work, and caught the train on the run.

He rode the Union Pacific up through the heart of the West he had written so many millions of words about. It was the last time he would ride through it, and perhaps some inkling of this came to him. His letters and notebook entries show his mind going back to his first days with Dorothy, to his trip across the country to rescue her from marriage to another man, and to his boyhood days in the valley. He was evidently thinking of the trains crashing through into his youthful consciousness out of this same West, becoming symbols of the outer world he wished to explore. Now he had explored almost all of that world, and yet it seemed he had discovered almost nothing. Perhaps there were one or two things worth mentioning. "You are going to be," he had written to Jane before leaving, "a citizen of a glorious continent where decency, cleanliness, friendship, faith, courage, truth, and beauty, beauty, beauty are the only actualities. All other things, all dirt, all treachery, all cruelty, all stupidity, and all of the so-called realities of this unhappy century, will someday be as unsubstantial as dreams."

But in his notes for the poem about Prometheus he had written, "This is the secret that Prometheus stole from heaven. He could return and tell humanity that of all things death is the most beautiful; but if this were known, humanity would rush at once to extinguish itself, embracing its greatest gift. And then the gods, fixed and cold in their immortality, would no longer have sight of the marvelous and terrible changes in the spirits of men, the unforgettable gestures of the partially blinded creatures that rise out of the earth and return to it."

He mailed Dorothy a cheerful letter from Cheyenne, asking her to send photographs of all the children which, as usual, he had forgotten to bring along. He was drinking double Scotches "to kill the cold," topping them off with a few chapters from Army Field Service Regulations and a passage or two of Dante.

"I think you could have endured poverty and hard work if you had been sure my work was something to be proud of," he said, and concluded, "The shadows begin to draw out long, and they are pointing toward the cold Eastern winter, but I can't help hoping that out of the cold and everything that lies beyond it I may come out a better man. I think this is the chance. Don't you?"

His going left the family devoid of men. John was already in service and on his way overseas, as was Jane's husband. The women would cluster at 317 Burlingame Avenue and wait. Included was Dorothy's sister, who was undergoing psychiatric treatment and whom Faust was supporting.

23.

FAREWELL TO NEW YORK

FAUST reached New York on February 21, 1944, quite ill with flu, to find good news. Brandt had sold a book-length serial, *After April*, to *The Saturday Evening Post* for $15,000. Faust had been dreading having to face Brandt and admit that Hollywood had ruined his talent for fiction.

After April, one of his best efforts, is transitional from the tale telling of an earlier period to the serious fiction he now wanted to write. The story centers in France and England. The time is 1940. Peter, a young Hollander who escaped from Rotterdam the day after the Germans bombed it, believes his wife to have been killed by the Nazis. He is now a fighter pilot with an RAF squadron in France. On a Paris street he catches sight of a beautiful young woman who reminds him strongly of his wife. He traces her to a house occupied by a strange company of men and women who have lost something precious, such as a lover, a husband, a country. The girl is introduced to him as Adrienne, "one of the lost." She remembers nothing of her past, and her past has evidently been horrible. Before he can be sure of her identity, the Germans are at the gates of Paris. Peter and Adrienne are separated. The remainder of the story is his physical search for her, through southern France to Bordeaux and eventually to England, and his emotional search for her and their lost love.

The story was suggested by an inch-long newspaper clipping handed Faust by Belle Folsey, his secretary at Warner Brothers.

As welcome as the sale was the interest expressed by the *Post* in seeing anything he should write at the front. Brandt was busy among the editors of other magazines, too, arranging a luncheon with members of the *Reader's Digest* staff, which he hoped would lead to the *Digest*'s using Faust's front-line writing. He estimated a thousand dollars a month might come from this source. With *Harper's* and *The Infantry Journal* also in the picture as Faust's sponsors, things looked promising. There were also the newspapers. Brandt arranged for Faust to send dispatches through the North American Newspaper Alliance, an arrangement which would open doors abroad and lend prestige at home.

Faust took to his bed at the Plaza, bothered by a hacking cough and running a high fever. He drank quantities of hot tea and took opiate pills prescribed by Dixie Fish, while getting to work on fiction Brandt wanted for *This Week* and *Collier's*.

Feeling better, he went shopping and outfitted himself for the front at Abercrombie & Fitch and Brooks Brothers. When he looked at the hundred and fifty pounds of equipment piled on the floor of his hotel room, he ruefully recalled the days when the Army of Northern Virginia had traveled with nothing but one blanket and a change of socks. Fish had even found him a rubber air-mattress to go under his sleeping bag and a non-magnetic waterproof wristwatch, two items all but unobtainable in wartime civilian markets.

The success of *After April* was countered by negative reaction to his Civil War novel. Canfield felt that the two-hundred-page sample needed further work, though he was sure the novel as a whole promised "real distinction." After four years of research and writing, it was a hard blow for Faust. Coupled with the rejection of *The Squadron*, it made thousands of hours seem wasted. On the brighter side, Canfield encouraged him to take one of Shakespeare's great plays, *Hamlet* or *Othello* or *Lear*, and write something for the modern reader—write it as he talked it to Canfield and others—making Shakespeare come alive as though he were a man on the street in the twentieth century. Faust wanted to begin with *The Tempest*, which he had been examining critically line by line in correspondence with a young writer he was helping, and Canfield agreed. Faust was carrying a copy of *The Tempest* in his luggage as well as copies of Chaucer and Homer.

There were many friends to see pending final clearances and sailing arrangements. He lunched with Polly Howard, Sidney's widow—there were four children—whom he described as touchingly gallant; and he paid a visit to ex-police commissioner Edward Mulrooney, "very old now, kindly, and extremely wise"; and there were the Bacons; the Tunneys; the Myerses; the Tim Cowards—she Willis Goldbeck's sister; the Schoolcrafts; and Marya Blow. He went for a Sunday to Jane and Cass Canfields' in the country, and to tea with three friends from Katonah days, Mrs. Granville Emmett, Moppy Iselin, and Eleanor Lapsley. Alice Lee Myers came to the Plaza to nurse him, clapping a mustard plaster on his chest. On Dorothy's urging, he visited Dr. Halsey, who took a cardiogram and measured his heart.

There was a dinner at the Oak Room at the Hotel St. Regis, where he was host to the Carl Brandts and the Vincent Sheeans. Brandt grimly warned Faust against the rigors of front-line life, quoting firsthand reports of correspondents and observers who had found the going very rough. Sheean, who had seen the war in North Africa, reenforced these warnings from personal experience. But Faust insisted that neither of them understood the value of relaxing, of "breathing with the diaphragm," and of proper muscular balance, as he claimed to have learned them from Boyd Comstock while training Italian Olympic athletes.

He was not well at all. He needed three pillows at night to enable him to breathe while lying down, and there were the familiar nightmares of being buried alive under loads of coal. Halsey had found "the heart failure more pronounced"; but Faust reported glowingly to Dorothy, "The heart has grown from 14 centimeters, which was one less than half the diameter of the chest, to 19, which is four more than half. It seems that in fibrillators there are cases, one in a million, where the heart, with its deteriorated muscle begins to build fresh muscles not improved in quality but sufficiently strong to replace the original virtues of the uncontaminated flesh by bulk. My heart therefore, it seems, is less good per ounce, but there are more ounces, and whereas most enlarging hearts are token of desperate and dangerous weakness mine is one of the lucky few and is a sign of increasing strength. Can you believe such a good interpretation?"

Dorothy clashed with him bitterly, suggesting that he was enjoying himself in New York, implying he was seeing his mistress again. He raged back, saying she drove him to wrongdoing by lack of faith.

They conducted such lovers' quarrels by long distance telephone two or three times a week, and at the end of one of them he asked her to collect the poetry he had left behind and send it to Brandt. "With what I have here, it might make a thin little volume that Cass Canfield or Tim Coward would publish." The volume was eventually published by Dodd, Mead with the addition of excerpts from Faust's notebooks and letters.

Faust's last night in New York was appropriately typical. He had planned to dine quietly and alone with Grace Flandrau; but at the last minute he met a young Navy serviceman in a bar and invited not only him but his girlfriend and his girlfriend's father and mother, and his girlfriend's girlfriend, to join them at Voisin's, one of the most expensive restaurants in town. Under Faust's influence, the company of more or less total strangers soon became intimate friends. He bought corsages for all the women and ordered the finest wines.

As the evening progressed he discovered that the girlfriend's girlfriend was a Barnard College English major with a special interest in Chaucer. Then nothing would do but that Faust should read Chaucer aloud.

> Whan that Aprille with his shoures soote
> The droghte of March hath perced to the roote,
> And bathed every veyne in swich licour
> Of which vertu engendred is the flour . . .

rang out through Voisin's. In the twenty-eight years since the same voice had rung out at Busy Jack's, its surroundings had changed considerably.

Faust caught the train at Pennsylvania Station by an eyelash, according to Grace Flandrau, hurrying in through the gate, bare-headed, wearing his usual loose gray suit with coat unbuttoned, a porter agonizingly laboring behind him, loaded with heavy bags.

In Washington, he stopped to change trains, planning to see Colonel Joseph Greene, editor of *The Infantry Journal*, but found no hotel room available so spent the night in Union Station, in company with many other wartime travelers. Next morning he had a bath in a fifty-cent lavatory and visited Greene, whom he found "a charming fellow, not old, a professional soldier, terribly keen. We chatted about the Civil War, Freeman's disgraceful attack on Stonewall Jackson in *Lee's Lieutenants*, and in short had a bully good time."

Always capable of one more misstep, he telephoned his former mistress, now married and living in the Washington area, and received a final rebuff.

The remainder of the trip to Camp Patrick Henry near Richmond was uneventful. After a quarter of a century Faust was back in an army camp in Virginia.

24.

OUTWARD BOUND

FAUST found that the Army had changed since 1918. "They really know what they're doing now, and they make you comfortable when they do it to you," he informed Dorothy. "Good food and clean sheets. Still, I'm haunted by the feeling I'll step on the wrong boat and wind up at Murmansk or Melbourne. In the meantime I'm pursuing shoeshining kits, sewing kits, khaki-colored towels, insignia—which seems supremely silly for this old man. However, it is army regulations and the best tactics are to remain safely inside the rules. War correspondents are unpopular enough in any case."

He sailed in late March in company with three other correspondents, William Randolph Hearst, Jr.; Russell Hill, of the New York *Herald Tribune*; and Gordon Grant, who represented a group of Florida newspapers. Hearst later recalled the passage to Casablanca on the "USS William Mitchell" as being relieved by Faust's pleasant, thoughtful, kindness and gruff exterior. On his part, Faust asked to see some of Hearst's dispatches and reported them "better than he had expected," and decided to like the young man "despite my aversion to his father."

"I'm in a compartment 19 x 9," he added, "which accommodates twelve people in three tiers of bunks, among whom my bad luck has placed me on the bottom row." Those bunking with him included a hypnotist belonging to a USO troupe of entertainers, a character actor, an accordion player, a tumbler forty-three years old, "but still made of Indian rubber," a master-of-ceremonies, a musical comedian, a juggler, three Office of War Information people, and a radio and radar expert.

The ship was carrying a large contingent of Negro troops, and Faust became so interested in them that he decided to go into combat with a Negro unit if possible. He took many notes, conducted interviews, wrote individual biographies at all levels from private to colonel, and decided he was becoming "increasingly fond of my countrymen every minute—black or white."

He found himself by no means unknown. Armed services paperback editions, the first paperback books mass-produced in the U.S., had placed his novels in the hands of millions of servicemen, and his Kildare films had become irrevocably identified with wartime in the minds of a generation of film goers. The public had taken Dr. Kildare to heart so keenly that, according to *Newsweek*, pictures in which Lew Ayres starred as Kildare were sometimes banned at local theaters, because of popular resentment against Ayres, who had refused to bear arms when drafted. (Ayres later served more than three years as a non-combatant medical assistant and chaplain's aid.)

In addition to Kildare films, others with which Faust's name was identified were reaching the screen in large numbers. Between May 6, 1943, and April 26, 1944, roughly the last year of his life, a total of seven major pictures were released, equaling his record established in 1921–22.

For a variety of reasons, it had been impossible for him to preserve his incognito as he went overseas. To obtain certifications and clearances, and to gain objectives, he had had to reveal his true identity. For the first time he was being regarded publicly as a celebrity, but he found it helpful in developing the necessary influence as he went along.

From Casablanca he reported that by using influence he had escaped from a barbed-wire-surrounded, dust-blown encampment at the edge of the city and was staying in a flea-infested hotel downtown, waiting for space on a plane to Algiers. Being near the Mediterranean excited him. "The unripened immature life in our country, though it irritates our friends when we speak of it," he told Dorothy, "is just as real as it was in 1925 when we sailed for Europe." He hoped that the two of them might spend their declining years in a small villa in Italy, something two servants could take care of whether they were there or not. "It might be in the hills near Siena. It might better be near Florence. And you'll have to be prepared for a lonelier life than you've ever had before, because I'm going to want you chiefly to myself. I'm going to work steadily, from now forward, and when I'm through working with paper, I'll want to work in a garden, with you, or with you at hand. I can think of potting plants for hours, with you reading aloud."

He asked her to telephone Richard Aldington. "The thought of him is like an oasis in this desert."

He flew on to Algiers, where two assignments developed from conferences with Russell Barnes, head of the Office of War Information in the Mediterranean area. The first was a series of character sketches of U.S. allies and enemies. It meant writing brief portraits of typical Russians, English, French, Italians, Australians and New Zealanders, Poles, Czechs, "and a few other of the smaller allies, more in brief"; and then the Germans and Japanese. O.W.I. experts would fill in gaps which might occur through Faust's lack of technical knowledge or lack of mastery of G.I. jargon.

The second assignment concerned the desire of many U.S. soldiers to go home after they had seen a certain amount of fighting. To remedy this widespread condition, Faust proposed to interview a German prisoner of war who had spent years away from home, fighting in Russia or North Africa, and present his strenuous history in detail, suggesting that to defeat such an enemy, U.S. soldiers would have to be as enduring or more so. Another aspect of the project was to locate a New Zealander who had fought through the arduous North African campaigns of the past three years and tell his story, with a view to showing that some Allied soldiers were perhaps more willing to take hard knocks than Americans.

Faust pounded his typewriter at odd moments and in odd

The Faust family, Katonah, New York, 1933.

Venice, 1935. Faust, left, with Dr. George Winthrop ("Dixie") Fish, the real-life Dr. Kildare.

written at New York, N.Y., U.S.A.

METRO-GOLDWYN PICTURES CORPORATION;

By _Edward Loewe_

Witness:

Dorothy S. Faust

Frederick Faust (SEAL)

(Max Brand)

Faust signs a contract with MGM and Dorothy is a witness.

Carl Brandt, Faust's literary agent and close friend.
(Carol Brandt.)

ARGOSY

Action Stories of Every Variety

Volume 258   CONTENTS FOR AUGUST 24, 1935   Number 1

SERIALS

Silver Thaw (Three Parts—Part I) . . . Frank Richardson Pierce 38
Man fights man and Nature in the Northwest woods

Bed Rock (Three Parts—Part II) . . . . . Borden Chase 78
With sand hogs at work below Manhattan

The Sacred Valley (Six Parts—Part III) . . . . . Max Brand 106
A white Indian among Cheyenne warriors

The Blackbirds Sing (Six Parts—Conclusion) . . . Dennis Lawton 122
When the South Seas were young

COMPLETE STORIES

The Pearls of Bonfadini (Long Novelette) . . . . George Challis 2
Tizzo matches swords with Cesare Borgia

Men of Daring (True Story in Pictures) . . . . Stookie Allen 64
Captain Edgar G. Hamilton, American officer of the Legion

The Rattler Whirs (Short Story) . . . . . Foster-Harris 66
Fighting rattlesnakes and human rattlers

Cure for a Headache (Short Story) . . . . Houston Day 118
A headsman's sword swings in inner China

OTHER FEATURES

Wonders of the World—No. 34 . . . . . Alfred George 37
"The only survival of a once luxurious empire"

Well Guarded Gold . . . . J. W. Holden 63

America's Vanished Sea . . . . Delos White 77

The Load on Our Minds . . . . . Joseph W. Skidmore 105

Tricks of Boilers . . . . Melville C. Whitman 141

Argonotes 142

Looking Ahead! 143

This magazine is on sale every Wednesday

THE FRANK A. MUNSEY COMPANY, Publisher   280 BROADWAY, NEW YORK

WILLIAM T. DEWART, President   RICHARD H. TITHERINGTON, Secretary

MESSAGERIES HACHETTE   PARIS: HACHETTE & CIE.
3, La Belle Sauvage, Ludgate Hill, London, E.C.4   111 Rue Beaumur

Published weekly and copyright, 1935, by The Frank A. Munsey Company. Single copies, 10 cents. By the year, $4.00 in United States, its dependencies, Mexico and Cuba; $7.00 to Canada; $7.00 to other foreign countries. Remittances should be made by check, express money order or postal money order. Currency should not be sent unless registered. Entered as second class matter November 28, 1896, at the post office at New York, under the Act of March 3, 1879. The entire contents of this magazine are protected by copyright, and must not be reprinted without the publishers' permission. Title registered in U. S. Patent Office. Copyrighted in Great Britain.

Manuscripts submitted to this magazine should be accompanied by sufficient postage for their return if found unavailable. The publisher can accept no responsibility for return of unsolicited manuscripts.

A 1—24   1

In a weekly issue of *Argosy*, Faust appears as Max Brand, Dennis Lawton, and George Challis. (Reprinted from *Argosy*, copyright 1935, Popular Publications.)

Joel McCrea and Barbara Stanwyck in *Internes Can't Take Money*, the first of the Dr. Kildare pictures, 1937. (Culver Pictures, Inc.)

Thomas B. Costain, while a magazine editor, bought Faust's work and became a warm friend. (Wide World Photos.)

Cass Canfield, president of Harper and Brothers, encouraged Faust's serious writing while publishing his western novels. (Wide World Photos.)

James Stewart and Marlene Dietrich in *Destry Rides Again*, 1939.
(Universal–Culver Pictures, Inc.)

From left to right, Robert Young, Laraine Day, Lionel Barrymore, and
Lew Ayres in *Dr. Kildare's Crisis*, 1940. (MGM, Lew Ayres, Clarence
S. Bull.)

Richard Aldington was Faust's closest friend in Hollywood. (Wide World Photos.)

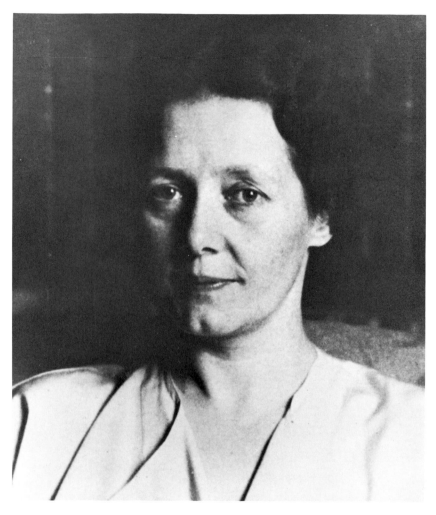

Dorothy Faust, 1941. (Frederick Faust.)

Last portrait, 1943. Faust as a grandfather.

Rita Hayworth and Gene Kelly in *Cover Girl*, 1944. (Columbia Pictures–Culver Pictures, Inc.)

A Decca album was made from the original Broadway musical, *Destry Rides Again*, 1959. (David Merrick Productions.)

Richard Chamberlain (left) and Raymond Massey played "Dr. Kildare" and "Dr. Gillespie" in the Dr. Kildare television series, beginning in 1961. (Metro-Goldwyn-Mayer.)

places, "crosslegged on the ground with the machine on my lap, astraddle a bunk, on a stool, and standing up to a high mess table." He kept his luggage packed for instant departure and tried to be patient.

In Algiers at this time was a writer Faust admired very much but had never met. He too had sometimes patiently and sometimes impatiently cut through every obstacle that stood between him and combat, including the objection that he was too old to be at the front. He was the French aviator, Antoine de St. Exupéry, the author of *Night Flight* and *Wind, Sand and Stars*, books Faust greatly admired. St. Exupéry had put the poetry of flight into fiction as well as into philosophy and had embodied the life of action coupled with art, much as Faust had.

By an odd quirk of circumstance, the two men resembled each other in physical appearance; but they were not to meet.

By the intervention of Colonel Reagan (Tex) McCrary of General Eaker's staff, to whom Faust carried a letter of introduction from Lovett, St. Exupéry was allowed to join an Anglo-American photo reconnaissance unit based on Sardinia. From there, flying a Lockheed P-38—manufactured not far from Jim Jeffries' Barn in San Fernando Valley—St. Exupéry took off on a mission over German-occupied France from which he never returned.

Faust moved on toward the front almost faster than he had hoped. After only four days in Algiers he was "winging over hills that were big and brown in the sun with curving terraces carved out of their sides and I knew that for the first time in almost six years I was looking at Italy again. It made my heart jump. And then we were swinging in towards a Naples airfield with a glimpse of the bay off to the left before we landed."

He was billeted with Gordon Grant and Ed Johnson of the Chicago *Sun* staff in a villa high above the bay "with a glorious view of Vesuvius and everything else out to Capri." Learning that Colonel Nee of Warner Brothers days was nearby, he telephoned him. Nee sent a car and an officer escort, and they brought Faust

245

to dine with Nee and General Tristram Tupper at O.S.S. head-quarters at San Lencio, after which Faust went to Fifth Army headquarters for his assignment.

Though he had requested duty with a Negro combat unit, he was assigned to the all-white 88th Infantry Division, then facing the enemy in rugged terrain not far north of Naples. Tempering his disappointment was the fact that the 88th was composed en-tirely of draftees and, in the forthcoming offensive, would be the first such division to see action. He would be participating in something new and different, and the performance of the raw draftees would be of keen interest to Army authorities as well as to the general public.

On April 22 Faust was taken to the command post of the 351st Infantry Regiment at Carinola by Major Walker, assistant chief of staff of the 88th Division, and introduced to Colonel Arthur S. Champeny, of Wellington, Kansas, the regimental commander. Champeny began by reminding him good humoredly that cor-respondents were not normally allowed forward of regimental headquarters.

"I suppose you think I'm crazy," Faust replied, "but I've come to write the true story of the infantry. People back home have almost no idea what's going on. They need to know. They read a lot about the war. But very little of what they read is real—down to earth—inside men's skins. I want to get inside your men, know what makes them tick, see how they behave in a crisis, and tell the people back home the truth."

"You know we're a green division, haven't had our baptism of fire yet?"

"So I understand. That's why I'm glad to be with you. Then I'll be on a level with your men all the way and know what I'm writing about."

Champeny outlined the past history of the regiment from its training days at Camp Gruber, Oklahoma, through Louisiana maneuvers to its present location; and plans were made for Faust to accompany the regiment's third battalion forward into the line on the following night.

The forward movement began by truck convoy. Faust thought it a lovely night, "Jupiter showing his brightest face right in the middle of the sky and Sirius getting bluer and bluer over in the West and Betelgeuse and some of the other familiar names scattered around." They seemed nearer and more congenial in the Italian sky. His column of jeeps and trucks followed the smooth highway that runs north along the coast from Naples toward Rome, and Faust began to notice, under the headlights, the shrubbery along the roadside "all powdered white with dust. It was the first step into war, and from then forward we seemed to be leaning into a new kind of world exactly like leaning through a window into a new view."

Behind him the long stream of trucks loaded with troops followed the windings of the road, "watching us with only one dim eye apiece," as headlights went off and black-out-lights came on. The vehicles were, he thought, like so many beetles glowing in the dark, and he remembered how earlier, when they were loading up, he had watched the men file slowly into the fields toward the trucks, "dim people in the half light," and been struck by "an odd touch of compassion, as though they were all blind and helpless."

They left the vehicles and walked, Faust stumbling along in the darkness in his new shoes, feet hurting, a little breathless in his overeagerness to keep up; and off among dark hills to the northeast he saw flashes of white light that looked like sheet lightning but were German guns at work. They walked across the Garigliano River on a sagging bridge supported by pontoons, feeling the bridge sway a little and jog up and down under their feet. Soon they were among their own artillery, the guns going off with great flashes, so loud and impressive that Faust thought they must be six- or eight-inchers but learned with chagrin that they were only three. Before long the guns were behind them, and when they fired he heard for the first time the shells "go wandering across the sky. The sound seems to press right up against the sky and it's a combination of a tearing noise with a pulsating howl, or perhaps, it is a very audible whisper. But it's not a complaining sound, as some people have called it. No, it's a wild and free and crazy noise of something going—it doesn't know where and doesn't give a damn."

They came into the battered hill town of Minturno about two in the morning. In the cellar of a bombed-out house, Faust inflated the rubber mattress Dixie Fish had found for him in New York, climbed into his bag, and fell wearily asleep, reflecting that a modern infantry battalion had more striking power than Napoleon's entire Grand Army. "It has artillery that lies ready to strike from a distance as accurately as the blows of a blacksmith's hammer, connected by a complicated system of telephone and radio with every part of its extended front where observation posts and the frontline infantry watch the enemy, ready to call down the artillery power like a fly-swatter on a fly."

He had been carrying about forty pounds for five hours but had managed to keep up, and no one suspected his heart condition.

25.

COMBAT CORRESPONDENT

FAUST was in battalion headquarters, and next morning he began to look into various parts of the organization of Headquarters Company, interviewing where he could. Everyone proved co-operative. That evening he dropped in to watch the supply officer receive rations brought from the rear and apportion them to the companies, at the same time taking in charge some soldiers who had been absent without leave. "There was a bit of confusion because some of the supply train had taken the wrong turning. And waiting and planning, and backing, and finally all was in order again. And in the midst of this there was a German air attack on a great city [Naples] to the south, and a hill of red, winking fire grew up in the sky, there, with great white flares going up now and then. The huge mountain of anti-aircraft fire would shrink away, and then climb higher than Mt. Everest; and enormous search-lights scooted through the confusion, and laid their hands on invisible things, and followed them slowly through the sky."

He got in an hour's sleep between one and two in the morning and then was called to go down and watch the cooks prepare breakfast. "Imagine three men stripped to the waist in a temperature of about 140° and an atmosphere choked with fumes of the gasoline heating units from three field kitchens—or field cooking stoves. Units so powerful that they can boil thirty gallons of water in an hour. They have to burn from yellow to blue before they are efficient, and this burning down was done on the floor of a small room with every window and door thoroughly blocked for fear of letting out a ray of light that German eyes—from the hills

249

that overlook us—might see." Faust tried to make notes, but gagged and had to leave, returned again and again, but it was no good. "Finally, at 4:30, the big tubs of food were put out and the company began to file past in the dark—strange how much one can see at night—poking out their mess kits at the shadow men who were serving, and receiving invisible spoonfuls of porridge and scrambled eggs, etc., and then finding a place to sit cross-legged on the ground and fumble at the breakfast. I suppose they were not very sure of anything except the coffee, strong and sweet with lots of evaporated milk."

He got to bed finally and slept late, and that afternoon when lunch had ended, had a long talk with the chaplain, "a very good man of thirty plus, certainly called to his vocation, modest, determined, no pretense, strong sense of direction, and I think, the possibility of giving great comfort to unhappy or injured men. While I was talking with him the Germans threw some shells in our direction—nothing closer than a couple of hundred yards at the nearest, I'm sure, but enough to make a lot of the men scamper for cover."

Chaplain W. W. Thompson's account of the occasion was somewhat different. "I was sitting talking with Faust one afternoon when several shells struck some distance beyond us. Hearing the whistle of the first, and of course not knowing where it would land, I hit ground. Mr. Faust continued to sit on the tree stump where he was, never moving a muscle."

In the evening Faust talked with a soldier of special daring in intelligence and reconnaissance who had been described to him by Colonel Champeny during the briefing at regimental headquarters. The young man was known as a daredevil and brought in prisoners by day as well as by night. "He looks like a soft young boy but has the restless way of a cat, a quick soft step, and a wildness like that of a random bullet." As they talked, Faust found that the supposed hellcat was living in an agony of suspense about his wife, who had suffered a complete mental breakdown when he was sent overseas and was confined to a mental hospital. The boy had been encouraged by his wife's letters, which constantly improved, until at last one came that was quite lucid and filled with affection. He could not understand the recent silence. The fact was, as the battalion had been informed, that his wife had had a serious relapse and was again confined to the hospital, and no one had the courage to tell him the truth. "This may be war and brutality on the whole, but in this instance I've never seen men use more affectionate delicacy than these fellows are doing with my young friend."

Faust found more compassionate understanding than he dreamed existed among the unlettered draftees, the kind of people he had fled from as a boy, and most of his grown life. He skimmed the filth off their speech and found a kind of poetry below. He decided he might become of use to them. "Something flows from the old to the young, I trust and believe."

The men began to trust and believe in him and to talk with him. They were to some degree flattered by the fact that a correspondent—they knew him as yet only as a correspondent—should care to share their hardships and risks; but they soon accepted him at his face value as one of themselves, to make good or not, as they were doing.

He accompanied a night patrol to the forward outpost line. "Everybody was lending me something, from combat trousers to mud-boots, a light sort of mukluk, very warm on the feet." It was a cold and clammy spring night. With a knife at his belt for self-defense and a pair of "neat little grenades" in his trench-coat pocket, and wool-lined trousers over his shoulders, to be donned for warmth during the long hours of standing in a foxhole, Faust trudged forward for an hour with the combat group. At last he reached a foxhole in the outpost line. He found it quite an establishment, with roofed-over sections and even a division into two chambers. His party of fifty-seven men with their six light machine guns were spread over a half-mile front, to close a gap in the line and guard against infiltration by the enemy.

"It seemed at first glance we were a pitiable little sacrifice to the first German attack. Actually we were playing an intelligent part in modern war, which holds ground lightly but develops floods of firepower."

He was permitted to take notes by the use of a green artillerist's light, jotting down amusedly the names of other foxholes connected to his by telephone. "Ours was Ruth, to our left flank was Winnie, extremely hesitant in speaking back, and away off to our right was Betty, not saying a damn word." Two men were dispatched into the darkness to determine what was the matter with Betty. "Just a pair of infantrymen, mind you, but these American G.I.'s have learned to turn their hands to everything. The country will be filled with ready-fingered mechanics of all sorts when the war has ended." However, the ready-fingered repairmen were not needed. Betty had simply hooked up her wires wrong, and soon corrected the difficulty herself.

Faust then "had the whole face of the sky to write about, and the frogs singing out in choruses and blacking out and coming in again, and a damned wind that got colder and colder the longer the night lasted, and a tree that always had a voice even when there seemed to be no wind at all. We had a moon up there too, usually just enough of it to make the sky blacker. To the right there was a low hill, pitch black, and always lifting and running toward us like a wave; and there was a lot of shrubbery that picked itself up, now and then, and came closer."

The damp ground chilled him. The wind covered him with gooseflesh. Feeling that the night must be nearly over he looked at his watch. It was ten-thirty. Five and a half hours of increasing misery, sharpened by suspense, lay ahead. Faust realized that bullets were one of the minor disasters of war.

The enemy finally provided distraction by opening up with artillery and even small arms. The sergeant who was with Faust found it necessary to seek the bottom of the hole, but Faust remained upright watching the display of shells, and the sergeant overheard the remark, "Beautiful!"

Legends began to grow, but the night's ordeal nearly finished

Faust. He had been up until three o'clock the night before getting the story of the young daredevil. By four of this night he was barely able to climb out of his hole, slipping and staggering down muddy paths, and falling flat twice. "You can fall from a walk in Italian mud as hard as from the back of a galloping horse in Ireland. I've tried both and know!" And he added that in the last cold morning hours when his blood was congealing and the clock standing still, the sergeant had insisted on lending him a canvas shelter half, "though I had not mentioned being cold and I don't think I looked it. But these soldiers have instinctive insight, which stems from their own experience with hardship, and such a kindness as won't fit in a book."

He found that the men preferred being in the front line to being in rest camp where they were safe but had to stand reveille and drill and much else they considered nonsense. "They prefer danger to boredom."

He had been assigned to Company "L," commanded by Captain Harold B. Ayres of New Orleans, Louisiana. Company headquarters was located in a farmhouse on the road running through shreds of grapevines and olive trees and fields of volunteer wheat and wildflowers, from Minturno to the next hill town eastward, Castelforte. The left flank of the division's line was anchored on the Gulf of Gaeta just south of Scauri, and its three regiments— the 351st in the center—held a 10,000-yard bridgehead front lying north of the Garigliano River. The line rose eastward from the seacoast through mountainous country to the heights of Damiano.

As Faust looked westward on clear days he could see the shore of the Gulf of Gaeta where Odysseus may have landed. Certainly Greeks of the sixth and seventh centuries B.C. had landed there. Not far away was Cumae where, according to poetic legend and myth, Aeneas had spoken with the Sybil and been guided by her to the underworld.

Overlooking the Allied line in this sector was high ground occupied by elements of the German 94th and 71st Infantry Divisions. The Germans had been entrenching themselves since the previous autumn. Their emplacements were part of what was known as the Gustav Line, and they were under command of Field Marshal Kesselring, one of the ablest of German commanders. His quick countermoves and stubborn resistance had sealed off the U.S. beachhead at Anzio north of Gaeta and held up the Allied advance for months at Cassino. The defending Germans in the 88th Division sector had a clear view of most American positions on the lower slopes opposite, and the movement of even one man was apt to draw fire. Central to the German position was the village of Santa Maria Infante, a pivotal strongpoint.

"There is billions of fiction, here," Faust wrote Brandt, "but for the present fact comes first"; and to Fish, "There's the pleasure of the return to the world of men. I hope to share some of it with you after the war." The tables had been turned at last—he was experiencing war and Fish was not.

On May 3, 1944, Faust heard General Mark Clark, U.S. Fifth Army Commander, address troops of the regiment in a sheltered natural amphitheater near Carinola and promise them, "It will not be long." Everyone knew that a big push by the American Army and its ally on the east, the British Eighth Army, was imminent.

Captain Ayres, the "L" Company commander, said he saw Faust on more than one occasion walking among the men in the foxholes in the front-line outposts, bending over them, giving each a word of encouragement. He was generally referred to as "the old boy," or "the old man." It pleased him. He had a sense of coming home, of fatherhood.

Few of them knew him at first except as Mr. Faust, correspondent for *Harper's Magazine*, but gradually the truth about his identity filtered down from rear areas. "Hardly one of us but hadn't read his books or seen his films," Sergeant Jack Delaney, later division historian, reported. Adding to the impact of his presence was the fact that General Dwight D. Eisenhower, the supreme commander in Europe, had said publicly that Max Brand was one of his favorite authors. Many years later, following his seventh heart attack, Eisenhower was treated successfully for fibrillation with a new drug, lidocaine, from which Faust might also have benefited.

Faust was becoming acquainted with other generals. He made a daylight tour of the front with General Paul W. Kendall, assistant commander of the 88th, who was some ten years his junior and had the reputation of trying to walk visitors' legs off. Faust's wind was gone and his eyes were half-blind from exhaustion, he said, when a dozen Italian mules led by their masters came down the trail with empty ammunition cases. "The general damned the interruption but it saved my life. By the time the last of the mules had gone by, sidling and waddling, I could breathe again, and just as I was about to perish once more there would be some other timely interruption, such as the view of a German position off to the side, or something on the plain we were climbing above. I must admit that when the end was in sight I did frankly call his attention to the view, and then leaned against a tree and gasped." Kendall had a good laugh. "We proceeded in the best of spirits and visited two battalions on high places and some of the company CPs."

All along the line, the stalemate which had existed for so many months was about to break up.

On May 10, D-Day minus one, Faust flew in a small observation plane that took off at 50 miles per hour and cruised at 75 and 80, above territory where the attack would be made next day. Allied smoke pots were at work along the Garigliano River to cover the bridges with a screen of smoke, and the pots sent up a mist that looked like water and made the valley resemble an inlet of the sea. The plane came near the German lines, and a bright red stream of tracer bullets burned past the window. The pilot dipped the Piper Cub into a slide that made Faust's stomach somersault, and they zoomed away to safety at tree-top level.

"It was such a perfect evening that I persuaded him to cruise around a while, low over the fields. There was a road, marble white, with its dust on the bushes, and we flew above that just fast enough to keep a good wind in the face." It was also fast enough to prevent the feeling of suffocation that still plagued him, and to let him drink deeply of the spring evening. "There isn't any reason that this countryside should seem more beautiful than thousands of others, except that it is Italian, but that word makes the difference."

Back among the men, he noticed that the hands of most of them were what his hands had been at their age, "thick fingered, and bent up a little crookedly at the wrists, the hands of men who have done manual labor. Now that the battle is not far from them, it's curious to see how little they change. They're just a little more tense but they don't sit around and brood. They don't sit in corners with their thoughts, but carry on about as usual."

He said they faced the situation realistically. "They appreciate the combat qualities of the Germans and they realize they are attacking a naturally strong position. They hope to win but there is no logic that convinces them they will win." He said that the mysterious and very beautiful fact was that they wanted to do their duty, make a good fight of it, and then have the war end for them, through death, or through wounds, or through victory. "I have talked to so many of them, now—best of all I've been silently in the corners of rooms while they were talking—that I'm confident this is the average feeling of these green troops, who have been hardened by little more than patrols. This is more than I expected to find, of course. I came hoping that I'd find our American boys better than the sour reports we've heard about our spiritless army, with its head in a sack stuck in the Italian mud; but I didn't dream that I'd run into this simple and elevated attitude. . . . Dimly, but deeply, these men see that Hitlerism cannot be permitted to exist in the same world with our ideas, and without passion, really without hate, they are willing to go out and die, doing the things they believe must be done."

256

His last words were for Dorothy, "No matter what is happening, there's one part of me that never stops thinking of you, particularly of the first, breathless days."

26.

THE STUFF OF DREAMS

D-DAY, May 11, was soft and warm, the real Italian *primavera*. There was a scent of jasmine in the air, and a faint smell of the sea. Poppies were blooming in the fields. The second platoon of "E" Company had assembled in a graveyard a short distance north of Minturno on the road leading up toward the enemy strongpoint, the village of Santa Maria Infante. The graveyard was overgrown with olive trees, and the men had shade and concealment as they whiled away the time cleaning weapons, checking equipment, writing last letters home. Faust moved among them, dropping an encouraging word here and there, listening. They remarked later how he had made them feel that what they said was important.

He had transferred to "E" Company of the 351st's Second Battalion a few days before, on learning that it was to spearhead the attack while "L" Company remained in reserve. Attempts had been made at various levels to discourage this exposure to extreme risk, but he had insisted. "The first attack is the cream and I want to be part of it," he told Colonel Champeny.

He was then assigned to the Second Platoon of "E" Company, commanded by Lieutenant Herbert Wadopian, of Asheville, North Carolina. Faust spent three days getting acquainted with Wadopian's men, especially Private Hendrick F. Rodriguez, a Mexican-American from the Southwest. Rodriguez apparently had no use for the Army or its discipline. Twice Wadopian had promoted him to corporal and twice had had to reduce him. "Rodriguez interested Faust more than any other member of the platoon," Wadopian said later. "Faust even spent a night or two in his foxhole. Apparently he wanted to see whether the maverick was going to deliver when the chips were down."

Lieutenant Colonel Raymond E. Kendall, who commanded the Second Battalion, visited Faust several times before the attack, and according to Wadopian they established a strong rapport, Kendall expressing concern for Faust's welfare and trying to dissuade him from accompanying the first wave of the assault.

Wadopian had also tried to dissuade Faust, urging him to remain back until the first objective was taken. According to the account Sergeant Jack Delaney published later in *Harper's*, Faust replied, "I feel that the only way to get the reactions of the men is to go in with them—take part in the assault. By my own feelings, my reactions, my thoughts—I'll know theirs."

Wadopian next attempted to dissuade him from accompanying the scouts who were to lead the attack. What finally convinced Faust he should accept a position at the rear of the platoon was the argument that he might be in the way up front. Actually, either position was extremely hazardous, though those who went first risked more.

But now there was concern among the men because Faust was going into the assault unarmed. They said his correspondent's shoulder patch would be no protection at all, especially in the dark. "I've got to abide by the rules," he replied. "Correspondents can't carry weapons." They insisted he carry a rifle or pistol but he shook his head. "I'm a bum shot. I'd likely do more damage to you than to the enemy." To appease them he finally agreed to carry a club which they cut from the branch of an olive tree. The men jokingly referred to it as his olive branch of peace.

H-hour was 2300, eleven P.M. The word had been passed around just before dark. The members of the platoon used the twilight hours to roll their packs, receive their issue of atabrine, halazone, canned "D" ration, and packaged "K" ration, and make ready last details. Faust carried several ampules of spirits of ammonia, which, when crushed between thumb and forefinger and held under his nose, might revive him in case of heart attack. "After dark we lay around and talked in whispers," Wadopian said later, "trying to draw as much comfort as possible out of the fellow next you." The tension that had been building for days reached a climax, and some of the men were nervous and even jittery. "Faust moved about talking to the boys and you could hear the little ripples of laughter that followed his movement," Wadopian continued. "He himself was as calm and collected as if it were a Sunday school picnic, and the men and I drew much courage from him."

After staking a path with white tapes that they could follow through a minefield, Sergeant Richard W. Courtney came back to shake hands with Faust and wish him good luck.

The last cigarette time was 2245, allowing fifteen minutes to hike to the jump-off line about 300 yards forward along the road toward Santa Maria Infante. Club in hand, Faust followed the line of silent men, each guiding on the dark silhouette of the man ahead and on the white stripe painted at the back of the helmet.

"We reached the line of departure precisely at 2300 as planned," Wadopian said, "just as all hell broke loose. In all my months of combat I had never seen a barrage like the one that we laid down that night—it was a continuous roar for thirty minutes that shook us almost as much as it must have shaken Jerry."

The barrage was officially described as the heaviest since the battle of El Alamein. "We followed closely behind," Wadopian continued, "to take advantage of the confusion it was causing and things were going wonderfully well—until we reached the outskirts of Santa Maria—then Jerry started giving it to us, and it seemed to me that he gave us as much as we had given him plus interest. Naturally we were having casualties, and it wasn't long before we were pretty well disorganized and rather decimated." This was an understatement. "I halted the platoon for a moment to try and reorganize it and of the 41 men I had started with I could find only 12 and among the 12 was Faust." Faust still had his club in his hand, but he was breathing very heavily. Though it was a black night and Wadopian could not see clearly, he sensed there was something wrong. "I asked if he had been hit and he said he thought he had been hit in the chest because he felt rather numb there and it was getting hard to breathe. I told him to lie down and take it easy as the medics were coming right behind us and they would take care of him and I left him there to continue the attack."

Faust did as Wadopian told him, the time being then about 12:30 A.M. Two medics found him soon after. They saw he was bleeding from a shell-fragment wound in the chest. He told them he was all right, to take care of two G.I.'s who were lying near. "They're worse off than I. I feel pretty good." A few minutes later the aid men returned, picked up Faust, and carried him back to the drift line, the line the litter-bearers were supposed to follow to evacuate the wounded.

When they put him down, he told them he was not in pain and felt fine. "Go on back up," he said, according to Sergeant Delaney, "I'll be seeing you later."

Faust did not see them later because when the litter-bearers found him he was dead.

He was buried at the divisional cemetery at Carano, facing the mountains he had been climbing when he was killed. They clearly and finally stood for all the heights he had attempted to scale. Faust had said that he wished to spend his last days in Italy and to die and be buried there. Though the notes he had taken at the front, as well as the poetry on which he was at work, and other personal belongings were lost, he seems to have been carrying, on his person or in his luggage, a copy of *The Tempest*. It contained the passage, "We are such stuff as dreams are made on."

The battle of Santa Maria Infante lasted sixty hours. Wadopian and the surviving men of "E" Company fought their way into the village. They were cut off there, and Wadopian was wounded. Colonel Kendall, the battalion commander, died in the counter-attack that finally took the stronghold. In all, the regiment lost more than 500 men, and "E" Company practically ceased to exist. So had Santa Maria Infante almost ceased to exist. Its wrecked, hollow houses, like open gray honeycombs, commanded the entire German position. Its capture broke the Gustav Line at this key point and opened the way to Rome and eventual victory in Italy.

The 88th Division continued to the Arno River and joined British and French units in the liberation of Florence. Thus by proxy Faust achieved a final dream. The men of the 88th indeed became proxies of which he could be proud. The once raw draftees of questionable promise developed into seasoned veterans renowned for spearheading attacks; and, until killed in action, one of the most courageous of them was Private Rodriguez, in whose foxhole Faust had spent much time during the last hours before the jump-off.

The division continued its victorious progress throughout the length of Italy and ended its fighting career at the Austrian border.

Faust's body was reinterred at the Nettuno-Anzio American Cemetery where it remains. The cemetery, situated on a southern slope open to the sun, is surrounded by grapevines and olive trees. Men and women working in the fields nearby can be heard talking and singing.

The night he was killed, Dorothy had a dream in which she heard him say her name very clearly, once, as if he were near at hand and needed her. The dream was so vivid it woke her. Next morning, she told Jane and the others about it at breakfast. In the afternoon they heard on the radio that he had been wounded. Next day, Dixie Fish telephoned from New York to say that he was dead. He died seventeen days before his fifty-second birthday.

EPILOGUE

THE publicity attendant on Faust's death did much to dispel the mystery surrounding the man and his work and to allow both to appear in true light. The Associated Press account began, "Frederick Faust, who thrilled millions with his fiction of adventure under the name of Max Brand, died in the forefront of battle within thirty minutes after the Allied offensive opened last Thursday night, the seventeenth war correspondent killed in the war"; and continued with a description of Faust as "King of the Pulps" and author of the Dr. Kildare stories and films and of a vast body of literature written under many names.

The *New York Times* carried the AP account at least twice in its edition of May 17, 1944, once in full, once in brief below a feature story by its own correspondent with the U.S. Fifth Army, Milton Bracker. Bracker said of Faust, "Technically he was just another accredited war correspondent attached to the Fifth Army. But in effect he was an over-age infantryman who had reported to Fifth Army headquarters a month ago and said that the only way to write about war was to write about the human beings who really fight it."

Time for May 29, 1944, Faust's birthday, carried a portrait of General De Gaulle on its cover with the caption, "Beyond the beaches 40,000,000 judges await him." The Normandy landings were a week away. The issue contained a column-long article on Faust, stating that he had written "some 30,000,000 words—115 published books and an uncharted quantity of magazine material, including at least 350 serials and novelettes." *Time* quoted Faust as saying, "No one is more than 40 to 50% efficient,

263

but when a man is backed into a corner by a man who intends to kill him, he can be as high as 90% efficient." *Time* added that Faust never explained who or what kept backing him into his productive corner.

Faust would probably have been amazed at the amount of attention he was receiving. The *San Francisco Chronicle* published a locally researched article including considerable detail about his college days and recalling his campus nickname, Fabulous Faust. There were editorials and tributes in *Harper's, The Infantry Journal, The Saturday Review of Literature, Publisher's Weekly, The London Times,* and elsewhere.

While the accounts of his death were still being published, *The Saturday Evening Post* began serializing *After April;* and additional original magazine stories continued to appear throughout the 1940's. It was all indicative of interest in Faust and his work that was to grow. Brandt searched the files for unpublished material, while keeping reprint houses supplied with successful novels from past years. Faust gradually reached a greater readership than he had enjoyed while living.

Dodd, Mead continued to issue at least two hardback western novels a year while arranging for paperback reprints. Harper continued original westerns in hardback under the Evan Evans pseudonym and arranged for their release in softcover; and Harper also issued hardback historical novels under the George Challis pseudonym *(The Firebrand, The Bait and the Trap),* dealing with the Renaissance Italy that had so strongly appealed to Faust.

There were parallel developments abroad, where Faust's work continued to be translated into all the major languages and to appear in both hard and soft covers.

In 1949 Edward H. Dodd, Jr., of Dodd, Mead was quoted in the *New York Herald Tribune* as saying there were 125 Max Brand novels yet to be published in book form, roughly enough to last for sixty years at the rate of two issues a year. They were chiefly serials that had originally appeared in *Western Story*. To them could be added unpublished manuscripts in the possession of the Brandt agency and the Faust family. It became clear that Faust was going to go on indefinitely. By 1969, a total of 179 of his books had been published.

Adding to the momentum have been anthologies, omnibuses, and "western roundups" of various descriptions, as well as Max Brand colored comic books, a *Max Brand Western Magazine* containing reprints and adaptations of favorite stories and novels, syndicated newspaper reprints, and similar marginalia.

Reader and fan interest has grown in proportion. In the late 1940's a Baptist minister living in Kentucky, Darrell C. Richardson, began publishing a fan magazine called *The Fabulous Faust Fanzine* and later published a book, *Max Brand: The Man and His Work*. These not only popularized Faust further but helped to dispel the mystery surrounding his many pen names and his way of life.

It is now clear that Faust was published under at least nineteen names in addition to his own: Frank Austin, George Owen Baxter, Lee Bolt, Max Brand, Walter C. Butler, George Challis, Peter Dawson, Martin Dexter, Evin Evan, Evan Evans, John Frederick, Frederick Frost, Dennis Lawton, David Manning, M. B., Peter Henry Morland, Hugh Owen, Nicholas Silver, Henry Uriel.

The process of shedding light on Faust and his work continued into the 1950's. In 1955 Quentin Reynolds devoted considerable space to the subject in a book, *The Fiction Factory,* the story of the Street and Smith publishing firm and some of its outstanding writers. Reynolds substantiated the almost incredible stories about Faust's performances, and earnings, while working for *Western Story*. "No man ever lived who could invent so many plots (not even Balzac) or so crowd a few thousand words with action as Max Brand," Reynolds said.

Also in 1955, Martha Bacon published an article in the *At-*

lantic Monthly, titled *Dionysus and Destry,* which added further dimensions to the slowly appearing true figure and served to introduce Faust to an audience that knew little about him.

The 1957 publication of his *Notebooks and Poems,* edited by John Schoolcraft, revealed Faust further. It contained considerable biographical material. It also contained perhaps his best short poem, which begins:

> What love is there on earth remaining
> Compared to all that has passed beyond our seeing . . . .

and ends:

> But love shall not forget.
> By the pomegranate I shall know you,
> The seeds bitter and sweet,
> And by your brightness among shadows,
> For not the less do you shine
> On the dead who adored you to the last day, the last
>   breath,
> Than on those who taste on earth
> The sweetness of your breath and the comfort
> Of your April.

Dorothy Faust's death in 1960 removed certain restraints. It also released materials previously unobtainable. By her wish, the Bancroft Library at the University of California in Berkeley became a central repository for material by and about Faust.

In the mid-1960's, articles devoted to Dixie Fish and his relationship to Faust and to Dr. Kildare appeared in *The Saturday Review,* in the Sunday newspaper supplement *Parade,* and elsewhere; and in 1967 Dodd, Mead published a collection of Faust's best stories with a biographical sketch that helped outline his complex figure. Also in 1967, Frank Gruber's book, *The Pulp Jungle,* threw more light on Faust's Hollywood days, as well as on his pulp writing career.

By 1968, increasing interest among fans and collectors resulted in the scheduled publication of a new fan magazine, *The Faust*

Collector, published and edited by William J. Clark, a U.S. government computer expert and statistician, headquartered at Arlington, Virginia.

So the matter has grown. Today it might take not one but two computer experts to total Faust's reading audience alone. His western novels regularly sell from 3,000 to 5,000 in hardcover, from 300,000 to 500,000 or more in soft. His historical romances continue to be popular, and his Dr. Kildare novels are frequently reprinted. A number of favorites, such as *The Untamed, Destry Rides Again, Singing Guns, Fightin' Fool,* and *The Border Kid,* have neared or passed the million mark, as have several Kildare titles. It is estimated that in the past twenty-five years, 20,000,000 of his books have been sold in the U.S. and many more millions abroad.

Perhaps the question of exactly how much Faust wrote will never be answered. Early records have been lost. Complicating the problem are known collaborations and ghost writing with John Schoolcraft, Kenneth Perkins, Robert Simpson, and perhaps others. It is certain that he was published under twenty names, but there may have been more. He himself said early in 1934 that he had written between twenty-four and twenty-five million words in the previous seventeen years, or the equivalent, at 70,000 words a book, of about 350 novels; but he wrote several million words after his 1934 statement. We have the assertion by Edward H. Dodd, Jr., in the March 26, 1938, *Publisher's Weekly,* that Faust had by that date published approximately twenty-five million words. Other authorities, including Carl Brandt, have put Faust's total printed output at between twenty-five and thirty million words. A recent reevaluation by William J. Clark, who says he has counted ninety-eight per cent of the words Faust published since college days, finds approximately twenty-two million words. This breaks down into 628 separate items, including 196 novels 50,000 or more words in length, 226 novelettes of from 20,000 to 50,000 words, 162 stories of less than 20,000 words, and 44 poems.

It seems safe to say Faust wrote between twenty-five and thirty million words and published about twenty-five million.

It seems probable that he published more varieties of prose fiction than anyone else on record. It seems certain that the bulk of this production took place in a remarkably short period of about seventeen years.

To evaluate Faust's work presents unusual difficulties. No critic has ever done so. No critic has known its full extent. It has been evaluated as Faust has been, by bits and pieces, under various aliases.

To begin with his prose, it is rather amusing to see how the reviewers responded to work published under various pseudonyms. *The New York Times,* for example, said this about *Brothers on the Trail* when it appeared in 1934, "For Western tales that are rough, swift, tense, and gripping, Max Brand is a top-notcher. He is prolific and uneven. Sometimes he grows careless about his plots and his writing. But this new yarn proves that he can take a fresh grip on himself and take pains with his work, for it is altogether the best written story of the last half dozen from his pen. It has conciseness, clarity, wit, punch, and hardly a superfluous word."

The *Times* said about Walter C. Butler's *The Night Flower,* when it appeared in 1936, "Action gets strongly under way on the first page of this exceptionally solid crime novel with the hold-up of an armored truck . . . The manifold intricacies of the plot are worked out with flawless skill and what is extremely rare in a tale of this genre, one can never positively foresee just what will happen next, or correctly conjecture what the conclusions will finally bring forth. The reviewer confidently chooses this book —he keeps an eye closely on the field—as the best written, most artfully constructed and thoroughly interesting crime-adventure novel published thus far within the year."

And about *Secret Agent Number One,* by Frederick Frost, also published in 1936, the *Times* reviewer said, "The story . . . stirs the pulse . . . and gives the reader a happy hour or two of vicarious excitement and that, no doubt, is what the author set out to do."

In 1937 the *Times* was saying about George Challis' *Golden Knight,* "If you like a rousing adventure story about one of the few great historical personages whose glamor has defied time . . . you will find 'the Golden Knight' wholly delightful."

In other newspapers as in the *Times,* the reviews of Faust's books were as a rule relatively extensive, well displayed, and favorable. The reviewers seem to have been as completely mystified as to the true identity of the author as were most of Faust's readers.

In later years when he was generally identified as Max Brand —and generally credited with having produced a wide variety of work under many pen names in addition to the well-known westerns and Kildares—critics tended to refer to him as one of the titans of popular literature. More recently, the publication of his collected best stories, which surprisingly included only one western, served to extend his reputation.

Still, no one was on solid ground when discussing Faust or his work. The subject was like an uncompleted picture puzzle. Quentin Reynolds, the official biographer of the Street and Smith publishing firm, said that *Western Story* once carried five Faust offerings in a single weekly issue. This is probably in error. There is no record of one issue of *Western Story* carrying more than three Faust contributions; however, this occurred approximately twenty times. *Argosy* once carried three contributions in the same week. In at least three consecutive monthly issues, *The American* carried two Faust offerings; the dates were November and December, 1937, and January, 1938.

As for Faust's poetry, the picture puzzle was relatively simple, since most of his verse was published under his own name. Such early verdicts as those of Benét and Le Gallienne—that the poetry contained promise and excellence but lacked mastery— applied at the end; when Bacon said of *Dionysus in Hades* in *The Saturday Review* for May 27, 1944, that it was "nobly planned, nobly felt, nobly written," while noting that it found little acceptance.

Now that the true dimensions of the subject are known, what can be said of Faust's work as a whole? The effort seems unparalleled in variety and extent. It covered practically every subject, genre, and locale that prose fiction can deal with: love, fantasy, westerns, mysteries, spy stories, adventure, the Arctic, the South Seas, big cities, the desert, the jungles, war, historical romance, aircraft, sailing ships, science fiction, animal stories, crime, high society, big business, and big medicine. For good measure there were the plays and the lyric and epic poetry on classical as well as contemporary themes, and some serious short stories. It represented a variety of influences from Homer to Kipling and a style that found acceptance at practically every level of readership.

There probably has been nothing else like it, nor will changing times permit it to occur again.

When his production of motion picture stories and screen plays is added, the range and versatility of Faust's talent become the more remarkable.

Among that notable cluster of American writers born in the decade between 1890 and 1900, which included some of the most capacious we have produced—MacLeish, Fitzgerald, Faulkner, Wilder, Hemingway, Benét, and Wolfe—Faust can reasonably be called the unknown giant. In various guises, he filled the empty spaces among his illustrious contemporaries and in a way embraced them all. He was serious and popular, poetry and prose, wine and corn, highbrow and lowbrow, American and cosmopolitan. None of them performed on a more gigantic scale and probably none reached a larger audience.

Grace Flandrau said a definitive word about the motivation for Faust's writing. "It had to pour out like automatic writing, like the material of a dream." She said it had to be fiction, written out of some disassociated fragment of youthful personality, or else it had to be highly conscious verse, during the writing of which "he probably thought too much, or rather, too exclusively. So that, distinguished as it was, it suffered from the absence of his daemon."

She said it was in his personality, not in his work, that Faust was at times a completely undivided being. Here Cass Canfield joined her. Speaking of Faust's memorable personality, Canfield said, "Our first meeting was on a squash court, and like any encounter with Faust it was unforgettable. I remember his size, his agility and his enormous enthusiasm. He played as if his life depended on it, and I felt that here was a man to whom squash must be an all-consuming interest.

"Then we had dinner and I have never seen anyone enjoy himself with greater gusto. The business of eating and of discussing the food and wine with rare discrimination utterly absorbed him.

"After dinner Faust talked. He talked for hours, wonderfully well, about literature and people and the values he prized. His range of knowledge and understanding seemed to me extraordinary. He discussed the classics as one would the writings of contemporaries. He made the great men of Greece so vivid that all at once they became old personal friends.

"At the end of this day with Faust, I knew that I'd had the luck to meet an extraordinary man with the spark of genius. I had been refreshed by his vitality, and his gargantuan appetite for life. And he had amazed me with his versatility and knowledge.

"Later as I got to know him well I learned to value many other qualities in Faust. He was the finest of companions with a lavish generosity and a capacity for friendship rarely found."

It is easy, perhaps too easy, to see that much of the motivation for the person and the writer came from the need to compensate for childhood deprivations and later bad health. The valley and the West also unquestionably helped give a physical integrity and a largeness of scope to almost everything that he did. The spirit of the times should be considered, too. Faust was to the writing of his era what Babe Ruth and Red Grange were to sports, Charles Lindbergh to flying, Henry Ford to industry: the expression of an expansive time, when horizons seemed larger and possibilities less limited.

Whatever drove him—whatever it was that *Time* said was forever backing him into a corner and trying to kill him—it drove him not only to uniqueness and to greatness but finally to the self-realization he sought.

There can be little doubt that in the final moments he was at one with himself, not twenty men but one. He was united at last. He had completed a great circle. He was back once more with the kind of men he had fled from most of his life—but who had read him and whom he had, after all, done most of his writing for. He was a people's writer and he died with the people he wrote for, and of. He had discovered new truth in them and they in him.

A FAUST BIBLIOGRAPHY

(Based on an index prepared by William J. Clark and containing material from Brandt & Brandt files and Faust family records.)

THE following entries refer to original U.S. publication only. To have included U.S. reprints, English originals, and English and other foreign reprints of Faust's work—whether in hard cover or soft—would have lengthened this bibliography unduly. For the same reason, Faust's school and college work has been omitted. Thus a reader may come across a year or two in the past ten or twenty when no Faust books appear to have been issued. This simply means that all issues for that year were reprints. In fact, Faust books have appeared uninterruptedly since 1919.

Entries are in chronological order. They are grouped under the headings "Magazine and Newspaper Work" and "Books."

In the case of magazine or newspaper publication, entries consist of the title of the work, followed by the author name (a complete list of Faust pen names is given on page 265), the nature of the work (whether poem, story, novelette, or serial), the name of the magazine or newspaper, and the date of publication.

In the case of book publication, the title, the name used by the author, the name of the publisher, and the place and date of publication are given. Faust's two books of poetry published in the U.S. have a (p) beside their titles. All other books are prose fiction.

To simplify listing, the following abbreviations have been used:

(p) = poem
(s) = story—work less than 20,000 words in length
(nt) = novelette—work 20,000 to 50,000 words in length
(bln) = book-length novel of approximately 50,000 words

(sl) = serial—work published serially and 50,000 or more words
    in length unless otherwise indicated, the date given being
    the publication date of the first installment

AA = Argosy-All Story Weekly
AC = American Cavalcade
AD = Adventure
AF = All-American Fiction
AH = Ace-High
AM = American Magazine
AR = Argosy
AS = All-Story Weekly
AW = American Weekly
BB = Blue Book
BE = Brooklyn Eagle
BM = Black Mask
CE = The Century
CG = Country Gentleman
CH = Country Home
CM = Cosmopolitan
CO = Collier's Weekly
CW = Complete Western Book
DB = Double Detective
DD = Dime Detective
DF = Detective Fiction Weekly
DS = Detective Story Magazine
DW = Dime Western
EM = Elk's Magazine
ES = Esquire Magazine
FD = Flynn's Detective Fiction
FF = Fabulous Faust Fanzine
FW = Far West Illustrated
GH = Good Housekeeping
HM = Harper's Magazine
IL = Illustrated Love Magazine
LM = Liberty Magazine
MA = MacLean's Magazine
MC = McCall's Magazine

MM = *Mavericks Magazine*
MU = *Munsey Magazine*
PM = *Photoplay Magazine*
RR = *Railroad Man's Magazine*
SE = *Saturday Evening Post*
SN = *St. Nicholas*
SP = *Sport Story Magazine*
SS = *Short Stories*
SW = *Star Western*
TM = *This Week Magazine*
WM = *West Magazine*
WS = *Western Story Magazine*

1917

MAGAZINE AND NEWSPAPER WORK

The Secret, Faust, (p), *CE,* February.
Convalescence, Faust, (s), *AS,* March 31
The Gambler and the Stake, Faust, (s), *AS,* April 28.
Mr. Cinderella, Brand, (s), *AS,* June 23.
Fate's Honeymoon, Brand, (sl), *AS,* July 14.
Your Country Needs You, Faust, (s), *AS,* August 4.
The Sole Survivor, Brand, (s), *AS,* September 15.
Dragon Teeth, Brand, (p), *AS,* September 22.
One Glass of Wine, Brand, (nt), *AS,* October 6.
The Adopted Son, Brand, (s), *AS,* October 27.
The Sword Lover, Brand, (sl), *AR,* November 10.

1918

MAGAZINE AND NEWSPAPER WORK

Who Am I? Brand, (sl), *AS,* February 23.
Silence, Brand, (p), *AS,* April 27.
A Rendezvous with Death, Brand, (nt), *AS,* May 18.
John Ovington Returns, Brand, (s), *AS,* June 8.
Devil Ritter, Brand, (nt), *AS,* July 13.
The Ballad of St. Christopher, Brand, (p), *AS,* July 20.
Above the Law, Brand, (nt), *AS,* August 31.
My Heroes, Faust, (p), *SN,* September.
Woodward's Devil, Brand, (s), *AS,* September 15.
Bad-Eye, His Life and Letters, Brand, (s), *AS,* October 19.

No Partners, Brand, (nt), *AS,* October 26.

The Double Crown, John Frederick and Peter Ward, (sl), *AR,* October 26.

Harrigan! Brand, (sl), *RR,* November 2.

The Great Stroke, Brand, (s), *AS,* November 16.

The Untamed, Brand, (sl), *AS,* December 7.

1919

MAGAZINE AND NEWSPAPER WORK

Victory, Brand, (s), *AS,* February 1.

That Receding Brow, Brand, (s), *AS,* February 15.

The Hammer, Frederick, (sl), *AR,* March 1.

Children of Night, Brand, (sl), *AS,* March 22.

The Ghost, Brand, (s), *AS,* May 3.

The Higher Strain, Frederick, (nt), *AR,* May 31.

The Laughter of Slim Malone, Brand, (s), *AS,* June 14.

The Fear of Morgan the Fearless, Brand, (s), *AS,* June 28.

Hole-in-the-Wall Barrett, Brand, (s), *MU,* August.

Luck, Frederick, (sl), *AR,* August 9.

"It Was Like This—," Brand (s), *AS,* August 30.

The House That Steve Built, Brand, (s), *AS,* September 27.

The Sacking of El Dorado, Brand, (s), *AS,* October 11.

Brain and Brawn, Frederick, (s), *AR,* November 1.

Trailin', Brand, (sl), *AS,* November 1.

BOOKS

The Untamed, Brand, G. P. Putnam's Sons, New York, March 14.

1920

MAGAZINE AND NEWSPAPER WORK

The Lost Garden, Brand, (s), *AS,* January 3.

Crossroads, Frederick, (sl), *AR,* January 31.

Out of the Dark, Brand, (s), *AS,* March 13.

Clung, Brand, (sl), *AS,* April 10.

The Frigate Bird, Bolt, (sl), *AS,* May 29.

Pride of Tyson, Frederick, (sl), *AR,* July 3.

A Sagebrush Cinderella, Brand, (s), *AS,* July 10.

The Ghost, Brand, (s), *AA,* July 24.

The Whisperer, Brand, (s), *AA,* August 21.

The Night Horseman, Brand, (sl), *AA,* September 18.

Jerry Peyton's Notched Inheritance, Baxter, (nt), *WS*,
    November 25.
The Consuming Fire, Brand, (s), *AA*, November 27.
The Man Who Forgot Christmas, Frederick, (nt), *WS*,
    December 25.

BOOKS
    Trailin', Brand, G. P. Putnam's Sons, New York, March 19.
    Riders of the Silences, Frederick, H. K. Fly, New York,
        September 25.
    The Ten-Foot Chain or Can Love Survive the Shackles?
        Brand (with Achmed Abdullah, E. K. Means, P. P. Sheehan),
        Reynolds Publishing Co., Inc., New York, September 28.
    The Night Horseman, Brand, G. P. Putnam's Sons, New York,
        November 5.

1921

MAGAZINE AND NEWSPAPER WORK
    Tiger, Brand, (sl), *AA*, January 8.
    The Cure of Silver Cañon, Frederick, (nt), *WS*, January 15.
    Iron Dust, Baxter, (sl), *WS*, January 29.
    His Back Against the Wall, Frederick, (nt), *WS*, March 12.
    White Heather Weather, Frederick, (sl), *AA*, April 9.
    Donnegan, Baxter, (sl), *WS*, April 16.
    "Jerico's" Garrison Finish, Frederick, (nt), *WS*, May 21.
    When the Wandering Whip Rode West, Frederick, (nt),
        WS, June 18.
    Bullets with Sense, Brand, (nt), *WS*, July 9.
    When Iron Turns to Gold, Baxter, (nt), *WS*, July 30.
    Bull Hunter Feels His Oats, Brand, (nt), *WS*, August 13.
    The Guide to Happiness, Brand, (sl), *AA*, August 13.
    Madcap of the Mountains, Baxter, (sl), *WS*, September 13.
    Outlaws All, Brand, (nt), *WS*, September 10.
    The Wolf Strain, Brand, (nt), *WS*, September 24.
    The Seventh Man, Brand, (sl), *AA*, October 1.
    Bull Hunter's Romance, Brand, (nt), *WS*, October 22.
    Ronicky Doone, Champion of Lost Causes, Manning, (sl),
        WS, October 29.
    The Gauntlet, Baxter, (nt), *WS*, November 12.

Riding Into Peril, Frederick, (nt), *WS*, November 19.
Sheriff Larrabee's Prisoner, Dexter, (nt), *WS*, December 3.
The Man Who Followed, Baxter, (nt), *WS*, December 10.
Black Jack, Brand, (sl), *AA*, December 10.
The Gift, Brand, (nt), *WS*, December 24.

BOOKS

Free Range Lanning, Baxter, Chelsea House, New York,
    October 15.
The Seventh Man, Brand, G. P. Putnam's Sons, New York,
    October 21.

1922

MAGAZINE AND NEWSPAPER WORK

Ronicky Doone and the Cosslett Treasure, Manning, (sl),
    WS, January 7.
The Fugitive's Mission, Baxter, (nt), *WS*, January 14.
The One-Way Trail, Baxter (nt), *WS*, February 4.
The Emerald Trail, Frederick, (nt), *WS*, February 25.
Gun Gentlemen, Brand, (sl), *AA*, February 25.
Jim Curry's Compromise, Brand, (nt), *WS*, April 1.
Three Who Paid, Baxter, (sl), *WS*, April 8.
The Garden of Eden, Brand, (sl), *AA*, April 15.
Jim Curry's Test, Brand, (nt), *WS*, April 22.
King Charlie and His Long Riders, Frederick, (nt), *WS*, May 6.
Jim Curry's Sacrifice, Brand, (nt), *WS*, May 20.
King Charlie—One Year Later, Frederick, (nt), *WS*, May 27.
The Unhallowed House, Frederick, (nt), *AH*, June.
His Third Master, Brand, (sl), *AA*, June 3.
Alcatraz, Brand, (sl-nt), *CG*, June 17.
The Shadow of Silver Tip, Baxter, (sl), *WS*, June 17.
King Charlie's Hosts, Frederick, (nt), *WS*, June 24.
Slumber Mountain, Frederick, (nt), *WS*, July 8.
Ronicky Doone's Reward, Manning, (sl), *WS*, July 15.
The Painted Alibi, Baxter, (nt), *DS*, July 22.
Walking Death, Silver, (nt), *DS*, July 29.
The Bill for Banditry, Frederick, (nt), *WS*, August 5.
The Cross Brand, Brand, (nt), *SS*, August 25.
Mountain Madness, Baxter, (nt), *WS*, August 26.

Old Carver Ranch, Frederick, (sl), *WS*, August 26.

The Night Rider, Silver, (nt), *DS*, September 9.

Over the Northern Border, Baxter (nt), *WS*, September 16.

The Black Muldoon, Dawson, (nt), *WS*, September 30.

Rubies of Guilt, Silver, (nt), *DS*, October 7.

Joe White's Brand, Baxter, (nt), *WS*, October 14.

Without a Penny in the World, Frederick, (nt), *WS*, October 21.

The Hopeless Case, Silver, (nt), *DS*, November 4.

Wild Freedom, Baxter, (sl), *WS*, November 11.

Jargan, Brand, (nt), *SS*, November 25.

Kain, Brand, (sl), *AA*, December 2.

Sealed for Fifty Years, Silver, (nt), *DS*, December 9.

The Cabin in the Pines, Frederick, (nt), *WS*, December 9.

A Christmas Encounter, Silver, (nt), *DS*, December 23.

The Power of Prayer, Frederick, (nt), *WS*, December 23.

Stolen Clothes, Silver, (nt), *DS*, December 30.

Phil, the Fiddler, Baxter, (nt), *WS*, December 30.

BOOKS

The Village Street, (p), Faust, G. P. Putnam's Sons, New York,
June 30.

1923

MAGAZINE AND NEWSPAPER WORK

Winking Lights, Frederick, (nt), *WS*, January 6.

Under His Shirt, Brand, (nt), *WS*, January 27.

Hired Guns, Brand, (sl), *WS*, March 10.

Two Sixes, Baxter, (nt), *WS*, March 17.

Black Shadows of Sawtrell House, Silver, (sl), *DS*, March 17.

"Sunset" Wins, Baxter, (nt), *WS*, April 7.

The Darkness at Windon Manor, Brand, (sl-nt), *AA*, April 21.

Gold King Turns His Back, Frederick, (nt), *WS*, April 28.

The Bandit of the Black Hills, Baxter, (sl), *WS*, April 28.

The Abandoned Outlaw, Frederick, (nt), *WS*, May 26.

His Name His Fortune, Brand, (nt), *WS*, June 9.

Little Sammy Green, *"Lucky Gent,"* Brand, (nt), *WS*, June 30.

Dan Barry's Daughter, Brand, (sl), *AA*, June 30.

Galloping Danger, Brand, (sl), *WS*, July 14.

Black Sheep, Baxter, (nt), *WS*, July 28.

"Safety" McTee, Brand, (s), *WS*, August 25.
Rodeo Ranch, Brand, (nt), *WS*, September 1.
Seven Trails to Romance, Baxter, (sl), *WS*, September 1.
Wooden Guns, Brand, (sl), *WS*, September 15.
Slow Bill, Frederick, (nt), *WS*, October 13.
Soft Metal, Baxter, (nt), *WS*, October 20.
The Stranger at the Gate, Brand, (sl), *AA*, November 3.
"Timber Line," Brand, (nt), *WS*, November 24.
The Whisperer of the Wilderness, Baxter, (sl), *WS*, December 1.
Uncle Chris Turns North, Brand, (nt), *WS*, December 8.
The Boy Who Found Christmas, Frederick, (nt), *WS*, December 22.

BOOKS

Donnegan, Baxter, Chelsea House, New York, January 15.
Alcatraz, Brand, G. P. Putnam's Sons, New York, January 26.
The Long, Long Trail, Baxter, Chelsea House, New York,
    September 15.

1924

MAGAZINE AND NEWSPAPER WORK

Master and Man, Brand, (nt), *WS*, January 5.
The Rock of Kiever, Brand, (nt), *WS*, January 19.
The Blackmailer, Brand, (nt), *AA*, January 26.
Train's Trust, Baxter, (sl), *WS*, January 26.
Bulldog, Brand, (s), *CO*, February 23.
Cuttle's Hired Man, Brand, (nt), *WS*, March 1.
Four Without Fear, Frederick, (sl), *WS*, March 8.
The Man in the Dark, Brand, (s), *AA*, March 22.
Lazy Tom Hooks Up with Skinny, Brand, (nt), *WS*, March 22.
One Hour Past Moonrise, Brand, (sl), *SS*, April 10.
The Welding Quirt, Brand, (nt), *WS*, April 12.
Saddle and Sentiment, Brand, (sl), *WS*, April 19.
Bared Fangs, Baxter, (nt), *WS*, May 10.
Argentine, Baxter, (sl), *WS*, May 31.
The Gambler, Brand, (sl), *WS*, June 7.
The Girl They Left Behind Them, Frederick, (nt), *WS*, June 21.
A Wolf Among Dogs, Frederick, (nt), *WS*, July 5.
The Red Rider, Silver, (nt), *WS*, July 12.
The Boy in the Wilderness, Baxter, (nt), *WS*, July 19.

The Brute, Baxter, (nt), *WS,* July 26.
The Love of Danger, Brand, (sl), *WS,* August 2.
The Race, Baxter, (nt), *WS,* August 9.
Hired by Dad, Baxter, (nt), *WS,* September 6.
The Conquering Heart, Brand, (s), *AA,* September 13.
Blackie and Red, Brand, (nt), *WS,* September 13.
Larramee's Ranch, Baxter, (sl), *WS,* September 13.
Clovelly, Brand, (sl), *AA,* September 27.
When "Red" Was White, Brand, (nt), *WS,* October 4.
In the Hills of Monterey, Frederick, (sl), *WS,* October 4.
Champion of Lost Causes, Brand, (sl), *FD,* October 11.
Chick's Fall, Brand, (nt), *WS,* November 15.
Billy Angel, Trouble Lover, Baxter, (nt), *WS,* November 22.
The Third Bullet, Brand, (nt), *WS,* December 13.
Mountain Made, Baxter, (sl), *WS,* December 13.
Fortune's Christmas, Brand, (nt), *WS,* December 20.
Dark Rosaleen, Brand, (sl-nt), *CG,* December 27.

BOOKS

Dan Barry's Daughter, Brand, G. P. Putnam's Sons, New York, January 18.
The Range-Land Avenger, Baxter, Chelsea House, New York, September 22.
Bull Hunter, Manning, Chelsea House, New York, December 19.
Bull Hunter's Romance, Manning, Chelsea House, December 26.

1925

MAGAZINE AND NEWSPAPER WORK

The Black Rider, Brand, (nt), *WS,* January 3.
Beyond the Outposts, Morland, (sl), *WS,* January 24.
The Crime by the River, Brand, (sl-nt), *DS,* February 21.
Blackie's Last Stand, Brand, (nt), *WS,* March 7.
Señor Jingle Bells, Brand, (sl), *AA,* March 7.
The Black Signal, Brand, (nt), *WS,* March 21.
Lew and Slim, Brand, (nt), *WS,* April 4.
In the River Bottom's Grip, Brand, (nt), *WS,* April 11.
In Dread of the Law, Baxter, (nt), *WS,* April 18.
Going Straight, Baxter, (nt), *WS,* May 2.
The Battle for Mike, Baxter, (nt), *WS,* May 16.

The Survivor, Brand, (sl), *WS*, May 23.
The Outlaw Redeemer, Baxter, (nt), *WS*, May 30.
His Fight for a Pardon, Baxter, (nt), *WS*, June 27.
The Squaw Boy, Morland, (sl), *WS*, July 4.
On the Trail of Four, Brand, (sl), *WS*, August 15.
Fire Brain, Baxter, (sl), *WS*, September 12.
Sammy Gregg's Mustang Herd, Brand, (nt), *WS*, October 3.
Gregg's Coach Line, Brand, (nt), *WS*, October 17.
The Runaways, Baxter, (sl), *WS*, October 24.
Sammy Gregg and the Posse, Brand, (nt), *WS*, October 31.
Not the Fastest Horse, Frederick, (nt), *WS*, November 7.
The Range Finder, Morland, (nt), *WS*, November 14.
Brother of the Beasts, Brand, (nt), *WS*, November 28.
The White Cheyenne, Morland, (sl), *WS*, December 12.
No Man's Friend, Brand, (nt), *WS*, December 26.

BOOKS

The Bronze Collar, Frederick, G. P. Putnam's Sons, New York, February 14.
Jerry Peyton's Notched Inheritance, Manning, Chelsea House, New York, May 9.
Jim Curry's Test, Manning, Chelsea House, New York, May 16.
King Charlie's Riders, Manning, Chelsea House, New York, May 16.
The Shadow of Silver Tip, Baxter, Chelsea House, New York, June 6.
Beyond the Outpost, Morland, G. P. Putnam's Sons, New York, October 23.
The Black Signal, Manning, Chelsea House, New York, December 5.
Wooden Guns, Baxter, Chelsea House, New York, December 26.

1926

MAGAZINE AND NEWSPAPER WORK

The Tyrant, Challis, (sl), *WS*, January 9.
Sandy Sweyn Comes Out of the Wilds, Brand, (nt), *WS*, January 16.
The Good Bad-Man, Baxter, (nt), *WS*, January 30.
Bluejay, Brand, (sl), *WS*, February 20.
The Man He Couldn't Get, Baxter, (nt), *WS*, February 27.

The White Wolf, Frederick, (sl), *WS*, March 6.
The Vamp's Bandit, Baxter, (nt), *WS*, March 20.
A Son of Danger, Brand, (sl), *WS*, April 17.
Trail of the Stone-that-Shines, Morland, (sl), *WS*, May 29.
The Thunderer, Brand, (sl-nt), *CG*, June 4.
Acres of Unrest, Brand, (sl), *WS*, June 12,
Bad Man's Gulch, Baxter, (nt), *WS*, July 17.
The Fugitive, Brand, (nt), *WS*, July 24.
Western Tommy, Frederick, (sl), *WS*, July 24.
The Valley of Jewels, Brand, (nt), *WS*, August 21.
Trouble Trail, Baxter, (sl), *WS*, August 28.
The Border Bandit, Brand, (nt), *WS*, September 25.
The Border Bandit's Indian Brother, Brand, (nt), *WS*, October 2.
The Border Bandit's Prize, Brand, (nt), *WS*, October 9.
Jokers Extra Wild, Brand, (nt), *SS*, October 10.
The Iron Trail, Brand, (sl), *WS*, October 30.
The Bells of San Filipo, Baxter, (sl), *WS*, November 6.
Comanche, Brand, (sl), *FW*, December.
Werewolf, Brand, (nt), *WS*, December 18.

BOOKS

Blackie and Red, Manning, Chelsea House, New York, March 13.
Fire Brain, Brand, G. P. Putnam's Sons, New York, March 19.
The Splendid Rascal, Challis, Bobbs-Merrill, Indianapolis, May 14
The Brute, Manning, Chelsea House, New York, May 29.
Train's Trust, Baxter, Chelsea House, New York, June 19.
Ronicky Doone, Manning, Chelsea House, New York, July 24.
The White Wolf, Brand, G. P. Putnam's Sons, New York,
    September 17.
Monsieur, Challis, Bobbs-Merrill, Indianapolis, November 11.
Ronicky Doone's Treasure, Manning, Chelsea House, New York,
    November 20.
The Whispering Outlaw, Baxter, Chelsea House, December 4.

1927

MAGAZINE AND NEWSPAPER WORK

The Canyon Coward, Brand, (nt), *WS*, January 15.
Smiling Charlie, Brand, (sl), *WS*, February 12.
Flaming Fortune, Baxter, (nt), *WS*, February 19.

Lightning Lumberjacks, Frederick, (nt), *WS*, March 12.
The Western Double, Baxter, (sl), *WS*, March 26.
Thunder Moon, Baxter, (sl), *FW*, April.
Peter Blue, One-Gun Man, Brand, (nt), *FW*, June.
The Desert Pilot, Brand, (nt), *WS*, June 4.
The City in the Sky, Brand (sl), *WS*, June 11.
The Terrible Tenderfoot, Baxter, (nt), *WS*, July 2.
The Gentle Desperado, Baxter, (nt), *WS*, July 16.
Tiger, Tiger! Baxter, (nt), *WS*, July 30.
Sawdust and Sixguns, Brand, (sl), *FW*, August.
The Silver Stork, Brand, (sl), *WS*, August 13.
Red Wind and Thunder Moon, Baxter, (nt), *WS*, August 27.
Thunder Moon—Pale Face, Baxter, (nt), *WS*, September 17.
Thunder Moon—Squawman, Baxter, (sl), *WS*, September 24.
A Lucky Dog, Frederick, (s), *WS*, October 22.
Pleasant Jim, Brand, (sl), *WS*, October 22.
Forgotten Treasure, Baxter, (nt), *WS*, November 19.

BOOKS

On the Trail of Four, Manning, Chelsea House, January 15.
The Mountain Fugitive, Manning, Chelsea House, New York, March 19.
The Blue Jay, Brand, Dodd, Mead, New York, March 26.
The Trail to San Triste, Baxter, Chelsea House, New York, April 2.
The Sword Lover, Frederick, Henry Watterson Company, New York, May 10.
Western Tommy, Manning, Chelsea House, New York, June 18.
Bandit's Honor, Manning, Chelsea House, New York, July 23.
The Outlaw Tamer, Manning, Chelsea House, New York, August 13.
The Mustang Herder, Manning, Chelsea House, New York, November 19.

1928

MAGAZINE AND NEWSPAPER WORK

Weakling of the Wild, Brand, (sl), *WS*, January 14.
Tragedy Trail, Baxter, (sl), *WS*, February 25.
The Path to Plunder, Brand, (sl), *WS*, March 17.

Outlaw Valley, Brand, (sl), *FW*, April.
The Magic Gun, Frederick, (nt), *WS*, April 7.
The Gun Tamer, Baxter, (sl), *WS*, April 28.
Three on the Trail, Brand, (sl), *WS*, May 12.
Coward of the Clan, Morland, (nt), *WS*, May 19.
The Man from the Sky, Morland, (nt), *WS*, June 2.
Prairie Pawn, Morland, (nt), *WS*, June 16.
The Brass Man, Baxter, (sl), *WS*, June 23.
Fugitive's Fire, Morland, (nt), *WS*, June 30.
Gunman's Goal, Brand, (nt), *WS*, July 14.
Pillar Mountain, Frederick, (sl), *WS*, August 4.
The Bright Face of Danger, Brand, (nt), *WS*, August 18.
Riders for Fortune, Baxter, (sl), *WS*, September 15.
Through Steel and Stone, Brand, (nt), *WS*, September 29.
The House of Gold, Brand, (nt), *WS*, October 13.
Silver Trail, Brand, (sl), *WS*, October 27.
Thunder Moon Goes White, Baxter, (nt), *WS*, November 3.
The Lion's Share, Baxter, (nt), *WS*, December 1.
Singing Guns, Baxter, (sl), *WS*, December 15.
The Flaming Rider, Morland, (nt), *WS*, December 29.

BOOKS

Pleasant Jim, Brand, Dodd, Mead, New York, January 28.
The Trap at Comanche Bend, Manning, Chelsea House, New York, February 18.
Gun Gentlemen, Manning, Chelsea House, New York, April 14.
Señor Jingle Bells, Manning, Chelsea House, New York, June 16.
Lost Wolf, Morland, Macy-Masius, New York, August 24.
Pillar Mountain, Brand, Dodd, Mead, New York, September 14.
Children of Night, Brand, L. Harper Allen Co., New York.

1929

MAGAZINE AND NEWSPAPER WORK

The Stranger, Brand, (sl), *WS*, January 12.
Mistral, Brand, (sl), *AW*, January 27.
Hunted Hunters, Baxter, (nt), *WS*, February 16.
The Winged Horse, Frederick, (sl), *WS*, February 16.
The Trail to Manhood, Brand, (sl), *WS*, April 13.
Blood and Iron, Brand, (sl), *MU*, May.

Strength of the Hills, Baxter, (sl), *WS*, May 25.
The Return of Geraldi, Brand, (nt), *WS*, June 29.
Rustlers' Rock, Manning, (sl), *WS*, July 6.
Chinook, Frederick, (sl), *WS*, July 13.
While Bullets Sang, Brand, (nt), *WS*, August 17.
Happy Valley, Baxter, (sl), *WS*, August 24.
Geraldi in the Haunted Hills, Brand, (nt), *WS*, August 31.
The Danger Lover, Manning, (nt), *WS*, September 7.
The Duster, Brand, (nt), *WS*, November 2.
Two Bronchos, Baxter, (sl), *WS*, November 9.
Twisted Bars, Brand, (nt), *WS*, November 16.
The Duster's Return, Brand, (nt), *WS*, November 30.
The Horizon of Danger, Morland, (sl), *WS*, December 21.

BOOKS
The Gun Tamer, Brand, Dodd, Mead, New York, January 4.
Tiger Man, Baxter, The Macaulay Company, New York, February 15.
Mistral, Brand, Dodd, Mead, New York, June 14.

1930

MAGAZINE AND NEWSPAPER WORK
Twelve Peers, Brand, (sl), *WS*, February 1.
Cayenne Charlie, Baxter, (nt), *WS*, February 22.
Tiger's Den, Frederick, (sl), *WS*, March 15.
Two Masters, Brand, (nt), *WS*, April 5.
The Golden Coyote, Manning, (s), *WS*, April 12.
White Hunger, Manning, (s), *WS*, April 26.
Happy Jack, Baxter, (sl), *WS*, April 26.
Sixteen in Nome, Brand, (nt), *WS*, May 3.
Battle's End, Brand, (nt), *WS*, May 10.
"Mother," Manning, (s), *WS*, May 17.
Shiver-Nose, Manning (s), *WS*, May 24.
Yellow Dog, Manning, (s), *WS*, May 31.
Back to His Own, Manning, (s), *WS*, June 7.
The Stingaree, Brand, (sl), *WS*, June 7.
The Golden Cat, Brand, (sl), *AW*, July 13.
Daring Duval, Baxter, (sl), *WS*, July 19.
The Mask of Ching Wo, Brand, (sl), *RR*, August.

Trouble's Messenger, Baxter, (sl), *WS*, September 6.
Rippon Rides Double, Brand, (sl), *WS*, October 18.
On Fortune's Back, Baxter, (sl), *WS*, December 6.

BOOKS

Mystery Ranch, Brand, Dodd, Mead, New York, January 4.
Destry Rides Again, Brand, Dodd, Mead, New York, August 22.

1931

MAGAZINE AND NEWSPAPER WORK

Chip and the Cactus Man, Brand, (nt), *WS*, January 10.
Chip Champions a Lady, Brand, (nt), *WS*, January 24.
Chip Traps a Sheriff, Brand, (nt), *WS*, January 31.
Twenty Notches, Brand, (sl), *WS*, March 14.
Golden Day, Brand, (s), *LM*, April 25.
Duck Hawk's Master, Baxter, (sl), *WS*, April 25.
Valley Vultures, Brand, (sl), *WS*, May 30.
Treasure Well, Baxter, (nt), *WS*, June 27.
Outlaw's Conscience, Baxter, (nt), *WS*, July 11.
The Rancher Returns, Frederick, (sl), *WS*, July 21.
Clean Courage, Baxter, (nt), *WS*, July 25.
The Rose of India, Brand, (s), *CH*, August.
Golden Lightning, Brand, (sl), *WS*, August 22.
Gun Pearl Trail, Baxter, (sl), *WS*, September 12.
Spot Lester, Brand, (nt), *WS*, October 17.
Tamer of the Wild, Morland, (sl), *WS*, October 24.
Nine Lives, Brand, (nt), *WS*, October 31.
Torture Canyon, Brand, (nt), *WS*, November 14.
Tramp Magic, Brand, (sl), *WS*, November 21.
Hawks and Eagles, Baxter, (nt), *WS*, December 5.
Black Snake and Gun, Baxter, (nt), *WS*, December 19.

BOOKS

Smiling Charlie, Brand, Dodd, Mead, New York, January 2.
The Killers, Baxter, The Macaulay Company, New York, June 4.
The Happy Valley, Brand, Dodd, Mead, New York, June 19.

1932

MAGAZINE AND NEWSPAPER WORK

Black-Snake Joe, Baxter, (nt), *WS*, January 2.
Dogs of the Captain, Brand, (sl), *WS*, January 2.

The Lightning Runner, Frederick, (sl), *WS*, January 9.
The Three Crosses, Baxter, (nt), *WS*, January 23.
White-Water Sam, Morland, (nt), *WS*, January 30.
Speedy — Deputy, Brand, (nt), *WS*, February 13.
White Wolf, Baxter, (sl), *WS*, February 13.
Outlaw Crew, Brand, (nt), *WS*, February 20.
Rancher's Legacy, Morland, (sl), *WS*, February 20.
Seven-Day Lawman, Brand, (nt), *WS*, February 27.
The Best Bandit, Manning, (nt), *WS*, March 5.
Speedy's Mare, Brand, (nt), *WS*, March 12.
Carcajou's Trail, Brand, (nt), *WS*, March 26.
The Golden Spurs, Manning, (sl), *WS*, March 26.
Speedy's Crystal Game, Brand, (nt), *WS*, April 2.
Lucky Larribee, Baxter, (sl), *WS*, April 2.
Mountain Raiders, Morland, (nt), *WS*, April 9.
Red Rock's Secret, Brand, (nt), *WS*, April 16.
Rawhide Bound, Morland, (nt), *WS*, April 23.
Speedy's Bargain, Brand, (nt), *WS*, May 14.
Greaser Trail, Morland, (nt), *WS*, May 21
Range Jester, Brand, (nt), *WS*, May 28.
Paradise Al, Manning, (nt), *WS*, June 4.
The Geraldi Trail, Brand, (sl), *WS*, June 11.
The Nighthawk Trail, Brand, (nt), *WS*, July 9.
Paradise Al's Confession, Manning, (nt), *WS*, July 16.
Mighty Lobo, Baxter, (sl), *WS*, July 23.
Outlaws from Afar, Brand, (nt), *WS*, August 20.
Torturous Trek, Brand, (sl), *WS*, August 27.
The Law Dodger at Windy Creek, Brand, (nt), *WS*, September 24.
All for One, Baxter, (sl), *WS*, October 1.
Thunderbolt, Brand, (sl-nt), *SP*, October 25.
Smoking Guns, Brand, (nt), *WS*, October 29.
The Invisible Outlaw, Brand, (sl), *WS*, November 5.
The Two-Handed Man, Baxter, (nt), *WS*, December 3.
Cat Hill Fugitive, Brand, (sl), *WS*, December 10.
The Longhorn Feud, Brand, (sl), *AR*, December 10.
BOOKS
Valley Vultures, Brand, Dodd, Mead, New York, January 2.

Twenty Notches, Brand, Dodd, Mead, New York, June 17.
The Jackson Trail, Brand, Dodd, Mead, New York, October 28.

1933

MAGAZINE AND NEWSPAPER WORK

Señor Billy, Baxter, (nt), *WS*, January 7.
Montana Rides, Evan, (sl), *WS*, January 14.
Speedy's Desert Dance, Brand, (nt), *WS*, January 28.
Steel Cut Steel, Brand, (sl), *DF*, January 28.
The Red Bandanna, Baxter, (nt), *WS*, February 4.
Printed Bait, Frederick, (s), *DS*, February 25.
Luck and a Horse, Brand, (sl-nt), *AW*, February 26.
Death Rides Behind, Brand, (nt), *DW*, March.
The Wolf and the Man, Baxter, (sl), *WS*, March 4.
The Stolen Stallion, Brand, (bln), *WS*, March 11.
The Masterman, Brand, (sl), *AR*, March 18.
Silvertip, Brand, (bln), *WS*, March 25.
Mercy Anne, Brand, (s), *IL*, April.
The Man from Mustang, Brand, (bln), *WS*, April 15.
Gunman's Gold, Frederick, (sl), *WS*, April 22.
Brothers of the West, Brand, (bln), *WS*, April 29.
The Quest, Brand, (nt), *WM*, May.
Silver's Strike, Brand, (bln), *WS*, May 20.
Horseshoe Flat's Speedy Stranger, Brand, (bln), *WS*, June 10.
Kingbird's Pursuit, Baxter, (sl), *WS*, June 10.
Black Thunder, Brand, (nt), *DW*, July.
The Trail of the Eagle, Brand, (nt), *WM*, July.
The False Rider, Brand, (bln), *WS*, July 1.
Riding Straight in Danger, Brand, (bln), *WS*, July 22.
Guardian Guns, Brand, (nt), *DW*, August.
The Iron Collar, Brand, (bln), *WS*, August 5.
The Fighting Four, Brand, (bln), *WS*, August 26.
Jingo, Brand, (bln), *WS*, September 9.
The White Indian, Brand, (sl), *AR*, September 9.
The Happy Rider, Baxter, (sl), *WS*, September 9.
Silver's Search, Brand, (bln), *WS*, September 23.
Only the Young Fear Death, Faust, (p), *HM*, October.
Valley Thieves, Brand, (sl-bln), *WS*, October 28.

Paston's Glory, Brand, (s), *AD*, November.
Reata, Baxter, (nt), *WS*, November 11.
Reata's Danger Trail, Baxter, (nt), *WS*, November 25.
Reata's Desert Ride, Baxter, (nt), *WS*, December 9.
Blue Water Bad Men, Brand, (sl-bln), *WS*, December 16.
The Red Pacer, Baxter, (sl), *AR*, December 16.
The Dark Peril, Brand, (sl), *DF*, December 16.
Reata and the Hidden Gold, Baxter, (nt), *WS*, December 23.

BOOKS

Slow Joe, Brand, Dodd, Mead, New York, January 3.
Montana Rides! Evans, Harper & Brothers, New York, June 1.
The Longhorn Feud, Brand, Dodd, Mead, New York, June 16.
The Return of the Rancher, Austin, Dodd, Mead, New York, July 28.
The Outlaw, Brand, Dodd, Mead, New York, October 13.
The Thunderer, M.B., Derrydale Press, New York, November 6.

1934

MAGAZINE AND NEWSPAPER WORK

The Wedding Guest, Faust, (s), *HM*, January.
Stolen Gold, Baxter, (nt), *WS*, January 6.
Reata and the Overland Kid, Baxter, (nt), *WS*, January 20.
A Special Occasion, Faust, (s), *HM*, February.
The Tough Tenderfoot, Brand, (sl), *WS*, February 3.
The Naked Blade, Challis, (sl), *AR*, February 10.
Reata's Peril Trek, Baxter, (nt), *WS*, March 17.
Brother of the Cheyennes, Brand, (sl), *AR*, March 17.
X, the Murderer, Brand, (sl), *DF*, March 17.
Beyond the Finish, Brand, (s), *CO*, March 24.
Gun Gift, Brand, (sl), *WS*, March 24.
Gunman's Bluff, Brand, (s), *SW*, April.
Montana Rides Again, Evans, (sl), *AR*, April 28.
Lawmen's Heart, Brand, (s), *SW*, May.
Man Beyond the Law, Brand, (s), *SW*, June.
Valley of Vanishing Men, Brand, (sl-bln), *WS*, June 2.
Challenger, Brand, (s), *AM*, July.
Gallows Gamble, Brand, (s), *SW*, July.
Cross Over Nine, Brand, (sl), *DF*, July 7.

The Flood, Brand, (s), *SS*, August 25.

One Man Posse, Brand, (s), *MM*, September.

Gunless Gunman, Brand, (s), *SW*, September.

Sleeper Pays a Debt, Brand, (s), *MM*, October.

Outcast Breed, Brand, (s), *SW*, October.

Wet Money, Brand, (s), *DD*, October 1.

Scourge of the Rio Grande, Brand, (sl), *AR*, October 20.

Satan's Gun Rider, Brand, (s), *MM*, November.

Gunman's Rendezvous, Brand, (s), *SW*, November.

Nine Parts Devil, Brand, (s), *DD*, November 1.

Man of the West, Brand, (sl), *WS*, November 10.

The Unnumbered Door, Brand, (s), *DD*, November 15.

The Firebrand, Challis, (sl-nt), *AR*, November 24.

The Sun Stood Still, Brand, (s), *AM*, December.

Sleeper Turns Horse-Thief, Brand, (s), *MM*, December.

Bad News for Bad Men, Owen, (s), *WS*, December 8.

Name Your Price, Brand, (sl-nt), *LM*, December 15.

The Red Well, Owen, (s), *WS*, December 29.

BOOKS

Timbal Gulch Trail, Brand, Dodd, Mead, New York, January 3.

Call of the Blood, Baxter, The Macaulay Company, New York, January 22.

The Sheriff Rides, Austin, Dodd, Mead, New York, March 14.

The Rancher's Revenge, Brand, Dodd, Mead, New York, June 20.

Montana Rides Again, Evans, Harper & Brothers, New York, September 21.

Red Devil of the Range, Baxter, The Macaulay Company, New York, October 25.

Brothers on the Trail, Brand, Dodd, Mead, New York, November 1.

1935

MAGAZINE AND NEWSPAPER WORK

The Captain, Brand, (s), *MC*, January.

The Strange Villa, Brand, (s), *DF*, January 5.

The Little Father of Death, Brand, (s), *DF*, January 12.

The Scarred Back, Brand, (s), *DF*, January 26.

The Fighting Coward, Owen, (s), *WS*, January 26.

Charlie, Brand, (s), *AM*, February.

The Great Betrayal, Challis, (sl-nt), *AR*, February 2.

Rifle Pass, Brand, (s), *AR*, February 9.

The Man in the Shroud, Brand, (s), *DF*, February 9.

Sun and Sand, Owen, (s), *WS*, February 16.

Crazy Rhythm, Brand, (s), *AR*, March 2.

Island of Safety, Brand, (s), *MC*, April.

Gun-Fighters in Hell, Brand, (s), *SW*, April.

The Storm, Challis, (sl-nt), *AR*, April 6.

Treason Against a King, Brand, (nt), *DF*, April 13.

The Gilded Box, Brand, (s), *DF*, April 27.

Paradise, Brand, (s), *EM*, May.

Wings over Moscow, Brand, (s), *DF*, May 11.

The Downfall, Brand, (s), *DF*, May 25.

The Cat and the Perfume, Challis, (s), *AR*, June 8.

Hummingbirds and Honeysuckle, Brand, (s), *ES*, July.

Claws of the Tigress, Challis, (nt), *AR*, July 13.

The Blackbirds Sing, Lawton, (sl), *AR*, July 20.

The Bait and the Trap, Challis, (s), *AR*, August 3.

The Sacred Valley, Brand, (sl), *AR*, August 10.

The Pearls of Bonfadini, Challis, (s), *AR*, August 24.

The Dew of Heaven, Challis, (sl), *AR*, September 7.

"—Murder Me!," Brand, (sl), *DF*, September 21.

Beggar My Tailor, Brand, (s), *AD*, October 1.

Thoroughbred, Brand, (s), *CO*, November 30.

The Bamboo Whistle, Brand, (sl), *DF*, December 7.

Perique, Lawton, (sl), *AR*, December 14.

BOOKS

The Seven of Diamonds, Brand, Dodd, Mead, New York, January 2.

King of the Range, Austin, Dodd, Mead, New York, January 17.

Hunted Riders, Brand, Dodd, Mead, New York, July 17.

Brother of the Cheyennes, Baxter, The Macaulay Company, New York, October 4.

Rustlers of Beacon Creek, Brand, Dodd, Mead, New York, October 23.

Cross Over Nine, Butler, The Macaulay Company, New York, December 20.

1936

MAGAZINE AND NEWSPAPER WORK

The Streak, Brand, (sl), *AR*, January 25.

The Small World, Brand, (s), *CO*, February 8.

Internes Can't Take Money, Brand, (s), *CM*, March.

The Song of the Whip, Evans, (sl), *AR*, March 28.

Big Game, Brand, (sl), *AR*, May 9.

Masquerade, Brand, (s), *AM*, June.

Wine in the Desert, Brand, (s), *TM*, June 7.

Fixed, Brand, (s), *CO*, June 13.

The Golden Knight, Challis, (sl), *AR*, June 20.

The Singular Horseman, Brand, (s), *CO*, June 27.

The Kinsale, Faust, (s), *SE*, June 27.

The Hound of the Hunter, Brand, (s), *MC*, July.

The Last Stretch, Brand, (s), *CO*, July 18.

The Granduca, Brand, (sl), *DF*, July 25.

The Black O'Rourke, Faust, (s), *SE*, August 8.

Seven Faces, Brand, (sl), *DF*, October 17.

Five Minutes to Twelve, Brand, (s), *CM*, November.

A Seabold Fights, Brand, (sl), *MA*, November 15.

BOOKS

Happy Jack, Brand, Dodd, Mead, New York, January 8.

Secret Agent Number One, Frost, Macrae-Smith, Philadelphia, April 15.

The Song of the Whip, Evans, Harper & Brothers, New York, May 20.

The King Bird Rides, Brand, Dodd, Mead, New York, June 30.

The Night Flower, Butler, The Macaulay Company, New York, July 24.

South of Rio Grande, Brand, Dodd, Mead, New York, October 28.

1937

MAGAZINE AND NEWSPAPER WORK

Bulldog, Brand, (s), *BM*, January.

Viva! Viva! Brand, (s), *AR*, January 2.

The American, Challis, (s), *AR*, February 27.

Johnny Comes Lately, Faust, (s), *SE*, March 6.

Pretty Boy, Brand, (sl), *AR*, March 20.
Dust Storm, Brand, (s), *CO*, April 3.
Six Golden Angels, Brand, (sl), *CO*, April 10.
War For Sale, Brand, (sl), *AR*, April 24.
The Face and the Doctor, Brand, (sl-nt), *DF*, May 22.
The Smoking Land, Challis, (sl), *AR*, May 29.
Devil Fly Away, Brand, (s), *AM*, June.
The Voice from the Record, Brand, (sl-s), *TM*, June 6.
Bottle in the Sea, Brand, (s), *AR*, June 12.
Just Irish, Brand, (s), *AR*, June 19.
The Platinum Watch, Brand, (sl-nt), *AW*, June 27.
To Meet in the Sun, Brand, (s), *AC*, July.
"Nifty," Brand, (s), *CM*, July.
The Death of Love, Brand, (s), *DF*, July 24.
The Nameless Member, Brand, (s), *AC*, August.
The Saint, Brand, (s), *AD*, August.
Outlaw Buster, Brand, (nt), *CW*, August.
Virginia Creeper, Brand, (s), *EM*, August.
Unhappy Landings, Brand, (s), *AC*, September.
Bright Danger, Brand, (sl-nt), *LM*, September 4.
Brothers in the Sky, Brand, (s), *AC*, October.
The Champion, Brand, (s), *AF*, November.
Three in the Dark, Faust, (s), *AM*, November.
Something Honest, Brand, (s), *DB*, November.
Dust Across the Range, Brand, (sl-nt), *AM*, November.
A Friend in the Night, Brand, (s), *TM*, November 28.
Lake Tyndal, Brand, (s), *AF*, December.
They Stand So Tall, Baxter, (s), *AM*, December.
Pringle's Luck, Brand, (s), *CM*, December.
The Hill of Gasquet, Brand, (s), *CO*, December 4.
BOOKS
Trouble Trail, Brand, Dodd, Mead, New York, January 6.
Spy Meets Spy, Frost, Macrae-Smith, Philadelphia, February 8.
The Streak, Brand, Dodd, Mead, New York, June 22.
The Golden Knight, Challis, Greystone Press, New York, October 5.
The Bamboo Whistle, Frost, Macrae-Smith, Philadelphia, October 18.
Six Golden Angels, Brand, Dodd, Mead, New York, October 27.

1938

MAGAZINE AND NEWSPAPER WORK

Blind Bluff, Brand, (s), *AF*, January.

Partners, Faust, (s), *AM*, January.

The Seventh Day, Brand, (sl), *MA*, January 1.

A Silence in Tappan Valley, Brand, (s), *TM*, January 9.

Eagles over Crooked Creek, Brand, (s), *WS*, January 29.

Forty-Cent Fare, Brand, (s), *TM*, January 30.

Whistle Thrice, Brand, (s), *AF*, February.

The Old Bean, Brand, (s), *CM*, February.

Turn of the Road, Brand, (s), *TM*, February 13.

The Silent Witness, Brand, (s), *BM*, March.

Nine Flights to Waterloo, Brand, (s), *AF*, March-April.

Whiskey Sour, Brand, (s), *CM*, April.

Flower of Hell, Brand, (sl-nt), *TM*, April 24.

The Bells of San Carlos, Brand, (s), *AR*, April 30.

What Price Story! Brand, (s), *AM*, May.

Speak No Evil, Brand, (s), *AF*, May-June.

The Living Ghost, Brand, (sl), *AR*, May 7.

Devil Dog, Brand, (s), *MA*, June 15.

Señor Coyote, Brand, (sl-nt), *AR*, June 18.

Fifteen Hundred Million, Brand, (s), *AF*, July-August.

The Flaming Finish, Brand, (s), *BB*, August.

Last Flight, Brand, (s), *BB*, September.

Late Summer Song, Brand, (s), *LM*, September 10.

The Return of the Man Who Was Killed, Brand, (s), *BB*, October.

Death and Jimmy Warner, Brand, (s), *CM*, November.

Young Doctor Kildare, Brand, (sl-nt), *AR*, December 17.

BOOKS

The Iron Trail, Brand, Dodd, Mead, New York, January 5.

The Naked Blade, Challis, Greystone Press, New York, June 2.

Singing Guns, Brand, Dodd, Mead, New York, June 18.

Dead or Alive, Brand, Dodd, Mead, New York, October 11.

1939

MAGAZINE AND NEWSPAPER WORK

True Steel, Brand, (s), *BB*, February.

Half a Partner, Brand, (s), *BB*, March.

Calling Doctor Kildare, Brand, (sl-nt), *AR*, March 25.
The Secret of Doctor Kildare, Brand, (nt), *CM*, September.
Miniature, Brand, (s), *GH*, September.
Level Landings, Brand, (s), *GH*, October.

BOOKS

Marble Face, Brand, Dodd, Mead, New York, January 3.
Fightin' Fool, Brand, Dodd, Mead, New York, June 20.
Gunman's Gold, Brand, Dodd, Mead, New York, September 19.

1940

MAGAZINE AND NEWSPAPER WORK

Doctor Kildare's Girl, Brand, (nt), *PM*, April.
Doctor Kildare Goes Home, Brand, (sl-nt), *AR*, June 1.
My People, Brand, (s), *CM*, August.
A Watch and the Wilderness, Brand, (s), *EM*, September.
Doctor Kildare's Crisis, Brand, (sl-nt), *AR*, December 21.

BOOKS

The Dude, Brand, Dodd Mead, New York, January 2.
The Secret of Dr. Kildare, Brand, Dodd, Mead, New York,
    February 7.
Danger Trail, Brand, Dodd, Mead, New York, June 18.
Calling Dr. Kildare, Brand, Dodd, Mead, New York, August 19.
Wine on the Desert and Other Stories, Brand, Dodd, Mead, New
    York, September 24. (Includes *Wine on the Desert, A Watch
    and the Wilderness, The Kinsale, Lew Corbin, Gentleman,
    The Luck of Pringle, The Small World, Hummingbirds and
    Honeysuckle, Internes Can't Take Money, Men Get Old, A
    Special Occasion, Charlie, The Wedding Guest, Fixed*, and the
    previously unpublished *Our Daily Bread* and *Oh, Wonderful!*)
Riders of the Plains, Brand, Dodd, Mead, New York, October 8.

1941

MAGAZINE AND NEWSPAPER WORK

Dead Man's Passport, Brand, (sl), *AW*, January 12.
Luck of the Spindrift, Brand, (sl), *BB*, April.
The People vs. Doctor Kildare, Brand, (nt), *CM*, May.
East Wind, Brand, (s), *AR*, July 5.
Cure for a Liar, Brand, (s), *TM*, August 31.

Seven-Mile House, Brand, (sl-nt), *AR*, October 4.

BOOKS

The Border Kid, Brand, Dodd, Mead, New York, January 7.
Young Dr. Kildare, Brand, Dodd, Mead, New York, February 11.
The Long Chance, Brand, Dodd, Mead, New York, June 17.
Dr. Kildare Takes Charge, Brand, Dodd, Mead, New York, August 19.
Vengeance Trail, Brand, Dodd, Mead, New York, October 7.

1942

MAGAZINE AND NEWSPAPER WORK

Distance, Faust, (p), *HM*, January.
Doctor Kildare's Hardest Case, Brand, (s), *CM*, March.
Taming of Red Thunder, Brand, (s), *ES*, September.

BOOKS

Silvertip, Brand, Dodd, Mead, New York, January 6.
Dr. Kildare's Crisis, Brand, Dodd, Mead, New York, January 20.
The Man from Mustang, Brand, Dodd, Mead, New York, June 16.
Dr. Kildare's Trial, Brand, Dodd, Mead, New York, August 11.
Silvertip's Strike, Brand, Dodd, Mead, New York, October 6.

1943

MAGAZINE AND NEWSPAPER WORK

The Freeing of Yovan, Brand, (s), *ES*, July.
Survival, Brand, (s), *AR*, September.

BOOKS

Dr. Kildare's Search, Brand, Dodd, Mead, New York, January 19.
Silvertip's Round-Up, Brand, Dodd, Mead, New York, February 9.
Silvertip's Trap, Brand, Dodd, Mead, New York, August 17.

1944

MAGAZINE AND NEWSPAPER WORK

"Mister Christmas," Brand, (sl-s), *BE*, January 23.
After April, Faust, (sl), *SE*, June 10.
By Their Works, Brand, (s), *AR*, August.

BOOKS

Silvertip's Chase, Brand, Dodd, Mead, New York, February 8.
The Fighting Four, Brand, Dodd, Mead, New York, August 22.

1945

MAGAZINE AND NEWSPAPER WORK

First-class Gentleman, Faust, (s), *LM*, January 27.

BOOKS

Silvertip's Search, Brand, Dodd, Mead, New York, February 7.
The Stolen Stallion, Brand, Dodd, Mead, New York, August 14.

1946

BOOKS

Valley Thieves, Brand, Dodd, Mead, New York, February 12.
Mountain Riders, Brand, Dodd, Mead, New York, June 18.

1947

BOOKS

The Border Bandit, Evans, Harper & Brothers, New York, January 8.
Valley of Vanishing Men, Brand, Dodd, Mead, New York, January 14.
The False Rider, Brand, Dodd, Mead, New York, June 23.

1948

MAGAZINE AND NEWSPAPER WORK

Honor Bright, Brand, (s), *CM*, November.
The King, Brand, (s), *TM*, November 21.
The West Wind, Uriel, (p), *FF*, December. (The text of this poem appeared originally, untitled, as part of the text of the novel *The Golden Knight*, by George Challis, which was published as a serial in *Argosy* in 1936 and as a book the following year. The poem is listed here because it appeared, titled, in the *Fabulous Faust Fanzine* under the name "Henry Uriel" and seems to be the only published use of the name under which Faust, as a young man, submitted several poems to editors.)

BOOKS

The Rescue of Broken Arrow, Evans, Harper & Brothers, New York, January 21.
Flaming Irons, Brand, Dodd, Mead, New York, February 9.
Hired Guns, Brand, Dodd, Mead, New York, July 19.

1949

BOOKS

Gunman's Legacy, Evans, Harper & Brothers, New York, January 5.
The Bandit of the Black Hills, Brand, Dodd, Mead, New York, January 10.
Seven Trails, Brand, Dodd, Mead, New York, May 9.

1950

BOOKS

Smuggler's Trail, Evans, Harper & Brothers, New York, January 4.
Single Jack, Brand, Dodd, Mead, New York, January 23.
The Firebrand, Challis, Harper & Brothers, New York, March 1.
Sawdust and Six Guns, Evans, Harper & Brothers, New York, July 5.
The Galloping Broncos, Brand, Dodd, Mead, New York, July 17.

1951

MAGAZINE AND NEWSPAPER WORK

The Thief, Brand, (s), *TM*, February 11. (This is a revision of *Our Daily Bread*, which appeared originally in Faust's first book of collected stories, *Wine on the Desert and Other Stories*, 1940.)

BOOKS

The Bait and the Trap, Challis, Harper & Brothers, New York, January 3.
The Hair-Trigger Kid, Brand, Dodd, Mead, New York, March 5.
Tragedy Trail, Brand, Dodd, Mead, New York, July 16.

1952

BOOKS

Border Guns, Brand, Dodd, Mead, New York, January 14.
Strange Courage, Evans, Harper & Brothers, New York, January 16.

1953

BOOKS

Outlaw Valley, Evans, Harper & Brothers, New York, January 7.
Smiling Desperado, Brand, Dodd, Mead, New York, February 2.
The Tenderfoot, Brand, Dodd, Mead, New York, August 17.

1954

BOOKS

Outlaw's Code, Evans, Harper & Brothers, January 6.

The Gambler, Brand, Dodd, Mead, New York, February 1.
The Invisible Outlaw, Brand, Dodd, Mead, New York, June 14.

1955

BOOKS

Speedy, Brand, Dodd, Mead, New York, January 31.
Outlaw Breed, Brand, Dodd, Mead, New York, June 20.

1956

BOOKS

The Big Trail, Brand, Dodd, Mead, New York, January 9.
Trail Partners, Brand, Dodd, Mead, New York, June 18.

1957

BOOKS

Lucky Larribee, Brand, Dodd, Mead, New York, February 8.
Notebooks and Poems of Max Brand, (p), Faust, Dodd, Mead, New York, May 20. (Includes the poems: "The Secret," "The Village Street," "A Song," "The Last Adventure," "On a Grecian Funeral Monument," "Sunday," "The Stars," "Only the Young Fear Death," "Distance," "Balin's Song to His Sword," "Song to Mars," Blondel's song from *The Golden Knight*, a passage from *Dionysus in Hades*, as well as the previously unpublished "I'll Have No Other Gods," "To My Soul," "What Love is There?" "Old Friends," "Rain," "So Poor," "The Island of Ios," "Time Gives Burdens," "I Wakened," "Dorothy Parker," "Ceyx and Halcyone," "La Belle France," "My Sweat," "Tom and Jerry," and passages from "Briareus," and "Gethsemane.")
Blood on the Trail, Brand, Dodd, Mead, New York, August 12.

1960

BOOKS

The White Cheyenne, Brand, Dodd, Mead, New York, January 11.
The Long Chase, Brand, Dodd, Mead, New York, June 15.

1962

BOOKS

Tamer of the Wild, Brand, Dodd, Mead, New York, February 26.
Mighty Lobo, Brand, Dodd, Mead, New York, June 18.

1963

BOOKS

The Stranger, Brand, Dodd, Mead, New York, January 14.
The Garden of Eden, Brand, Dodd, Mead, New York, October 14.

1964

BOOKS

Golden Lightning, Brand, Dodd, Mead, New York, January 13.
The Gentle Gunman, Brand, Dodd, Mead, New York, September 21.

1965

BOOKS

Torture Trail, Brand, Dodd, Mead, New York, February 22.
The Guns of Dorking Hollow, Brand, Dodd, Mead, New York, October 24.

1966

BOOKS

Ride the Wild Trail, Brand, Dodd, Mead, New York, February 21.
Larramee's Ranch, Brand, Dodd, Mead, New York, October 17.

1967

BOOKS

Max Brand's Best Stories, Brand, Dodd, Mead, New York, May 22. (Includes a general introduction, also brief prefaces to each of the following: *The King, Honor Bright, Wine on the Desert, Our Daily Bread, The Wolf Pack and the Kill* [from the autobiographical novel *Harrigan*], *Internes Can't Take Money, The Claws of the Tigress* [from the novel *The Bait and the Trap*], *The Silent Witness, The Kinsale, A Life for a Life* [from the novel *Calling Dr. Kildare*], *The Luck of Pringle, A Special Occasion, The Sun Stood Still.*)

1968

BOOKS

Rippon Rides Double, Brand, Dodd, Mead, New York, January 15.
The Stingaree, Brand, Dodd, Mead, New York, August 12.

1969 (first three months)

BOOKS

Thunder Moon, Brand, Dodd, Mead, New York, February 24.

FILM, RADIO,
AND TELEVISION APPENDIX

APPROXIMATELY a dozen films with which Faust was associated appeared after his death, among them *Three Men in White*, starring Lionel Barrymore, Van Johnson, and Ava Gardner; *Rainbow Over Texas*, with Roy Rogers and Dale Evans; *Branded*, with Alan Ladd and Mona Freeman; and *Destry Rides Again*—for the third time—starring Audie Murphy and Mari Blanchard.

Faust's peculiar contributions to film history included the perhaps still unequalled record established in 1921–22 when seven major films based on his work were released during a twelve-month period. The record was, as has been said, nearly equalled by him in 1943–44 when seven films with which his name was associated were released in a similar period. For good measure there were six films in eighteen months in 1939–40. He has, furthermore, been credited with creating a method of writing screen treatments which became standard. After Faust, they were frequently written in the present tense with action and dialogue as an integral part of the text, rather than as narrative with directions interpolated. As a further contribution, Faust authored the pivotal story, *Destry Rides Again*, which established a trend toward the reluctant western hero and the anti-hero, as well as toward satire, parody, and stage-show enjoyment of shoot-'em-up westerns.

In all, Faust can be identified with more than 70 films of various kinds, perhaps as many as 75, released over a period of 40 years, featuring more than four dozen stars and super-stars.

Radio broadcasts based on Faust's work began in the thirties and extended into the forties and fifties. In the beginning they were one-time-only programs based on individual stories and were aired on major stations in the New York area, such as WOR and WJZ. The stories included *A Silence in Tappan Valley*, which had appeared in *This Week*; *Whiskey Sour*, from *Cosmopolitan*; *What Price Story*, from *The American*; and *After April*, following its appearance in *The Saturday Evening Post*. CBS network broadcasts based on *Destry Rides Again* and on *Singing Guns* were aired in 1945 and in 1947. A Dr. Kildare weekly radio series began in 1949 and continued until 1952.

Faust's first stage show opened at the Imperial Theater on Broadway on April 23, 1959, in the form of David Merrick's production based on *Destry*. After a successful New York run, it toured the country and is still performed from time to time.

With the advent of television, Faust soon proved popular in a new medium. One-time-only telecasts began in 1949 when his exceptionally popular short story *What Price Story* was presented on the Colgate Theater of the Air. In addition to original magazine appearance and radio broadcast, *What Price Story* had been published under a new title, "Men Get Old," in the 1940 collection of stories, *Wine on the Desert*. It is characteristic of the qualities that made Faust's work popular in a variety of media. Burleigh is a celebrated war correspondent of legendary reputation but he is slipping; the spark has gone out of his work. Simmons is a cub reporter on his way up. They want the same girl. They are sent by the editor of their big city daily to run down a tip on the whereabouts of two most-wanted criminals. At the moment of truth, it is the supposedly fearless Burleigh with nerves of steel who funks out and gets killed, while the desperately frightened Simmons kills the two murderers in self-defense and gets the story—and the girl. In the excitement of a telephone report to his editor, Simmons finds himself acquiescing in the editor's assumption that it was of course the famous Burleigh who has killed the two thugs and nobly given his life, and not the inconspicuous Simmons. He realizes fiction is proving better than fact.

The myth is told under a four-column headline on next day's front page. Simmons gets a pat on the back from the editor and a twenty-dollar raise, but he and his girl know the truth.

What Price Story is a retelling of the myth of virtue and power passing from an aging and decadent father, or hero, to a courageous and deserving son, or successor. As ancient myth was supposed to do, it carried the seeds of life.

In 1955, Lux Video Theater televised an adaptation of the film scenario of *Branded*, based on *Montana Rides*, an Evan Evans novel.

303

The Dr. Kildare television series starring Richard Chamberlain and Raymond Massey, which began in 1961, was soon reaching a weekly audience estimated at more than 100 million in 33 countries. Chamberlain's fan mail was reported at 11,000 letters a week.

In 1963 a second Faust-based television series, this one suggested by *Destry*, began running concurrently with the Kildare series. Thus Faust was on national television twice weekly.

By the late sixties his public had taken on new dimensions. There were Dr. Kildare comic strips in daily newspapers and Kildare hosiery, toys, dolls, and chewing gum. Abroad, Faust had penetrated the Iron Curtain. According to *Time Magazine*, Polish Communist Party meetings had been rescheduled so as not to conflict with Dr. Kildare TV on Wednesday nights. There were also the films with which his name was associated, many of them reshown continually on television in the U.S. and foreign countries.

Twenty-five years after his death, Faust was very much alive, on the screen, on the stage, and in print.

A FAUST FILMOGRAPHY

THIS compilation is based on original work by William F. Nolan and has been expanded from various sources. Sources include the three volumes of the *Catalog of Copyright Entries, Cumulative Series: Motion Pictures,* for 1912–39, 1940–49, and 1950–59, respectively, published by the United States Copyright Office, The Library of Congress; the annual volumes 1937 to 1968 of the *International Motion Picture Almanac,* published by Quigley Publications, New York; *The Library of Congress Catalogs: The National Union Catalog, 1953–1957, Motion Pictures and Film Strips*; and *The Library of Congress Author Catalog, 1948–1952, Films*; as well as studio records, Library of Academy of Motion Picture Arts and Sciences archives, Brandt & Brandt agency records, and Faust memorabilia and correspondence. Listings include motion pictures based on or suggested by Faust's writings, pictures on which he worked while employed in Hollywood, and pictures associated with his name and work in various ways (for example, the fifteen-part serial entitled *Valley of Vanishing Men,* a title purchased from Faust). Though the filmography may seem extensive, it does not include at least 20 Faust stories and novels to which motion picture rights were sold but from which no films appear to have been made.

Year	Title of Film	Studio	Featured Players	Copyright or Release Date
1917	*The Adopted Son*	Metro Pictures Corp.	Francis X. Bushman Beverly Bayne	Oct. 17
1918	*Lawless Love*	Fox	Jewel Carmen Henry Woodward Edward Hearn	Aug. 25
1918	*Kiss Or Kill*	Universal	Herbert Rawlinson Priscilla Dean	Sept. 30

Year	Title of Film	Studio	Featured Players	Copyright or Release Date
1920	*The Untamed*	Fox	Tom Mix Pauline Starke	Sept. 5
1920	*A Thousand to One*	J. Parker Read, Jr.	Hobart Bosworth Ethel Grey Terry	Dec. 5
1921	*Tiger True*	Universal	Frank Mayo Fritzi Brunette Eleanor Hancock	Jan. 8
1921	*Children of the Night*	Fox	William Russell Ruth Renick	June 26
1921	*The Night Horsemen*	Fox	Tom Mix May Hopkins	Sept. 18
1921	*Shame*	Fox	John Gilbert Anna May Wong	Sept. 18
1921	*Trailin'*	Fox	Tom Mix Eva Novak Carol Holloway	Dec. 11
1922	*His Back Against the Wall*	Goldwyn	Raymond Hatton Virginia Valli	Jan. 3
1922	*Just Tony*	Fox	Tony Tom Mix Claire Adams	Aug. 20
1923	*Three Who Paid*	Fox	Dustin Farnum	Jan. 7
1923	*Mile-a-Minute Romeo*	Fox	Tony Tom Mix Betty Jewel James Mason	Nov. 18
1923	*The Gun Fighter*	Fox	William Farnum Doris May	Aug. 2
1924	*Against All Odds*	Fox	Charles Jones Dolores Rousse	July 27
1925	*Champion of Lost Causes*	Fox	Edmund Lowe Barbara Bedford Walter McGrail	Feb. 17
1925	*The Best Bad Man*	Fox	Tom Mix Clara Bow	Nov. 15
1926	*The Flying Horseman*	Fox	Buck Jones Gladys McConnell	Aug. 29
1928	*The Cavalier*	Tiffany-Stahl	Richard Talmadge Barbara Bedford Stuart Holmes	June 15

A Faust Filmography

Year	Title of Film	Studio	Featured Players	Copyright or Release Date
1930	*Fair Warning*	Fox	George O'Brien Louise Huntington George Brent	Dec. 25
1931	*A Holy Terror*	Fox	George O'Brien Sally Eilers Rita La Roy Humphrey Bogart	June 22
1932	*Destry Rides Again*	Universal	Tom Mix Claudia Dell Zasu Pitts Andy Devine	Apr. 4
1937	*Internes Can't Take Money*	Paramount	Barbara Stanwyck Joel McCrea Lloyd Nolan Stanley Ridges	Apr. 9
1938	*Young Dr. Kildare*	M.G.M.	Lew Ayres Lionel Barrymore Lynne Carver	Oct. 14
1939	*Calling Dr. Kildare*	M.G.M.	Lew Ayres Lionel Barrymore Lana Turner	Apr. 28
1939	*The Secret of Dr. Kildare*	M.G.M.	Lew Ayres Lionel Barrymore Laraine Day	Nov. 24
1939	*Destry Rides Again*	Universal	Marlene Dietrich James Stewart	Dec. 29
1940	*Dr. Kildare's Strange Case*	M.G.M.	Lew Ayres Lionel Barrymore Laraine Day	Apr. 12
1940	*Dr. Kildare Goes Home*	M.G.M.	Lew Ayres Lionel Barrymore Laraine Day	Sept. 6
1940	*Dr. Kildare's Crisis*	M.G.M.	Lew Ayres Lionel Barrymore Laraine Day Robert Young	Nov. 26
1941	*The People vs. Dr. Kildare*	M.G.M.	Lew Ayres Lionel Barrymore Laraine Day	May 2
1941	*Dr. Kildare's Wedding Day*	M.G.M.	Lew Ayres Laraine Day	Aug. 22

307

1941	*Dr. Kildare's Victory*	M.G.M.	Lew Ayres Laraine Day	Nov. 26
1942	*Powder Town*	RKO-Radio	Victor McLaglen Edmond O'Brien June Havoc	June 19
1942	*Calling Dr. Gillespie*	M.G.M.	Lionel Barrymore Philip Dorn Donna Reed	June 19
1942	*Dr. Gillespie's New Assistant*	M.G.M.	Lionel Barrymore Van Johnson Susan Peters Pamela Blake	Nov. 13
1942	*The Valley of Vanishing Men**	Columbia	Bill Elliott Slim Summerville Carmen Morales	Dec. 17
1943	*Dr. Gillespie's Criminal Case*	M.G.M.	Lionel Barrymore Van Johnson Donna Reed	May 6
1943	*The Desperadoes*	Columbia	Randolph Scott Glenn Ford Claire Trevor Evelyn Keyes	May 25
1943	*The Deerslayer*	Republic	Bruce Kellogg Jean Parker	Oct. 28
1944	*In Our Time*	Warner Bros	Ida Lupino Paul Henreid	Feb. 19
1944	*Cover Girl*	Columbia	Rita Hayworth Gene Kelly	Apr. 6
1944	*Uncertain Glory*	Warner Bros	Errol Flynn Paul Lukas Jean Sullivan Faye Emerson	Apr. 22

* A serial in fifteen episodes, each released separately: *Trouble in Canyon City*, Dec. 17, '42; *The Mystery of Ghost Town*, Dec. 24, '42; *Danger Walks by Night*, Dec. 31, '42; *Hillside Horror*, Jan. 7, '43; *Guns in the Night*, Jan. 15, '43; *The Bottomless Well*, Jan. 22, '43; *The Man in the Gold Mask*, Jan. 29, '43; *When the Devil Drives*, Feb. 5, '43; *The Traitor's Shroud*, Feb. 12, '43; *Death Strikes at Seven*, Feb. 12, '43; *Satan in the Saddle*, Feb. 26, '43; *The Mine of Missing Men*, Mar. 5, '43; *Danger on Dome Rock*, Mar. 8, '43; *The Door that Has No Key*, Mar. 10, '43; *Empire's End*, Mar. 12, '43.

1944	*Three Men in White*	M.G.M.	Lionel Barrymore Van Johnson Ava Gardner	Apr. 26
1944	*The Conspirators*	Warner Bros	Hedy Lamarr Paul Henreid Peter Lorre Sydney Greenstreet	Oct. 21
1944	*Between Two Women*	M.G.M.	Van Johnson Lionel Barrymore Gloria De Haven	Dec. 19
1946	*Rainbow Over Texas*	Republic	Roy Rogers Dale Evans	May 9
1947	*Dark Delusion*	M.G.M.	Lionel Barrymore James Craig Lucille Bremer	May 14
1949	*The Adventures of Don Juan*	Warner Bros	Errol Flynn Viveca Lindfors	Jan. 29
1950	*Singing Guns*	Republic	Vaughn Monroe Ella Raines	Feb. 28
1950	*The Gunfighter**	Twentieth-Century-Fox	Gregory Peck Helen Westcott	May 26
1951	*Branded*	Paramount	Alan Ladd Mona Freeman	**Jan. 16**
1951	*My Outlaw Brother*	United Artists	Mickey Rooney Wanda Hendrix	Mar. 15
1954	*Destry*	Universal	Audie Murphy Mari Blanchard	Aug. 18
1957	*The Hired Gun*	M.G.M.	Rory Calhoun Anne Francis	Sept. 1

* Retains the title but not the story of the Faust-based film released by Fox in 1923.

BOOKS ABOUT FAUST

INCLUDED here are books dealing wholly or in part with Frederick Faust and books primarily of Faust's own work that contain biographical or autobiographical material. Listings are chronological.

Brand, Max. *Harrigan*. London, 1926.

Bacon, Leonard. *Semi-Centennial*. New York, 1939.

O'Rourke, Frank. *"E" Company*. New York, 1945.

Maule, Harry E. (ed.). *Great Tales of the American West*, New York, 1945.

Delaney, John P. *The Blue Devils in Italy*. Washington, D.C., 1947.

Richardson, Darrell C. *Max Brand: The Man and His Work*, Los Angeles, 1952.

Reynolds, Quentin. *The Fiction Factory*. New York, 1955.

Schoolcraft, John (ed.). *The Notebooks and Poems of "Max Brand."* New York, 1957.

Jordan-Smith, Paul (ed.). *Poetry from Hidden Springs*. New York, 1962.

Easton, Robert (ed.). *Max Brand's Best Stories*. New York, 1967.

Gruber, Frank. *The Pulp Jungle*. Los Angeles, 1967.

Taylor, J. Golden (ed.). *Great Western Short Stories*. Palo Alto, 1967.

AUTHOR'S ACKNOWLEDGMENTS

I AM grateful to the late John Schoolcraft and Dorothy Faust, as well as to surviving members of the Faust family, for much of the material in this book.

Others to whom I am indebted include Carol Brandt; Dr. George Winthrop Fish; Martha Bacon; Dr. John Cooper; Herbert Wadopian; William J. Clark; William Randolph Hearst, Jr.; William F. Nolan; Kenneth Littauer; Riley H. Allen; the late Thomas B. Costain; the late Dwight D. Eisenhower; Wallace Downey; Adele Downey Tillson and other members of the Downey family.

I am also grateful to Waring Jones, J. H. Logan and the Accessions and Reference Division of the Public Archives of Canada; J. R. Cominsky, Althea E. Sedgwick, and the *Saturday Review*; Dodd, Mead and Company; Harper and Row; Elliott Morgan and the Research Department of Metro-Goldwyn-Mayer, Culver City; Ocean Wave Lucas; Robert H. Becker, Dale Morgan, Estelle Rebec, J. B. Tompkins, and other members of the staff of the Bancroft Library at the University of California, at Berkeley; likewise James R. K. Kantor, University of California Archivist, and the archives staff; Lillian Schwartz, Mildred Simpson, and members of the staff of the Academy of Motion Picture Arts and Sciences Library; Jack Delaney; Arthur S. Champeny, Harold B. Ayres, Richard Courtney, and the many officers and men of the 88th Division with whom Faust served in World War II and whose letters and reminiscences have proved invaluable; and the Historical Section, Department of the Army.

I am also grateful to Mrs. Mary M. Hirth, Librarian, The University of Texas; Paul H. Bonner, Jr., and Condé Nast Publications Inc.; Mrs. Molly Costain Haycraft; Ben Benjamin; Charles Schlessiger; Anthony W. De Fina; Haven Falconer, Norman Kaphan, and the staff of the Metro-Goldwyn-Mayer Research Department, New York; Thornton

Wilder; Gene Tunney; Archibald MacLeish; John R. O'Steen and Steve Goodman of the Warner Brothers staff; Carl Stucke; Belle Folsey; Larry Winship; J. W. Berry; Frank Gruber; Lew Ayres; Dennis Wilson and the Columbia Pictures Research Department; Josephine Green; Jack McDowell; and members of the staffs of the Santa Barbara Public Library and the University of California at Santa Barbara Library.

Books to which I am indebted include Leonard Bacon's *Semi-Centennial*; Charles A. Fenton's *Stephen Vincent Benét*; Darrell C. Richardson's *Max Brand: The Man and His Work*; Quentin Reynolds' *The Fiction Factory*; Frank Gruber's *The Pulp Jungle;* James K. Folsom's *The American Western Novel*; and Arthur Mizener's *The Far Side of Paradise*. Darrell Richardson's *Faust Fanzine* magazines have proved an important source of information about Faust and his work, as have copies of *Argosy, Western Story*, and *Harper's*. Two books on the development of the motion picture have been especially helpful: *Immortals of the Screen*, by Ray Stuart, and *The Western*, by George H. Fenin and William K. Everson.

I am particularly grateful to Davis Dresser, Jack Schaefer, and to Kenneth Millar for helpful critical comments.

I wish to thank the following for permission to quote or reproduce material from the copyrighted works listed. Dodd, Mead & Company for *Rupert Brooke: The Collected Poems*; Martha Bacon and *The Atlantic Monthly* for *Destry and Dionysus*; David Merrick Productions for the front cover of Decca Original Cast Album, DL 9075; and Metro-Goldwyn-Mayer, Inc., for material pertaining to the Dr. Kildare television series.

INDEX

Above the Law: 70
Ace-High Magazine: 94
Achilles, Homer's: 65
Acosta, Bert: 196
Acropolis, the: 188
Acton, Arthur: 116, 132, 164, 214
Acton, Harold: 132
Acton, William: 132
Adams, Claire: 91
Adopted Son, The: 58
Adventure: 180
Adventures of Don Juan, The: 229
Aegean Sea: 31, 148, 188
Aeschylus: 10, 97, 102, 123, 188
After April: sale of, 237; plot of, 237;
    success of, 238
Against All Odds: 100
Age of Pericles: 149
Ah, Wilderness: 205
Aiken, Conrad: 174
Ainslee's Magazine: 74
Albuquerque, N.M.: 190
Alcatraz: 91
Aldershot, Nova Scotia: 37
Aldington, Richard: 229–30, 233–34, 244
Alec (a trapper): 72
"Alexander's Ragtime Band": 55, 125
Algiers: 243–45
Alinari prints: 194
All For One: 161
All-Story Weekly: 45, 47, 49, 57–58, 61,
    65, 70, 86
Allen, Riley (editor): 28
American, The: 174, 177, 180
American, The (French Revolution
    story): 193
American Cavalcade: 197–98
American Club of Toronto: 36

American Weekly, The: 134, 163, 171,
    212–13
Amici-Grossi, Piero: 120
Amsterdam, Holland: 95
Anderson, Sherwood: 70
Andrews, Roy Chapman: 159
Andromache: 66
Andromeda: 123
Antibes, France: 110
Anzio, Italy: 231, 254
Apennines: 113, 132, 214
Aphrodite: 66
Arctic, the: 123
Argosy-All Story: 86, 94
Argosy Magazine: 56–57, 70–71, 99,
    155–57, 160, 164, 166, 168–69, 174,
    177–78, 180–82, 188, 197; Max Brand
    in, 57, 72; *Young Doctor Kildare* pub-
    lished by, 213
Aristophanes: 97
Army, U.S.: 36, 52, 61–62
Arno River: 112–13, 116, 126, 262
Art of War: 122
Aspasia: 54
Associated Press, The: 263
Athens, Greece: 149–50, 188
Atlantic Monthly: 144, 265–66
Auer, Mischa: 221–22
Austen, Jane: 205
Austin, Frank: 204, 265; *see also* Faust
    pseudonyms
Austin, Mary: 98
Ayres, Captain Harold B.: as company
    "L" commander, 253–54
Ayres, Lew: 127; in Kildare films, 215,
    226, 243; resentment of, 243; as non-
    combatant serviceman, 243

313

Bach, Johann Sebastian: 109
Bacon, Leonard: 17–18, 30, 70, 73, 91,
106, 116, 120, 214, 220, 224, 233–34,
239; at University of California, 17–18,
49, 53, 72; Pulitzer Prize winner, 17,
195; in military service, 60; epic poem
by, 100; Faust's "Rimini" criticized by,
107; psychoanalytic treatment of, 106–
108; in Italy, 144
Bacon, Martha (Leonard Bacon's
daughter): 120, 265–66; in *Atlantic
Monthly*, 144–45
Bait and the Trap, The: 264
Baker, George: 130
Baker, George Pierce: 82
"Balin": 92–94
Ballad of St. Christopher, The: 61
Baltimore Sun: 231
Balzac, Honoré de: 41, 48, 101, 125
Bancroft Library, Berkeley, Calif.: 266
Bandit's Honor: 122
Bangor, Maine: 38
Bank holiday of March, 1933: 167, 170
Barnes, Russell: 244
Barrett, Elizabeth: 113
Barry, Dan (fictional): 65, 69
Barry, Philip: 49, 59, 70, 83, 195, 209, 220
Barrymore, Lionel: 127; in Kildare
movies, 215, 226
Barton, Chandler: 114
Basutoland: 123
Bauer, Joe: 231
Baum, Vicki: 205
Baumgarten, Bernice: 163
Bavaria: 146
Baxter, George Owen: 74, 77–78, 204,
265; in *Western Story*, 74, 77, 157; in
other magazines, 94; *see also* Faust
pseudonyms
Bayne, Beverly: 58
Baynes, Dr. and Mrs. H. G.: 106–107,
110
Beatitudes, the: 228
Bedford, Barbara: 100, 127
Beer Is Best: 171
Beery, Wallace: 205
Beethoven, Ludwig van: 109
Ben Greet Company: 40
Benchley, Robert: 110
Benét, Laura: 48

Benét, Stephen Vincent: 49, 59, 70, 98,
154, 174, 195, 203, 220, 270; in military
service, 60; in Paris, 83; as Pulitzer
Prize winner, 195; death of, 233
Benét, William Rose: 42–44, 48–49, 56,
59, 70, 90, 98, 166, 195, 220; in military
service, 60; Faust poem criticized by,
92, 94
Benicia, Calif.: 49
Bent (fictional): 142–43
Beowulf: 21
Berenson, Bernard: 113, 126
Bergman, Ingrid: 205
Berkeley, Calif.: 14–16, 19, 24, 29–31, 40,
53, 106, 148, 185, 187, 220, 225
Best Bad Man, The: 127
Billy-the-Kid: 199
Blackbirds Sing, The: 189
Blackie and Red: 111
Black Jack: 111
Black Mask: 197
Blackness of McTee, The: 167
Black Rider, The: 127
Blackwell, Basil: 105, 151
Blackwell, Frank: 73, 76–79, 85, 105–106,
130–32, 134, 148, 153, 163–64, 167–71,
181; Faust writings rejected by, 154,
160–62, 166; "Hugh Owen" western
bought by, 178
Bloomfield, Howard: 163, 165, 171, 180
Blow, Dick: 120, 214, 233
Blow, Marya: 239
Blue and Gold, The: 22
Blue Book: 212
Bobbs-Merrill Company: 111
"Bob Davis Reveals" (newspaper
column): 73
Boccaccio: 114
Bogart, Humphrey: 127, 153, 226
Bolt, Lee: 265; *see also* Faust pseudo-
nyms
Bombi (fictional): 198
Border Bandit, The: 111
Border Kid, The: 267
Bosworth, Hobart: 81, 127
Bow, Clara: 127, 140
Bowery, the: 39–41
Boyer, Charles: 205
Bracker, Milton (war correspondent):
263

Brand, Max: 49, 77, 79, 94, 122, 137, 159–61, 164, 167–68, 171, 173, 179, 181, 198, 202–204, 215, 263–65, 268; in *Argosy Magazine*, 57, 72; in *Western Story*, 78, 157; in other magazines, 94; identity revealed, 203–204; as Dwight D. Eisenhower's favorite, 255; *see also* Faust pseudonyms
Brandt, Carl (agent): 154–61, 163–91, 194–203, 206, 208–13, 215, 217–18, 220, 227, 230–32, 237–39, 254, 264–65, 267
Brandt, Erdman: 165, 178, 202
Brent, George: 127, 153
Briareus (mythical): 170
British Army: 39
British Eighth Army, Italy: 233, 254
Bronze Collar, The: 127
Brooke, Rupert: 30–31
Brother John: 22
Brothers on the Trail: 268
Browning, Robert: 113
Brunette, Fritzi: 86
Brute, The: 111
Buchan, John: 45
Buffalo Bill: 198
Bull Moose ticket: 138
Bundy, Mary Sutton: 228
Bunyan, Paul: 198
Burnet, W. K.: 229
Burns, Robert: 105
Burroughs, Edgar Rice: 45
Bushman, Francis X.: 58, 127
Busy Jack's Lunch: 40–42, 241
Butler, Samuel: 45
Butler, Walter C.: 204, 265, 268; *see also* Faust pseudonyms
Bynner, Witter: 95

Cabell, James Branch: 57
California: 34, 49–50, 52, 72, 135–36, 159, 164, 202
California Institute of Technology: 225
Calling Dr. Kildare: 225
Camp Gruber, Okla.: 246
Camp Humphreys, Va.: 62, 64, 70, 88
Camp Patrick Henry, Va.: 241
Campbell, Bob: 217
Campbell, Campbell (fictional): 171–72; Faust revealed in, 172
Canada: 30–31, 206, 211

Canadian Army: 30, 33, 190; Faust in, 31–38; American Legion of, 36–37
Canby, Henry Seidel: 49, 59–60, 98, 165–66, 195
Canfield, Cass: 160, 164, 177, 194, 223, 227, 230–32, 234, 238–40, 271
Cannes, France: 110
Canterbury Tales: 96
Carmen, Jewel: 70, 127
Carnavalet Museum, France: 83
Carnegie Hall: 71
Carr, Rosemary (Mrs. Stephen Benét): 83
Carson Appeal, Carson City, Nev.: 44
Carver, Lynn: in *Young Doctor Kildare*, 215
Casablanca: 242–43
Cassino, Italy: 254
Cavalier, The: 45, 127, 153
Cave, Hugh B.: 75
Caxton's Chaucer: 172
Cellini, Benvenuto: 177–78
Century Magazine: 42, 47
Cervantes, Miguel de: 217
Challis, George: 78, 164, 182, 264–65, 269; *see also* Faust pseudonyms
Chamberlain, Richard: 128
Champeny, Colonel Arthur S.: 246, 250, 258
Champion of Lost Causes: 100
Chaplin, Charlie: 108
Chapmans, the Frank: 122
Chaucer, Geoffrey: 96–97, 130, 234–40
Cheetah: 206
Chelsea House: 91, 111
Chicago Daily News: 161
Chicago *Sun*: 245
Children of the Night: 86
Christ at Gethsemane (poem subject): 200, 238
Christopher of Luigi Pastorelli, The: 178
Churchill, Winston: 234
Civil War: 5, 241; novel of, 222, 227, 234–35, 238
Clark, General Mark: 254
Clark, Kenneth: 104, 122, 126
Clark, William C.: 267
Clark, William J.: 267
Clayton, Fred: 177, 188

Clung: 86
Cohn, Harry: 227
Cohn, J. J.: 207, 212, 216
Coleman, Ronald: 205
Coleridge, Samuel Taylor: 105
College Humor: 155, 159–60
"College Sonnets": 21
Collegeville, Calif.: 4
Collier's: 111, 115, 162–64, 167, 170, 174–75, 177, 179–80, 182, 184, 238; *Six Golden Angels* rejected by, 91; *Six Golden Angels* bought by, 194
Columbia Pictures: 194, 203; Faust working for, 226, 230
Columbia University: 81, 220
Comanche: 111
Coming Clean: 164
Company "C," 62nd Battalion, Canadian Expeditionary Forces: 34–35
Comstock, Boyd: 185–88, 190–91, 239
Comstock Lode, the: 44
Congressional Medal of Honor: 231
Conrad, Joseph: 45, 79
Conspirators, The: 229
Constitution, U.S.: 20, 123
Convalescence: 47
Cook prize: 22
Cook, Professor Albert Stanburrough: 22
Cooper, Courtney Riley: 75
Cooper, Gladys: 223
Cooper, James Fenimore: 110–11, 218
Cooper, John: 11
Corbelay, Kate: 208
Corbett, Jim: 159
Cornelius, Helen: 17
Cos, Greece: 149
Cosmopolitan: 178, 180, 182–83, 196, 198, 213, 217, 222
Costain, Thomas B.: 169–70, 173, 197–98
Cotton, T. G. (physician): 107
Country Gentleman: 84–85, 94, 111, 127, 155, 179–80
Cover Girl: 227
Coward, Tim: 239–40
Cozzens, James Gould: 163
Cram, Mildred: 178
Crane, Stephen: 151
Crawford, Joan: 209
Cronus: 32

Cuchulain: 66
Cue: 198
Culver City, Calif.: 204
Cumberland, Kate (fictional): 67
Curtis publications: 179
Cuthbert, C. D.: 69

Daily Californian: 22, 30
Dallas, Texas: 139
Dan Barry's Daughter: 69
Dangerfield, Charlotte (fictional): 143–44
Dangerfield, Elizabeth: 137–38
Dante: 20, 90, 99, 110, 114, 148, 151, 236
Dark Rosaleen: 127
Darrieux, Danielle: 217
Darwin, Charles: 41
Dashiell, Alfred: 169
Davis, Madge (Mrs. Robert H. Davis): 99
Davis, Robert H.: 44, 47–48, 51–54, 56–58, 60, 63, 69–70, 76–77, 79, 84–85, 90, 99, 134, 159; Munsey executive, 44–46; background of, 44–45; quits Munsey company, 73; as literary agent, 73; as *Sun* columnist, 73; back with Munsey, 73–74; on U.S. tour, 135–40, 142–44, 166
Dawson, Peter: 77, 94, 265; *see also* Faust pseudonyms
Day, Frederick Van Rennsselaer: 57
Day, Laraine: 127, 226
Dead Man Steer, The: 160
Dean, Priscilla: 71, 127
Declaration of Independence: 135
Deep South, the: 138
Deerslayer, The: 218
De Gaulle, General Charles: 263
de Haven, Gloria: 226
de Haviland, Olivia: 205
Delacorte, George, Jr.: 155
Delaney, Sergeant Jack (military historian): 254, 259, 261
Delineator, The: 155
Dell (publishers): 155
Dell, Claudia: 154
Dempsey-Carpentier fight: 84
Dempsey-Tunney fight: 100
Dere Mable: 99
Desperadoes, The: 226

Destry, Harry (fictional): 142–43
Destry Rides Again: 142, 205, 267; plot of, 142–43; movie versions of, 144, 154, 221–22; as musical comedy theme, 144
Detective Fiction Weekly: 111, 165–66, 173, 177, 179–81
Detective Story Magazine: 74, 94, 111, 163, 171
Devil Ritter: 70
Devil Walks, The: 167
Devine, Andy: 127, 154
Dewart, W. T.: 52–53
Dexter, Martin: 78, 265; *see also* Faust pseudonyms
Diana, Temple of: 190
Dice, Jeremy (fictional): 86
Dickens, Charles: 7
Dietrich, Marlene: 127, 174, 205; in *Destry Rides Again*, 144, 221–22
Dietrichstein, Jo: 214
Dietrichstein, Josephine and Leo: 122
Dionysus: 114, 121, 128, 145, 147, 152; mythical story of, 149–51
Dionysus and Destry: 266
Dionysus in Hades: 151, 158, 188, 269–70; published by Faust, 151; failure of, 151–52
Dionysus, theater of: 188
"Distance" (a poem): 228
Divine Comedy: 99
Dr. Jekyll and Mr. Hyde: 205
Dr. Kildare's Crisis: 225
Dodd, Edward H., Jr.: 203, 264, 267
Dodd-Mead, publishers: 99, 164, 167–68, 203–204, 240, 264, 266
Dolly: 208
Donat, Robert: 205
Donnegan: 91
Dostoevski, Feodor Mikhailovich: 228–29
Doubleday, Doran (publisher): 160
Double Crown, The: 57
Douglas, Melvyn: 205
Douglas, Norman: 113
Downey, Thomas: 9–11, 13, 16, 50, 93
Doyle, A. Conan: 74
Dreiser, Theodore: 74
Dublin, Ireland: 129
Dumas, Alexandre: 7
Du Maurier, Daphne: 217

Dumfries: 105
Dundee, Scotland: 105
Dunraven, Earl of: 129
Dursts, the Herbert: 131
Dyer, Deborah: 17

Eaker, General Ira: 233, 245
Eames, Claire (Mrs. Sidney Howard): 98
East 115th Street, Harlem: 40
Eaton, Lady: 116
Economic Warfare, Board of: 230
Eddy, Nelson: 205
Edinburgh, Scotland: 105
Egypt: 155
88th Division: 246, 254–55
Eikenberry, Kenneth: 218
Eilers, Sally: 127, 153
Eisenhower, General Dwight D.: 254–55
El Alamein, battle of: 260
Electric Torch, The: 179
Elia (the Fausts' butler): 118, 121–22, 126, 131
Elks Magazine: 198
Elliott, Bill: 226
El Paso, Texas: 71, 140
El Toro, Calif.: 231
Emerson, Faye: 229
Emery, Gilbert: 223
Embassy Theatre, Broadway, N.Y.: 127
Emmett, Mrs. Granville: 239
England: 99, 105, 147, 233–34
Ensenada, Mexico: 211
Ephesus: 190
Ephrata, Pa.: 135–36
Erewhon: 45
Esquire: 181, 220
Euripides: 97, 123
Eurydice: 150
Evan, Evan: 161, 167, 178, 181, 204, 264–65; *see also* Faust pseudonyms
Evan, Evin: 77, 166, 265; *see also* Faust pseudonyms
Evans, Evan (heart specialist): 89–91
Evans, Sir Arthur: 149
Everyman's Library: 217
Excitement & College Stories: 74

"Fabulous Faust": 54, 264; *see also* Frederick Schiller Faust
Fabulous Faust Magazine, The: 265

Faerie Queen: 97
Fairbanks, Douglas: 73, 127
Fair Warning: 153; *see also The Untamed*
Falmouth, Mass.: 174
Farmington Country Club: 174
Farnum, Dustin: 98, 127
Farnum, William: 98, 127
Farrar, Geraldine: 159
Far West Illustrated: 111
Fate's Honeymoon: 54, 81, 111; *see also A Thousand To One*
Father of the Bride: 99
Faulkner, William: 229, 270
Faust, Dorothy (Mrs. Frederick Faust): 55–56, 58, 60–62, 71, 79, 84, 87–89, 91, 94–96, 135, 139–40, 145–47, 159–65, 171, 173, 180–82, 184, 186, 188, 193–97, 200, 207–209, 211, 213, 220–21, 223–24, 227, 231, 235–36, 239–40, 242–43, 257; in Santa Barbara, 76; nervous breakdown of, 81, 147; song written for, 92–93; at Katonah, 96–101, 173, 182, 200; in England, 103–10, 130–31, 147; in France, 110–13; in Florence, 112–28, 130, 132, 134–35, 147, 160, 162, 200; in Ireland, 129, 147; in Italy, 144–45; leaves Faust, 147; reunited with Faust, 147–48; in Egypt, 155–57; in Virginia, 174; divorce considered by, 196; suicide attempt of, 218; dream of, 262; death of, 266; *see also* Dorothy Schilling
Faust, Elizabeth: 3; background of, 5–6; death of, 6
Faust, Frederick Schiller: 3–4, 6, 27, 39, 47–52, 55–58, 65, 69, 72–73, 78–85, 92–103, 152, 166–75, 177–85, 199, 214, 233; childhood of, 3–8, 33, 48, 55, 234–35; name problem for, 7, 39, 51, 100; high school years of, 9–14, 33, 83; college years of, 14–26; early writings of, 18, 23, 28–29, 35, 46, 53; in Hawaii, 28–30; in Canada, 31–39, 55, 61; philanderings of, 34, 50–51, 146–47, 195–96, 200–201, 218; in New York, 39–52, 54–55, 63, 73–81, 85, 134–35, 158–60, 162–65, 173, 191, 193–98, 213; poetry of, 42–44, 47–48, 58–61, 71, 73, 92–95, 101, 107, 110, 145, 150–51, 165–
69, 179–80, 188–89, 197, 201, 219, 234; with Munsey publications, 46, 49; as young writer, 48; Faust name reserved for poetry, 49–50; as lavish spender, 50, 101, 117, 228; motion picture work of, 54, 58, 70–71, 80–81, 86–87, 91–92, 95, 98, 100–101, 143–44, 153, 183–84, 194–95, 204–12, 217, 225; marriage of, 54; in U.S. Army, 61–64; westerns of, 61, 66–69, 73, 77–78, 80–81, 91, 98, 105, 142–43, 161, 166, 171, 178, 181–83, 197; mythology influence on, 66; in Southwest, 71–72; as Street and Smith writer, 74–78, 153–58; in France, 82–85, 87, 110–13; heart attacks of, 87–91, 125, 211, 218; in England, 103–10, 147; in Florence, 112–28, 131, 146–47, 157, 160, 190, 200; in Ireland, 129, 147; in Italy, 130, 140–41, 144, 154, 170, 176–81, 184–85, 199–200, 212; on U.S. tour, 135–40, 142–44, 166; in Greece, 147–49, 152, 185, 187–91; in Egypt, 155–57; in Virginia, 174; South Sea Island series of, 179–80; in Hollywood, 204–12, 266; in Los Angeles (Brentwood), 214–33; plot sources of, 219–20; correspondence of, 220–22; Modesto revisited by, 225, 234; University of California degree refused by, 225; love affair terminated by, 227; war enlistment efforts of, 230–32; 25 to 30 million words published, 234, 264, 268; associated with 60 or more films, 235; en route to war front, 234–44; heart report of, 239–40; last night in New York, 240–41; in Algiers, 244–45; at war front, 246; as war correspondent, 246–61; with "E" company, 351st's Second Battalion, 258; at battle of Santa Maria Infante, 260–62; death of, 261–63; buried at Carano, 261; reinterred at Nettuno-Anzio American Cemetery, 262; comments on, 263–72
Faust, Gilbert Leander: 3; character of, 4–6; background of, 4–6; death of, 7, 43
Faust, Gounod's: 63, 69
Faust, Heinie: *see* Frederick Schiller Faust
Faust, Jane: 60, 76, 122–23, 182, 195, 213,

235; in Vienna, 200; in Italy, 207; marriage of, 224–25; Dorothy Faust's dream told to, 262

Faust, John: 76, 122, 213; in school in England, 123, 173; in school in Switzerland, 162–63, 166; illness of, 166; in Hotchkiss School, Connecticut, 182, 195; in Vienna, 200; in Italy, 207; at Harvard, 222; in military service, 236

Faust, Judith: 131, 162, 195–96, 200, 214; in Italy, 207

Faust, Pauline: 64, 130, 132

Faust, Thomas Carlyle: 100

Fawcett Publications: 155

Fiction Factory, The: 265

Fiction Rodeo: 225

Fiddle (a mare): 142

Fielding, Sol: 205

Fifth Army headquarters: 246

Fightin' Fool: 267

Film Stories: 74

Fire Brain: 111

Firebrand, The: 177, 264

First Principles: 41

Fish, Dixie: *see* George Winthrop Fish

Fish, George Winthrop ("Dixie"): 31, 34, 83, 90–91, 198, 238, 248, 254, 266; in Canadian Army, 32–35; discharge of, 35, 37; in ambulance unit, 35, 37; in U.S. Air Corps, 60; as New York medical student, 81; in France, 81–82; intern at Roosevelt Hospital, 99, 183; as surgeon, 159; Faust's death reported by, 262

Fisher, Steve: 229

Fitch, Clyde: 95

Fitzgerald, F. Scott: 30, 70, 83, 101, 110, 195, 197, 206, 209, 270

Fitzimmons, Robert Prometheus: 45

5 Columbus Circle, New York: 80

Flandrau, Grace: 220, 222, 240–41, 270

Flanner, Hildegarde: 17

Flanner, Janet: 122; *see also* "Genêt"

Florence, Italy: 95, 112–14, 129, 131–32, 135–36, 140, 147, 159–60, 164, 166, 187, 190, 193, 200, 207, 213, 222–24, 232–34

Flower of Hell: 202

Flying Horseman, The: 127

Flynn, Errol: 229

Folsey, Belle: 237

Fools All: 20

Ford, Glenn: 226

Ford, Henry: 272

Fort Belvoir, Va.: *see* Camp Humphreys, Va.

Fortune: 17

Forum: 165, 197

49 East 10th Street, New York: 55

438 West 116th Street, New York: 81

Fox studios: 70, 86, 91, 100, 153, 167

Fox, William: 80–81

France: 30, 36–38, 60, 82–84, 99, 110–11, 178

Francis of Assisi, St.: 201, 211

Franklin, Chester: 206

Frederick, John: 57, 77–78, 86, 94, 156, 265; *see also* Faust pseudonyms

Freeman, Douglas Southall: 223

Fremont, John C.: 199

French Revolution: 81, 83, 180, 193

Friend in Need, A: 148

Froissart, by Berner: 105

Frost, Frederick: 204, 265, 268; *see also* Faust pseudonyms

Froude, James Anthony: 105, 110

Fullers, the Charles: 195

Gable, Clark: 205

Galileo: 10, 112

Gallagher, Francis: 209, 223

Gallico, Paul: 101

Gallipoli campaign: 31

Garbo, Greta: 205

Garden of Eden, The: 66, 85; as unique western, 111

Gardner, Ava: 205, 226

Garland, Judy: 205

Garson, Greer: 205

Gaslight: 205

Gates, Harvey: 206

Gayley, Charles Mills: 15, 22

Geiger, Frederic: 99

"Genêt": 17

Gentlemen Prefer Blondes: 100

Gettysburg Address, the: 123

Gibney, Al: 162, 177, 180

Gideon Bible: 42, 47

Gilbert, John: 86, 127

Gingrich, Arnold: 181

Goethe, Johann Wolfgang von: 7, 48, 109, 217

Goldbeck, Willis: 213, 215, 239

Golden Coyote: 78

Golden Knight, The: 179, 182, 269

Golden Spurs, The: 157

Gold Rush, The: 108–109

Goldwyn, Samuel: 86

"Golgotha": 42

Gone With the Wind: 205

Good-bye Mr. Chips: 205

Gramercy Park South, New York: 55

Grand Army of the Republic: 5

Grand Central Station, N.Y.: 173

Grand Hotel: 205

Grand Illusion: 203, 208, 230

Grange, Red: 271

Grant, Cary: 205

Grant, Gordon: 242, 245

Grant, Ulysses S.: 223

Graves, Robert: 109–10

Gray Charteris, The: 91

Great Enemy: 167

Great Gatsby, The: 101

Greece: 95, 114, 180, 187, 189; Fausts' trip to, 147–49, 152

Greeley, Horace: 130

Greely, Miss Florence: 223

Green Beetle, The: 169

Green, John Richard: 110

Greene, Colonel Joseph: 241

Greenwich Village: 43, 98

Grey, Dolores: 128, 144

Grey, Zane: 67, 69, 74, 143, 160

Griffith, Andy: 128, 144

Grinnell, George Bird: 169

Gruber, Frank: 229–30, 266

Grumman, Wildcats: 231

Guenevere: 54

Guerin, Jules: 55

Guest, Lady Charlotte: 129

Guadalcanal: 231

Gun Club, the: 19

Gun Fighter, The: 98

Gustav Line, the: 254, 262

Hadden, Britten: 59

Hades (mythical character): 150

Halcyon Club series: 198

Halliday, Richard: 174, 184

Halsey, Robert (heart specialist): 89–91, 98, 103, 130, 164, 183, 239

Ham, Roswell: 17, 220

Hamilton, Alexander: 123

Hamilton, Anthony (Faust agent): 180

Hamilton, "Tex": 231

Hamlet: 66, 96, 105, 124, 238

Hammett, Dashiell: 223

Hancock, Eleanor: 86

Hands Across the Border: 211

Harding, President Warren G.: 77

Hardtack and Coffee: 223

Hardy, Thomas: 17, 19, 29

Harper's Ferry, W. Va.: 136

Harper's Magazine (Harper): 160–61, 164–67, 171–72, 177–78, 180–81, 194, 202, 204, 220, 223, 228, 230, 232, 264; as Faust war correspondent sponsor, 232, 238, 254; Delaney's account of Faust in, 259; Faust tribute by, 264

Harrigan: 32, 111

Hart, Walter Morris: 151, 185; at University of California, 187, 220, 225

Hartman, Lee: 171

Harts, the Walter Morris: 148

Harvard University: 39–40, 82

Hastings Park Barracks, Vancouver, B. C.: 34

Hatton, Raymond: 86

Havermale, Hazel: 17

Hawaii: 28–29

Haycox, Ernest: 75

Hayworth, Rita: 127, 226–27

Hazard, Caroline: 72

Hazards, the Peace: 116

Hearn, Edward: 70

Hearst, William Randolph, Jr.: 242

Heath, A. M.: 107

Hellespont, the: 31

Hemingway, Ernest: 39, 70, 83, 100, 126, 270

Henreid, Paul: 229

Henry VIII: 136

Henry, O.: 45, 57, 74, 79

Hera: 150–51

Hermann and Dorothea: 3

Hermes: 150

Hepburn, Katherine: 205

Hill, Russell: 242

Hilton, James: 205, 229

His Back Against the Wall: 86
History of England from the Fall of Wolsey to the Defeat of the Spanish Armada: 105
History of Greece, J. B. Bury's: 16
History of the Jews: 130
History of Latin Christianity: 130
History of Rome: 130
Hitchcock, Alfred: 198, 217
Hitler, Adolf: 77, 200, 205, 214
Hodder and Stroughton (in England): 111
Holloway, Carol: 86
Hollywood, Calif.: 140, 142, 153–55, 164, 179, 184, 194–95, 197–98, 201–203, 205, 208, 212, 229, 234; Faust in, 204–12
Holme, Garnet (actor): 40, 43–44, 90
Holmes, Stuart: 127
Holy Terror, A.: 153; *see also Trailin'*
Homecoming of Lazy Purdue, The: 52
Homer: 20, 33, 66, 95, 123, 147, 149 51, 188, 203, 239
Honolulu, Hawaii: 28–30, 116
Hood, John Bell (Confederate general): 223
Hopkins, Gerard Manley: 195
Hopkins, May: 86
Horn, Roy de S.: 165
Hotchkiss School, Connecticut: 182, 195
Hough, Emerson: 75
House on the Hill: 177–78
House of Rulaki, The: 22, 46
Howard, Leslie: 205
Howard, Mrs. John L. (Sidney Howard's mother): 71, 122
Howard, Polly (Mrs. Sidney Howard): 239
Howard, Sidney: 17, 19, 30, 40, 60, 71, 92, 98, 110, 122, 203, 220; in Paris, 82–83; on *Life* staff, 82; in Switzerland, 83; Pulitzer Prize won by, 100; *Gone With the Wind* film story by, 205; death of, 233
Hugo, Victor: 7
Human Comedy: 205
Hume, David: 41
Hummingbirds and Honeysuckle: 18
Hunting Silver: 169
Huntington, Louise: 153
Husley, Thomas Henry: 41

Huston, Walter: 143
Huxley, Aldous: 113, 144, 205–206, 224, 227
Huxley, Maria: 224, 227
Huxley, Matthew: 224

I, Claudius: 109
"I Have a Rendezvous With Death": 40
Iliad: 16, 33, 66
India: 27–30
Indians: 168–69
Infantry Journal, The: 232, 238, 241; Faust tribute by, 264
"In Our Humiliation": 42
In Our Time: 229
Internes Can't Take Money: 183, 198, 203
Invisible Man, The: 179
Ionian Sea: 148
Ireland: 129, 147, 164
Irving Trust Company: 101
Irwin, Will: 39
Iselin, Mrs. Arthur: 182
Iselin, Moppy: 239
Italy: 84, 95, 130, 140–41, 144, 146, 148, 165, 177–78, 184–85, 191–92, 199, 212–13, 232
Ivanhoe: 6, 12

Jackson, Stonewall (General Thomas J. Jackson): 137, 241
Jackson Trail, The: 164
James, Henry: 113
Jane (in Tarzan series): 206
Japan: 200
Japanese Zero fighters: 231
Jerry Peyton's Notched Inheritance: 74
"Jester's Song, The": 42
Jesus, Judas and Pilate, dialogue of: 114–16
Jewell, Betty: 98
Jews, persecution of: 192
Jim Jeffries' Barn: 228, 245
Johnny Comes Lately: 197
Johnson, Ed: 245
Johnson, Jack: 228
Johnson, Van: 226
Johnston, J. E. (Confederate general): 137

Jomini, Baron Henri (military strategist): 122
Jones, Buck: 127
Jones, Charles: 100
Journal American, New York: 44
Joyce, James: 129, 217
Judo: 123
Jung, Carl: 106–109
Just Tony: 91

Kant, Immanuel: 41
Katonah, Westchester County, N.Y.: 95–98, 101, 173, 182, 200, 218, 223
Keats, John: 7
Kendall, General Paul W.: 255
Kendall, Lieutenant Colonel Raymond E.: 259
Kennecott, Don: 212
Kesselring, Field Marshal (German commander): 254
Keyes, Evelyn: 226
Kidnapped: 105
Kildare (hero of *The Naked Blade*): 164
Kildare, Doctor: 31–32, 99, 183, 198, 203, 212, 215, 243; MGM films of, 226; Dixie Fish relationship to, 266
Kildare stories: 213, 217–18, 222, 225, 263, 269; for films, 213, 217, 243; for magazine, book publication, 213, 220, 267
King, The: 223–24
King Arthur: 66, 104, 129
Kinsale, The: 184, 194
Kipling, Rudyard: 20, 74, 79
Kismet: 205
Kiss or Kill: 71
Knopf, Edwin: 195, 197, 201–202, 206–11
König Ottokar, Grillparzer's: 17
Kyne, Peter B.: 75

La Cossitt, Henry: 198
Ladd, Alan: 127
Ladies Home Journal: 154–55, 179
Lady Chatterly's Lover: 126, 224
Lake Bruin, La.: 138
Lakewood, N.J.: 90–91
Lamarr, Hedy: 229
Lamont, Miss Grace ("Monty"): 104–105, 129–30, 132, 144, 146, 162, 173, 196, 234

Lancelot: 92
Land of Little Rain: 98
Langford, Sam: 159
"La Pietra" (a villa): 116
Lapsley, Eleanor: 239
Lardner, Ring: 101
Last of the Medicis, The: 132
"Last Venture, The" (a poem): 94
Lawless Love: 70
Lawson, John Howard: 229
Lawton, Dennis: 182, 188, 265; *see also* Faust pseudonyms
Lausanne, Switzerland: 163–64, 166
Lawrence, D. H.: 113, 126, 224, 234
Lay of the Last Minstrel: 105
Lazy Purdue: 58
Lee's Lieutenants: 241
Lear, King: 96, 238
Lee, Robert E.: 137, 198, 223
Le Gallienne, Richard: 92, 94
Leigh, Vivian: 205
Le Roy, Rita: 153
Levin, Sam: 159
Lewis, Sinclair: 49, 101, 126, 205
Lewis, Sir Thomas: 103, 110
Lexington, Ky.: 137–38
Liberty (a book): 41
Liberty (a magazine): 155, 174–75, 177–79, 181, 198
Library of Congress: 204
Life for Life's Sake: 234
Liliuokalani, Queen: 28
Lindbergh, Charles: 197, 272
Lindsay, Vachel: 19, 152
Linforth, Ivan: 220
Literary Digest: 60, 95
Literary Review: 92
Littauer, Kenneth: 162–63, 165, 170–71
"Little Bobbie": 22
Little Women: 205
Live Wire, The: 45
Livius, Titus: 130
Locke, John: 41
Loeb classical library: 130
London, Jack: 18, 69, 74
London, England: 95, 103, 105–107, 231
London Times: 234, 264
Longstreet, James (Confederate general): 223
Loos, Anita: 100

Lorre, Peter: 229
Los Angeles, Calif.: 139–40, 214, 218, 234
Louvre Museum: 82–85
Love Story Magazine: 74
Love's Labour's Lost: 96
Lovett, Robert A.: 99, 195, 245; as U.S. assistant secretary of war for air, 233
Lowe, Edmund: 100
Lower East Side, New York: 40
Lowry, Howard: 234
Loy, Myrna: 223
Lubelle, Frieda: 198, 220–21
Lucas, Ocean Wave: 205
Luck: 111
Luck and a Horse: 163
Lucky Larribee: 157
Lupino, Ida: 229

Mabinogion, The: 129
Macauley (publishers): 204
McBride, Jesse: 121
McCall's: 155, 177, 180
McConell, Gladys: 127
Macrae-Smith: 204
McCrary, Colonel Reagan ("Tex"): 245
McCrea, Joel: 127, 198
McCreary, General Richard: 233
MacDonald, Jeanette: 205
McGeehan, W. O. ("Bill"): 49, 59
McLean, Pinckney: 231, 233
MacLean's Magazine: 198
MacLeish, Archibald: 59–60, 110, 270; as Pulitzer Prize winner, 195
Macmillan Company: 61, 99
McTee (fictional): 32
Madison Square Garden: 60, 91
"Madonna of the Rocks," Leonardo's: 84, 101
Main Street: 101
Majestic: 154
Malory, Sir Thomas: 7, 217
Man o' War: 137–38
Mann, Thomas: 207, 227
Mannes, Marya: 120, 214
Manning, David: 77–78, 94, 122, 157, 204, 265; *see also* Faust pseudonyms
Mannix, Eddie: 206
Marie Antoinette: 205
"Marijuana": *see Flower of Hell*

Marine Corps, U.S.: 36, 231
Marlborough: 34
Marlowe, Julia: 124
Marquand, J. P.: 70
Marriage in the Dark: 169
Mary, Queen of Scots: 105
"Mary Rogers": 32–33
Marx, Karl: 41
Mason, James: 98
Massey, Raymond: 128
Masterman, The: 164
Maule, Harry: 160, 167–68
Maupassant, Guy de: 29
"Maxbrand" (cable address): 169
Max Brand Western Magazine: 265
Mayer, Louis B.: 206
Mayerling: 203, 208, 230
Mayo, Frank: 86
M. B.: 265; *see also* Faust pseudonyms
Medici, Giulano de: 114
MGM: *see* Metro-Goldwyn-Mayer
Meloney, Mrs. William Brown: 182
Memoirs of an Aesthete: 132
Menton (on French Riviera): 110–11
Mephistopheles: 69
Merivale, Philip: 223
Merkel, Una: 221
Merritt, Abe: 163, 171, 312–13
Merrick, David: 144
Metro-Goldwyn-Mayer: 195, 197, 203–206, 211–13, 215–17, 230; Faust on leave from, 219; left by Faust, 226
Metro Pictures Corporation: 58
Metropolitan Museum of Art: 41, 214
Michael Carmichael: 159
Michaux's Travels Through Ohio, Kentucky and Tennessee: 126
Michelangelo: 109, 114, 144, 193
Mihailovich, Draža: 231
Mile-A-Minute Romeo: 98
Mill, John Stuart: 41
Millay, Edna St. Vincent: 83, 174
Millikens, the Robert: 225
Mills, Professor Frederick C.: 220
Milton, John: 7, 199
Minsk, Russia: 206
Miss Barry's American School (in Florence): 123
Mission Canyon, Calif.: 72

Miss Spence's finishing school: 182, 195
Mr. Christmas: 175
Mistral: 134
Mitchell, Lennon: 213
Mix, Tom: 68, 80–81, 86, 91, 98, 127;
  in *Destry Rides Again*, 144, 154
Modesto, Calif.: 9, 11–12, 101, 104, 142,
  177, 224–25
Modesto High School: 9–10, 14, 83, 112
Moffett, Clemens: 44
Moffett, Mrs. (sister of Mark Twain): 44
Mongolia: 123, 159
Monroe, La.: 138–39
Monsieur: 111
Montana Rides: 166, 171
Montmartre, France: 82
Moore, Don: 155, 165, 168–69, 196, 218
Moores, the Douglas: 83
Morales, Carmen: 226
Morgan, Angela: 95
Morgan le Fay: 66
Morland, Peter Henry: 78, 204, 265;
  see also Faust pseudonyms
Morse Code: 37
Morte d' Arthur: 7, 12
Morvich (a thoroughbred): 137
Motion Picture News: 58, 80, 100
Motion Picture World: 86, 221
Moving Picture World: 127
Mulrooney, Edward P.: 99, 122, 177, 239
Munsey Building, 280 Broadway, N.Y.:
  44, 56
Munsey, Frank A. (Munsey Company):
  44–45, 53–54, 73–74, 77, 135, 156, 158,
  162, 170, 177
Murphy, Audie: 144
Murphys, the Gerald: 195
Murray, D. L.: 234
Mussolini, Benito: 200, 205
Mwemba: 194
Myers, Alice Lee: 239
Myerses, the Dick: 83, 98, 195, 239
"My Heroes" (a poem): 61
Myron Selznick Agency: 202
Mytilene (city of Sappho): 188–89
Mytton, John (fictional): 176

Naked Blade, The: 164–65
Navy, U. S.: 36
Nazi Germany: 207

Nee, Colonel W. F.: 232, 245–46
Negli Ulivi Villa: 117, 129–30
Negri, Pola: 221
Negro troops, World War II: 243, 246
Nettuno-Anzio American Cemetery: 261
Nevada: 143
New Brunswick: 38
New Buffalo Bill Weekly, The: 74; *see
  also Western Story*
New Canaan, Conn.: 162
Newman, Cardinal John Henry: 41
News, New York: 44
New Story & All Around: 74
Newsweek: 60, 243
New York City: 30, 35, 39–47, 50, 52–54,
  63, 79, 85–86, 95, 101, 105, 125, 134,
  155, 158–59, 163–64, 177, 184–85, 193,
  208, 227, 234, 262; underworld of,
  171; February, 1944, arrival of
  Faust in, 237
New Yorker: 17, 122, 220
New York Herald, The: 85
New York Herald Tribune: 49, 165, 242,
  264
New York Public Library: 41, 204
New York Sun: 44, 73, 77, 135
New York Times: 44, 92, 263, 268–69
Nice, France: 110
Nick (a trapper): 72
"Nick Carter" stories: 57
Nietzsche, Frederick Wilhelm: 41
Night Flight: 245
Nightflower, The: 217
Night Flower, The: 170–71, 173, 268
Night Horseman, The: 68–69, 80, 86
Normandy: 233
North American Newspaper Alliance:
  238
Norton-Taylor, Duncan: 179–80
Notebooks and Poems: 266
Nova Scotia: 38, 42
Novak, Eva: 86

Oakland, Calif.: 20, 24, 30, 83
O'Brien, George: 127, 153
O'Brien, Howard Vincent: 161–62
Occident, The: 19, 21–23, 32, 46, 53
Ocean, The: 45
Odysseus: 66, 147, 188, 253
Oedipus Rex: 71

Of Mice and Men: 199
Offenbach, Jacques: 207–208
Office of War Information: 242, 244
Offner, Richard: 193
Oliphant, Tom: 160
Olympic Games, 1936: 190, 194
Olympic teams, Italian: 185, 188–89, 191
One of Cleopatra's Nights: 22
110 Morningside Drive, New York: 71
169 East 63rd Street, New York: 48, 51, 55–56
Only the Young Fear Death: 166
Oppenheim, E. Phillips: 45
Original Joe's (restaurant): 51
Orioli, Giuseppé (publisher): 126
Orpheus: 150
O'Sullivan, Maureen: 206
Othello: 96
Our Daily Bread: see The Thief
Oursler, Fulton: 174, 178
Overland Journey from New York to San Francisco in the Summer of 1859, An: 130–31
Ovid: 131
Owen, Hugh: 77, 178, 181, 265; *see also* Faust pseudonyms
Owens, Jesse: 191
Oxford, England: 105, 151

Paddock, Charles: 185
"Pagliacci": 63
Palace of Minos, Crete: 149
Pan: 66
Panama Pacific Exposition, San Francisco: 55
Paolo-Francesca theme: 99, 105
Parade: 266
Parade (a horse): 140, 166
Paramount Pictures: 174, 183–84; first Kildare story released by, 198
Parker, Jean: 206
Paris, France: 82–85, 87, 110, 113, 122, 147, 161, 180, 194, 213
Pasadena, Calif.: 204
Paxton, Harry: 179
Pazzi Villa: 112, 114, 116
Pelican, The: 22
Pelly: 23–24; *see also The Pelican*
Penn Relays: 185
Perkins, Kenneth: 79–80, 267

Perry, Professor Bliss: 22
Peters, Susan: 226
Petrarch: 114
Phi Beta Kappa: 24
Photoplay: 220
Pickford, Mary: 205
Pictorial Review: 175, 180
Picture Play: 74
Pillar Mountain: 66
Pitts, Zasu: 127, 154
Plaza Hotel: 44
Pocket Books Corporation: 197
Poe, Edgar Allan: 7
Popular Magazine: 74
Popular Publications: 166
Port Washington, Long Island: 49
Portland, Ore.: 33
Powell, William: 208, 223
Power, Tyrone: 205
Pride and Prejudice: 205
Princeton campus: 30
Princeton University: 39
Prison Shakes: 169
Prometheus: 150, 188; Faust poem on, 234; notes on poem of, 236
Pseudonyms, Faust: Max Brand, 49, 57, 72, 77–79, 94, 122, 137, 157, 159–61, 164, 167–68, 171, 173, 179, 181–82, 202–204, 215, 255, 263–65, 268; John Frederick, 57, 77–78, 86, 94, 156, 265; George Owen Baxter, 74, 77, 94, 157, 204, 265; David Manning, 77–78, 94, 122, 157, 204, 265; Hugh Owen, 77, 178, 181, 265; Evin Evan, 77, 166, 265; Peter Dawson, 77, 94, 265; Nicholas Silver, 78, 94, 265; Peter Henry Morland, 78, 204, 265; George Challis, 78, 164, 182, 264–65, 269; Martin Dexter, 78, 265; Evan Evans, 161, 167, 178, 181, 204, 264–65; Dennis Lawton, 182, 188, 265; Frank Austin, 204, 265; Frederick Frost, 204, 265, 268; Walter C. Butler, 204, 265, 268; Lee Bolt, 265; M. B., 265; Henry Uriel, 265
Publisher's Weekly: 203, 264, 267
Pulp Jungle, The: 266–67
Pulp magazines: 45, 47, 74, 133, 162, 167, 170, 181, 196–97, 203, 263

Putnam's Sons, G. P.: 59, 61, 86, 91–92, 99, 111
Pyle, Ernie: 232

Quest, The: 168
Quiet Birdmen Club, New York: 197

Rabelais, François: 29, 101, 172
Racehorses in Training: 105
Rai, Lajpat: 27, 31
Railroad Man's Magazine: 45
Raine, William MacLeod: 57
Range-Finder, The: 105
Rawlinson, Herbert: 71
Read, J. Parker, Jr., and Associated Producers: 81, 86
Reader's Digest: 191, 238
Rebecca: 217
Red Pacer, The: 155, 157
Reilly, Patricia: 159
Reinsch, Paul S.: 29
Rembrandt: 84, 109, 126, 193
Renaissance, the: 112, 114, 131
Renick, Ruth: 86
Reporter, The: 214
Return of the Native, The: 16
Reynolds, Quentin: 265, 269
Reynolds Tobacco Company: 137
Richard the Lion Hearted: 179, 182, 187, 203
Richardson, Darrell C.: 265
Richardson, Leon: 152
Richardson, Tracy: 37, 190
Richman, Philip: Max Brand identity detected by, 204
Riddle Stables, the: 137, 142
Ridolfi, the Marchese: 186–87
Rieber, Professor Charles: 55, 225
Rieber, Winifred: 55, 71, 90
Rifenbark, the Reverend Mark: 54
"Rimini": 107
Rinehart, Mary Roberts: 45, 74
Rin-tin-tin films: 206
RKO Radio Pictures: 155, 165, 203, 218
Roark, Aidan: 228
Rob Roy: 105
Robinson, Brailsford: 16
Robinson, Edwin Arlington: 92, 152
Rodriguez, Private Hendrick F.: 258
Rogers, Will: 205

Rome, Italy: 113, 146
Rome-Berlin axis: 200
Romeo and Juliet: 124
Ronicky Doone: 111
Ronicky Doone's Treasure: 111
Rooney, Mickey: 205
Roosevelt, Brigadier General Theodore, Jr.: 233
Roosevelt Division, the: 59
Roosevelt Hospital, New York: 61, 99, 183
Roosevelt, President Franklin D.: 163, 165
Roosevelt, Theodore: 138
Rousse, Dolores: 100
Runyon, Damon: 101
Ruskin, Harry: 213, 215
Russell, William: 86
Ruth, Babe: 271
Ryder, Arthur: 15–16
Rand, Ayn: 229

Sacramento, Calif.: 23–24
St. Christopher, legend of: 61
St. Exupéry, Antoine de: 245
St. Nicholas Magazine: 61
Salerno, Italy: 232
San Fernando Valley: 228–29, 245
San Francisco, Calif.: 16, 19–20, 25, 44, 53, 180, 207, 210, 212
San Joaquin Valley: 4–5, 177
Santa Barbara, Calif.: 72
Santa Monica, Calif.: 209
Santa Maria Infante: 254, 258; battle of, 260–62
Santa Ynez Mountains: 72
Santell, Alfred: 198
Sappho: 54, 101, 179, 184–85, 188–89, 197, 203; failure of Sappho poem, 188
Saroyan, William: 205
Satan (a horse): 69
Saturday Evening Post, The: 84, 154–55, 169–70, 173–74, 177–79, 184, 194, 196–97, 202, 213; Faust's *After April* bought by, 237; *After April* published by, 264
Saturday Review of Literature: 98–99, 165, 264, 269–70
Saxton, Gene: 194, 223
Schaefer, Jack: 143

326

Schafer, Lena: 13
Schary, Dore: 205
Schenck, Joseph M.: 198
Schiller, Johann Christoph Frederich von: 7
Schillig, Belle (Mrs. Lawrence Schillig): 54, 210
Schillig, Dorothy: 23–24, 27–29, 31, 34–37, 48, 50–51; in Yuba City, 52, 81; engagement broken by, 52; wedding of, 54; *see also* Dorothy Faust
Schillig, Lawrence: 54
Schoolcraft, John: 17, 41–42, 57, 91, 97, 107, 176, 220, 239, 265, 267; in military service, 60
Schultz, James Willard: 169
Scott, Randolph: 226
Scott, Sir Walter: 7, 105
Scrap Book: 45
Scribner's Magazine: 169
Sea Stories: 74
Seattle, Wash.: 5, 35, 132
"Secret, The" (a poem): 47, 60
Secret Agent Number One: 268
Seeger, Alan: 40
Seeger, Charles: 40
Selznick, David: 205
Semaphore: 37
Semele: 149–51
Semple, Ellen: 83
Señor Jingle Bells: 127
Sequoia: 206
Serbo-Croatian country: 231
Service for Authors Agency: 101
Service, Robert: 20
Seventh Day, The: 198
Seventh Man, The: 68–69, 80, 86
Shakespeare plays: 40, 97, 105, 130, 217, 238
Shakespeare, William: 7, 10, 66, 104, 107, 109, 123
Shame: 86
Shane: 143
Shanghai Express: 174
Sharkey, Tom: 228
Shaw, George Bernard: 74, 127
Shearer, Norma: 205
Sheeans, the Vincent: 239
Shelley, Percy Bysshe: 7, 144
Shenandoah Valley: 136

Sheridan, Phillip Henry (Union general): 223
Short History of the English People: 110
Short Stories: 111, 160, 167
Short Story Magazine: 94
Silver, Nicholas: 78, 94, 265; *see also* Faust pseudonyms
Silver Search: 171
Silvertip series (westerns): 166, 168–69
Simpson, Robert (editor): 56–57, 71–72, 91, 267
Sinatra, Frank: 205
Sinclair, Upton: 45
Singing Guns: 267
Six Golden Angels: 191, 193–94
Slow Joe: 167
Smith's Magazine: 74
Smithson, George A.: 21, 24
Smoking Land, The: 197
Snow, C. P.: 233
"Some Doubted": 115–16
Sophocles' plays: 71, 97, 123
Southern, Edward: 124
Southern Pacific Railroad: 9
Southey, Robert: 105
Southwest, the: 70–72
Special Occasion, A: 171–72
Speedy's Crystal Game: 157
Spencer, Herbert: 41
Spenser, Edmund: 97
Splendid Rascal, The: 111
Sports Story: 74
Sprangers, the John: 148
Sproul, Robert Gordon: 187
Spy, The: 218
Squadron, The: 231, 238
Stalin, Joseph: 205
Stanford University: 15, 18, 26
Stanwyck, Barbara: 127, 198
Star-Bulletin, Honolulu: 28
Starke, Pauline: 80
Stein, Gertrude: 83
Sten, Anna: 174
Stephens, Henry Morse: 24
Stevenson, Robert Louis: 105
Stewart, James: 127, 205; in *Destry Rides Again*, 144, 221
Stockbridge, Mass.: 81
Stock market crash of 1929: 148
Stockton, Calif.: 4, 9

Storm in the West: 205
Stout, "Cowboy": 231
Stout, Wesley Winans: 202
Stranger at the Gate, The: 111
Stratford, England: 104–105
Street and Smith syndicate: 74, 77, 153, 157, 160, 178, 265, 269
Streeter, Edward: 99
Stringham, Martha (Mrs. Leonard Bacon): 106
Sullivan, John L.: 159
Sullivan, Jean: 229
Summerville, Slim: 226
Sun Also Rises, The: 100
Sun Stood Still, The: 177
Swanson, H. N.: 155
Swarthout, Gladys: 122
Switzerland: 162–65
Sword Lover, The: 57
Sycamore, The: 13
Synge, John Millington: 129

Taft, William Howard: 14
Talmadge, Richard: 127, 153
Taming of Red Thunder: 220
Tannhäuser: 5
Tarzan: 206
Taylor, Bayard: 130
Taylor, Robert: 211
Teasdale, Sara: 60
Tell It to the Marines: 208
Tempe, Vale of: 149
Tempest, The: 123, 217, 238–39, 261
Tender Is the Night: 195
Tennyson, Alfred: 7
Terhune, Albert Payson: 57, 75
Terrill, Rogers: 166, 174–75
Terry, Ethel Grey: 81
Texas Negroes: 221
Thackeray, William Makepeace: 7
That Receding Brow: 70
They Knew What They Wanted: 19, 100
Thief, The: 41
Thin Man, The: 223
This Week: 182, 197, 220, 224, 238
Thomas, John Charles: 220
Thompson, Chaplain W. W.: 250
Thornton, Texas (a firefighter): 140
Thousand To One, A: 81, 86; *see also* *Fate's Honeymoon*

351st Infantry Regiment, command post of: 346
340 West 86th Street, New York: 87
"Three O'Clock in the Morning": 125
317 Burlingame Avenue, Brentwood, Calif.: 212, 223–24, 231, 236
Three Who Paid: 98
Thrill Book: 74
Thucydides (historian): 172
Thus Spake Zarathustra: 41
Thyone: *see* Semele
Tiffany-Stahl: 153
Tiger True: 86
Time Magazine: 59–60, 264, 272
Tintagel Castle: 104
Tippity Witchett: 160
Tip Top Magazine & Wide Awake: 74
"To a Lady" (a poem): 94
Tolstoy: 151
Tony (a horse): 91, 98, 127, 154
Top Notch Magazine: 74, 160, 167
Torquay: 104
Toronto, Canada: 36
Torreys, the Clair: 106
Towne, Gene: 218
Tracy, Spencer: 205
Trailin': 66, 73, 86, 153
Train's Trust: 111
Treadwell, Sophie: 49
Trevor, Claire: 226
Triple-X Western: 155
Tristan, Wagner's: 174
Tristram-Iseult theme, poem on: 31, 37, 59–60, 104
Trouble Trail: 111
True Confessions: 155
Trumbo, Dalton: 229
Tunney, Gene: 159, 198, 239
Tuolumne River: 11–12
Tupper, General Tristram: 246
Turner, Lana: 205, 226
Tuttle, W. C.: 75
Twain, Mark: 7, 44
Twentieth Century-Fox: 198
25 East End Avenue, New York: 196
Twelve Peers: *see* *Destry Rides Again*
Two-Faced Woman: 205
212th Marine Fighter Squadron: 231

Uncertain Glory: 229

Union Station, Los Angeles: 235
Universal studios: 71, 86, 143–44, 194, 205, 217, 222
University of California, Berkeley: 14, 18–19, 40, 53, 55, 85, 106, 148, 187; nonconformity in, 15, 22–23
University of California Chronicle, The: 22, 152
University of California, Los Angeles: 225
University of Chicago: 185
University Club, University of California: 53
University of Virginia: 174
Untamed, The: 61, 63, 65–69, 86, 156, 267; influence of, 68; sales of, 68; movie versions of, 80–81
Uriel, Henry: 265; *see also* Faust pseudonyms
Utah: 226

Valentino, Rudolph: 127
Valley of Vanishing Men: book title sold to Columbia pictures, 226
Valli, Virginia: 86
Vancouver, B. C.: 33, 35–36
Vanderbilts, the: 106
Van Doren, Ireta: 165
Variety: 153, 214
Veblen, Thorstein: 15
Velasquez: 193
Victoria, B. C.: 35
Victorville-Lancaster area, Calif.: 224
Victory: 45, 79
Vienna, Austria: 95, 132, 207, 214
Viking Book of Poetry of the English Speaking World, The: 234
Villa, Pancho: 15
Village Street, The: 92–95, 99–100, 114
Vinci, da, Leonardo: 114, 193
Virgil: 150–51
Virgin Mary: 149
Virginia Creeper: 198
Volunteer Ambulance Service: 39–40

Wadopian, Lieutenant Herbert: 258–60; account of Faust at Santa Maria Infante by, 259–60; account of Santa Maria Infante battle by, 260
Wagner, Richard: 109

Walker, Jimmy: 101
Wanamaker's department store: 40–41
Warner Brothers: 164, 231, 237, 245; Faust at, 228–30
Washington, D. C.: 37, 62, 230, 241
Washington, George: 137, 199
Way of All Flesh, The: 45
Wedding Guest, The: 172
Weeks, Carnes: 220
Weismuller, Johnny: 205
Wells, H. G.: 74
West: 160, 167
Western Story: 74, 76, 86, 105, 111, 132–34, 143, 153–57, 161, 163–68, 170, 174, 197, 265, 269; George Owen Baxter in, 74; circulation of, 77
Wheeler, Benjamin Ide: 23–28; commencement address of, 25
Wheelock, John Hall: 60
Whispering Outlaw, The: 111
White Indian, The: 169–70
White, Stewart Edward: 75
White Wolf, The: 111
Whitney, Jock: 174
Wilder, Thornton: 59, 270
Willards, the Charles: 106
Williams, William: 9–10, 112
Wills, Helen: 228
Wilson, Carey: 207, 212, 216
Wilson, Edmund: 83
Wilson, President Woodrow: 52, 58, 60
Winchester, England: 104
Wind, Sand and Stars: 245
Wine on the Desert: 182, 225; plot of, 182–83
Winston-Salem, N. C.: 137
Wister, Owen: 67, 70
Wodehouse, P. G.: 57
Wolfe, Thomas C.: 270
Woman (magazine): 45
Women Stories & Live Stories: 74
Wong, Anna May: 86, 127
Woodward, Henry: 70
Wordsworth, William: 105
World, New York: 44–45
World War I: 30, 223, 233; declaration of, 52
World War II: outbreak of, 221; U.S. entry into, 227, 230
Wykoff, Frank: 185

Wylie, I. A. R.: 178
Wyoming: 67

Yale University: 41, 49, 220
Yarrow, Bill: 120
Yeats, William Butler: 129
Young, Collier: 179, 202, 204, 206, 209–12, 218, 220, 228
Young Doctor Kildare: 213–15
Young, Robert: 226

Young, Valery: 220
You Only Die Once: 226
Yuba City, Calif.: 24, 52–54, 81, 140, 159
Yugoslavia: 231

Zaehnsdorf (bookbinder): 131
Zeus: 32, 66, 149–51
Ziegfeld's Follies: 101
Zimbalist, Sam: 211
Zola, Emile: 19, 29